Soul Shaping Tails

Soul Shaping Tails

A travel memoir

~

Christy Nichols

A Venture Within

First paperback edition June 2022

Editor
Marisa Zocco

Illustrations
Bartosz Tytus Trojanowski

Cover and Book Design
Cora McKenzie

978-1-7377116-5-0

www.venture-within.com

To all the named, name-changed, or unnamed characters within this book, thank you for being a part of the journey.

For those who are journeying now, I hope these stories serve as an uplifting and encouraging companion for you.

Thanks to the inspiring and vivacious members of my "Title My Damn Book" party: Nicklas, Adam, Natalie, Anna, Mateo, Mateo's papa, Josée, Olga, Joan, Adriana, and Ivana. Poster boarding has never been more entertaining, colourful, and fruitful.

A whole-hearted thank you to my proofreaders, Milton, Cheryl (mom), Tony and Carol. Your input, advice and opinions proved invaluable.

Thank you to my incredible editor, Marisa, who delivered not only fastiduous editing, but her personal coaching for my writing enabled the voice behind my words to be truly heard.

Thank you to my talented roommate, Bart, whose artistic abilities I am honored to have illustrate my first book.

And especially thanks to my Mom, my sister Cheri, and my brother Derek and his wife Lindsay, for the love, support, tolerance for my open travel bags messing up their floors during visits home and for all of the airport pick-ups.

And of course, a huge thank you to my many beautiful family and friends who are ever a part of my life stories. Thank you for listening to me, laughing with me, sometimes feeding me, and supporting me always.

Love you all.

Finally, this book is also dedicated to my 80-year-old future self. Decades ahead, she will know if I have held back my voice or failed to write as fully as I could have. And so it's for her that I have tried to be brave and true in relating these tales.

Christy

We write to taste life twice.
ANAÏS NIN

Table of Contents

Prologue

TO TRAVEL IS TO have an experience that is awakening.

Travel can be an experience that makes your heart pound out of your chest with excitement for all that is to come.

Travel can be lonely. Scary. Humbling at times when you'd rather feel confident.

Rejuvenating when your outlook feels low. Enlightening when you didn't expect it.

When travelling, I have found myself so completely happy with where I find myself that all I want is to crouch down low to the place I am in. Dig my fingers right into the soft, dark earth beneath my feet.

I spread my fingers wide and delve deep, past my knuckles and up to my wrists and keep pressing into the very core of the place where I am...feeling the familiar touch and move up along my skin.

I never want to let go of how this feels. I want to cling to the earth with my bare hands and hold precious in that earth the very essence of the moment.

I want to hold close the warm energy of people and vibrant faces—the spiced scent in the winds, the fire-lit guitar strings and barefoot rhythms, the sea salt and wine. I want all of it to wrap so tightly inside the caves of my heart that the moment stays anchored to me and my heart swells almost past the point of believing that the connection, the aliveness, the wonder of it all could be so real.

I didn't board my first plane expecting to return months later, seasoned with experience and muddy-footed knowledge of what being a traveller truly means on the deeper, soul-shaping kind of level. Nor did I understand there is a place within us where we truly discover what our life can be. But that's what happened. And I came back with an unquenchable thirst for more.

As I farewelled my friends at the departure gate, I pictured in my head the snapshots I would take of the places I had seen snapshots of. I envisioned the bustling city streets of London and grand cathedrals and red double-decker buses teetering through narrow, smoke-stained buildings. I anticipated spending coins imprinted with the profiles of a long-lived queen instead of a long-dead politician.

I anticipated my ears filling with the lilt of English colloquialisms, listening not so much to what strangers were saying to me but rather the sound of how they spoke. The rise and fall of pitch as each word left their lips.

I had planned a four-month trip overseas, which seemed a very long time to be away from home, so limited was my sense of travelling back then. However, seven years would have come to pass by the time I boarded my final one-way return flight out of London and to Los Angeles.

This is a story about those seven years.

This isn't a story about travel for the purpose of career exploration or the pursuit of love and hot summer romances, although those very much play a lively part in those years.

This isn't a story about seaside holidays and fruity cocktails, or camping expeditions and scenic mountain treks, or close encounters with wildlife and harrowing escapades, although these narratives weave their way throughout this story too.

This isn't a story about the brightness of life or the sudden darkness of death, but of course, you'll find that here too.

This is a story about travel and how it can open up a life in beautiful and tragic ways. How travel flips us upside down, propels us forward and sideways and wrong-ways and right-ways again.

And how it can hold us perfectly still in a crystal moment.

This is a story about how a trip becomes a journey and travel becomes an experience. A story about the ways travel seeps into the soul and gives it a good shaking. Or a good shaping.

I'm going to have to say I'm 50/50 on that one. Travel has shaken and shaped my soul to the very core.

Through these stories, I want to share with you just how that happened.

We'll traverse medieval landscapes in broken boots, traipse barefoot through olive tree-scented Italian towns, flirt with Greek lovers by the sea, survive Bulgarian mountain snowstorms, and embark on an epic Pilgrimage across Spain.

We'll meet the faces, hear the voices and join the chatter of every kind of person who stepped into my path and journeyed along with me for part of the way.

But first, let's start with the animals.

The Spanish Zebra

Years ago, I read an article in *The Guardian* about a world-famous flamenco player who had killed a man in a hit-and-run accident in Seville. The Gypsy artist was at the wheel of a BMW when he ran down a man crossing the street along a zebra crossing.

Now, the Spanish Zebra may not be featured in any Attenborough documentary, but how delightfully unexpected! Here I'd found him in the cosiness of a grey Sunday morning in the kitchen with my British flatmate, cups of tea, spread-out newspaper, and Paco Peña strumming Flamenco music in the background.

I lifted my head from the newspaper and, with childlike joy, glanced over the breakfast table at my companion. "I didn't know there were zebras in Spain," I exclaimed.

I hadn't yet learned that the dark and light stripes on the surface of the road were referred to as zebra crossings in the UK—a common crosswalk.

You know, it's not my flatmate's days-long, bellowing laughter that bothered me. It's the fact that had my flatmate not been teaching himself flamenco on his guitar, I never would have read parts of that particular article aloud to him. I would have taken in the information about the reckless performer, silently filed away—without question—the interesting new fact I had learned about the unexpected urban habitat of zebras and moved on to another news article. Somewhere down the road—months, maybe even years later—this little nugget of insider knowledge would have found its way into a conversation.

"Yes," I'd tell them, "it's true. There are wild herds of zebras so abundant in population that cities in Spain were forced to paint zebra crossings on the roads so that drivers knew to watch out for them."

Something would have triggered this memory—this misperceived, but long-held truth—and even though I might not have been able to remember exactly *how* I had heard about the Spanish Zebra, I, no doubt, would have been infuriatingly insistent upon this wildlife fact: Some zebras live in Spain. My belief would have been unshakeable.

Of course, there are zebras in Spain.

To be fair, there are also buffalo roaming islands in the Pacific, elephants grazing in the deep south, and foxes bounding along salty seashores. And once in a great while, a small whale might surface from the dirty Thames River in busy downtown London.

These are all truths. But I am getting ahead of myself.

The Spanish Zebra serves as a reminder of how much travel has to show us. It is a symbol of the undoing and perhaps the skewed retelling of our long-held beliefs—how easily we allow them to become inarguable "truths" without a pause.

Even though I had departed from the US equipped with a college degree, a history of love, and a few life-lesson scars, I had so much ahead to discover, and so much more to learn.

PART ONE

The Undoing of Long-Held Truths

The Castle, United Kingdom
2001

THERE WERE MANY TRUTHS I'd held long before I began my travels.

Truth: I believed I was in love. I'd led a carefully curated life complete with a soon-to-be spouse and a house. The future held weekend barbecues and family dinners neatly mapped out before me. With one heartbreak already logged in my past, I felt ready and eager for this well-planted relationship to fully bloom.

Truth: I believed that I hailed from a nation powered by "the good guys." From where I stood, the US was unquestionably flawless, altruistic in its politics, and directed only the best of intentions for humanity across the globe, focused in its crosshairs.

Truth: I believed that the God I grew up with was not my friend. His churches were peopled with hypocrites, and I had witnessed enough hate and rage, control, judgement and shaming from the Christians I knew to be convinced Christianity was not my path. Thus the world's religious spaces meant little to me, and I desired to experience them not at all.

This tapestry of truths had been woven with every thought and experience of my life so far. Each event had served to define my perspectives and opinions and had been tamped firmly to depict my own story as I knew it to be true at the age of 21.

Unbeknownst to me, my tapestry would soon unravel.

~

WE APPROACHED THE CASTLE from the upper wooded hillside, descending into a green, softly waiting valley. Aged nearly 600 years and half-encircled by a murky moat, the red bricks and stones of the castle stood impenetrably strong. Set low amongst bordered pastures and a quiet tree-lined village, the castle itself was kept company by the nearby aged copper domes of an observatory, a moss-shrouded stone church, and an elusive, troubled ghost.

We sleepy but clamorous North American invaders pressed our jetlagged faces and hands to our coach windows as it rolled down the lane past the castle's four tall towers, its turrets framing the flagged battlements, a staggering sight for our tired eyes. Any defenders that once might have pointed arrows towards us from the battlements had gone centuries ago, so it was only the castle's burnt-red image that peacefully reflected between the lily-padded waters in the moat. We were home.

"Look at all those moo-cows," I said. Heads turned from one window to look out the other, and from the lush field opposite the castle, the moo-cows turned their chewing faces lazily toward the coach to watch us pass.

And this is how it would be. It was as if our surroundings had been pulled straight from a storybook: The familiar and imagined encapsulated in the same moment in time, the simple juxtaposed with the grandiose. Our castle was enchanting.

For the next 15 months, my address would be Room 3, D Wing, Herstmonceux Castle, England. My roommates and classmates would mostly be Canadian.

What was it like to live in a castle? Magical. Inspiring. Unbelievable. And then, after a time, normal, familiar and common.

The yet-to-be-explored rising and prominent cathedrals dotted throughout Great Britain, as I later discovered, were captivating. So too were the abbeys, the bridges, the towers, and palaces; the battlefields of England, Scotland, France, and Belgium. The romantic settings etched in the weighty tomes of my history books and anthologies were brought to life more deeply and richly than any dreamscape.

But then, so were the smaller things. The stone churches were miniature in comparison to the vast cathedrals but no less enthralling. Glittering palaces and roped-off infamous art mesmerised me equally as much as the spacious, chilly acres of lush farmland hugged in fog. Every new scene and unfamiliar sound intrigued and excited me from the first giddy moment until my very last.

My first few months of soaking up all that I could of living fully in another country, learning its culture, studying its history, and befriending the locals was enriching and life-filling. I was living in another westernised, English-speaking country, sure. But despite a certain level of familiarity, the exhilaration I felt from experiencing a different version of life was unlike anything I'd ever imagined.

Living in the castle, the first few weeks were lived as if from within the gusts of a whirlwind. The energy held the feeling of the first year at university. Each new face became a fast friend with whom I'd share stories and adventures and overseas tourist experiences, complete with daily itineraries to follow and overpriced souvenirs to purchase.

My enthusiasm for these days never waned. But as the days stacked into weeks, life in the castle became easy and familiar. The weekend trips to London came to be as common a dinner conversation as the bland, boiled potatoes on our plates. My camera took fewer photos of the places I'd always wanted to see and more photos of the friends I'd had no idea I would meet.

What started as an innocent adventure to spend one semester abroad with a Canadian university auditing a few art history courses in Sussex rapidly became a pivoting point in my life. I had left one home, but with each passing day, I felt the castle, its inhabitants, and my life feeling more truly at home than I had felt in a long time.

Perhaps it had happened instantaneously, as we pulled up in front of the castle on that first day, or maybe it had been a steady flick of switches. But during those unforgettable, magical castle days, every light in my soul was turned on, and they lit up brightly.

Correspondence about this first solo trip abroad turned out to be narrated in two conflicting ways: One was through lengthy, elaborate, unforgivably misspelt and poorly punctuated email recountings of the adventures I had been having. These were full of excitement, comedy, and abundant energy passed from my thoughts and feelings into the keyboard. The other side of my story was narrated through tearful, often sobbing voice messages I'd leave at home.

I often called my mother, but I struggled to align my needy emotions with her time zone. Sometimes, I would call too late and would only reach her voicemail. I was living a fuller experience than I had expected, but I missed my family terribly. I missed being with everyone after so many passing weeks. My intentions to let her know I was okay were futile. I would break down and cry halfway through my message. I think she must have found my communication with home disconcerting at the least. In my emails, I was having the time of my life; via phone, I was lonely and heartsick.

But I didn't want to go back to that home. Not for a minute. I only sought to touch base, to gain enough confidence, comfort, and love from the call to refuel. And then, I could continue on my journey. When I reflect on truths and tapestries, perhaps these calls home were an attempt to tighten the slipping knots of already-unravelling long-held truths.

Love—solid, unbreakable love—would still be present in my life and something I could reach for in times of uncertainty or fear. But romantic love, politics, religion, life, friendships, all my untravelled opinions? These truths began to shift into new and unfamiliar stories. Upon arrival to Herstmonceux Castle, unbeknownst to me, my world had started to grow more expansive than the ocean I had just crossed.

Each day and with each adventure, I found my long-held truths tested in ways that left me feeling a little unsettled. But without a doubt, despite the discomfort of my unravelling, I found myself, too, yearning for more.

Clifftops & Castle Ducks

HERSTMONCEUX CASTLE WAS BUILT not atop a formidable cliff but nestled down in the heart folds of rolling hills. Long walks over the lush green acreage proved to be a lovely way to spend a chilly afternoon, as did touring local villages via heated van throughout the countryside. It was during my strolls that I could let my mind wander while my eyes soaked in the landscape. I could roll over in my mind all the thoughts and emotions ignited from each new experience as I gazed out the window, rounding slight turns past thick hedges and lush pastures beyond. There was so much to take in from my new surroundings as I learned more about history and culture through observing the way locals went about their business, doing their shopping, and popping into pubs.

During these tranquil outings, as I let each new connective experience permeate my heart a little deeper each day, something began to churn within me. I couldn't quite put my finger on it then, but I was taking in the blended energies of those things that had stood for centuries and would stand, for centuries to come, alongside a modern, present day existence. An existence I would only be a part of for a few months while I lived amongst the older dwellings and the new.

But there was something more going on. Something I began to notice, even if I couldn't immediately name it. I was captivated by the timeless, aged permanence of human constructions, farmhouses, cottages, churches—all rising from grassy fields, fields that changed with the weather and the season, where human footprints would tread and then fade.

I recognised with an electric frenzy that the next four months would be both exhilarating for me and also gone in a flash. This realisation, these colliding moments of permanence and impermanence, fused in me an urgency to pay attention and take in it all.

Within the first few days of my arrival, I'd joined a seven-hour tour of Sussex. I can't deny it: I was the stereotypical, bright-eyed, palms-pressed-on-the-van-windows, overly loud and boisterous American university student tourist. I couldn't help it.

I had spent four and a half years as an undergrad studying English Literature and History, and I was ecstatic watching the land-scapes and structures from my favourite novels and textbooks lift into life as they might in a pop-up book. The expected sights surpassed my expectations. Even the hidden, in-between pockets of off-the-map discoveries were full of bright cultural gems. For example, I would visit a pub famed for being frequented by a certain British author, but then I would find myself equally charmed solely by the names of the British pubs: The Queen's Head, The Druid's Head, The Shepherd and Dog, The Swan, The Mermaid Inn. My trip was full of unplanned trav-eller bonuses that deepened my connection with people and places in delightfully unexpected ways.

My first stop to a famous British landmark was a visit across the Downs to the Seven Sisters—a natural formation of high, white chalk cliffs bordering the southern edge of the shores overlooking the English Channel. On clear days, France was visible just across the choppy, cold sea—a fact that fascinated me. To view Europe with the naked eye from a clifftop across the water? From another country? I was super entertained by the notion of another country, a country harbouring its own history and language and culture, while still being visible from afar without the viewer actually being physically close to it or looking down from a plane window.

The slopes of the hillsides were blanketed in shaggy, wispy brown, deadening grass, which my new Canadian friends and I breath-lessly climbed, only to stand frigidly in the biting cold wind as we took in the scenery. From atop this chalky cliff, we could see the seven different cliffs bounding away from us on down the coast, just as they had for thousands of years.

The experience was beautiful and peaceful, but not necessarily calming. We were giddy and excited, freezing from the gusty winds, and chatty as ever as we appreciated the stark beauty of the cliffs we'd just clambered up.

There was no gift shop, surprisingly, so I decided to take my own souvenirs. I cemented my short-sighted touristy behaviour by completely ignoring the signs that said, "Please don't take the chalk or pebbles," and shoved two white pieces of chalk into my pockets.

Keeping pebbles and stones had always been a way for me to connect to the land with greater depth. Pebbles had been around long before my fingers picked them up, and they would be here long after I departed; that had always been my mindset. I hadn't yet learned to put responsible appreciation for a place above my own need to have tangible evidence that I had stood in some place amazing. And so, common theft from natural and historical landmarks and favourite pubs became a habit I refused to acknowledge as rude and selfish. I've since learned there are other ways to honour a place that snugly holds its own within my memory. But at the time, I just couldn't believe I had actually climbed to the top of the cliffs, taken in the view of the sea and of France, or handled the chalk with my fingers.

Most of the places I visited had this effect on me, and I was often moved to tears from the sheer excitement of it all. It was as if words on a page describing cliffs or a cathedral or a castle were no longer just words and visions in my mind. There was a realness to them now. I could lie on the wispy grass, feel the cold wind brutally blasting my skin; my eyes could take in turrets and stone churches that thousands of others had laid eyes on for hundreds of years. I felt I was a part of the history I had studied and loved so much.

In time, we can grow in the ways we all hope to; we learn and change our points of view. Today, I'm less likely to rebel against signage protecting history or nature and wouldn't have such a cavalier attitude towards rules or regulations. Now, I try to follow the "Take only photos, leave only footprints" etiquette of the seasoned traveller who has seen a place of beauty marred or diminished by too much of the taking.

On our tour of Sussex we also stopped to visit Pevensey Castle in the nearby town of Hastings, which had the same effect. Even though the town was a haven for modern-day drug dealers, in my young, romantically inclined mind, it still teemed with the ghosts from William the Conqueror's invaders and marauders. I couldn't believe I could lean against the walls of the 1000-year-old fortress, its ruins still an impressive sight. It was crumbled, but it hadn't fallen.

I couldn't help but marvel and wonder: *How could anything have been built so long ago, and the same walls still be touchable?* We could walk right up to the dilapidated structure and lay our hands on the stones; they remained solid though damaged and wouldn't tremble with something so insignificant as our present-day skin touching ancient minerals. Again, I was overcome by physically being in a place so old and overrun with characters and stories from my studies. I had never seen a place or edifice that was more than two or three hundred years old. How could something be so unfathomably old and retain so much of its strength and appeal?

The history of each place we visited in Sussex served to create an impression mixed with either overwhelming grandeur or quaint, aged charm. It captivated my imagination, and while in their presence, I had no other thoughts on my mind or feelings in my heart aside from the wonder at where I was. I immersed myself into every moment of it.

The excitement of discovery was something I never lost during that semester. Not once. It seems even though I could lay my eyes and hands on my own castle while living in Herstmonceux day after day, at my core, I held on to the knowledge that each of these moments was fleeting.

Four months, fifteen months, five hundred years. While the castles and churches I had been visiting still stood strong and stable, they were also reminders that all things pass away—particularly experiences. With this knowledge, I made a great effort to stay awake as much as possible. During those months, I wanted to see and feel and breathe in every minute of the time and opportunity I was given. I knew that the time would come when this chapter in my life would pass; these experiences would move beyond my reach, and these shiny, bright moments would gradually fade into warm memories.

~

AMIDST THE SPLENDOUR OF the mighty castles and chalky cliffsides I explored in my excursions, there was something much smaller charming my home in Herstmonceux Castle that caught my eye every day—one of these warm memories I'm so fond of returning to. Aside from the medieval history that I found myself immersed in daily, I also found myself delighted by the castle's darling family of ducks.

There were dozens of ducks, Canada geese, and I think even a couple of swans that considered Herstmonceux Castle to be their home too. In the spring, a brood of ducklings had been hatched by clever parents that, rather than nest in the reeds along the outer moat, had chosen to lay their eggs within the castle's courtyard walls.

Herstmonceux Castle is built like a fortress, with thick brick walls and iron gates that echo and clamour as the heavy metal doors are opened and shut. But once inside the gates, the space breathes out into a lovely green courtyard with flowering bushes manicured regally and completely protected from the elements, foxes, and hounds. These sleek, feathered ducks and their fuzzy duckling babies had made themselves a cosy little haven there—a royal abode of sorts.

Twice a day, about 14 young ducks would come waddling up the muddy bank from one side of the moat. They duck-walked in a crooked line, without fear, over the stone walkway along the side of the castle until they reached the main wooden entrance.

Upon their arrival, they would proceed to disrupt any peace with a loud, quacking fuss until someone from inside heard their racket and opened the wide, creaking, heavy door to let them in. With an air of royalty, they would dodder over the stone slabs with webbed feet in the reception area and on through another iron gate that led into the courtyard. Here, they would feast happily and unperturbed, on whatever insects they could find in the soft grass.

They were fuzzy little royals, walking in and out as if they owned the place. It struck me that they were there before us students and would remain residents after we left at the end of the semester. I got the feeling they were attended to far better than we students were at times. But, gosh, they were cute.

I developed a warm bond with these ducks—likely a one-sided bond, but I didn't mind. Every day, my routine included a friendly hello to them. Like me, they had travelled across the pond to live inside a castle that unexpectedly felt like home. Sure, their pond might have been a moat while mine had been the Atlantic Ocean. All the same, we shared the castle that kept us safe and away from the dangers of the outside world—dangers I would be exposed to soon enough.

And just as I found myself doing those early days of exploration and pebble-pocketing, so too did the ducks help themselves to pleasures without a second thought, taking advantage of what was offered to them.

Mostly, the first few weeks I lived in the UK, I ran amok visiting every nook and crevasse within the distance our minibus could take us. I visited cottages and towns and pubs and beaches I had never heard of, only to discover they were the location of familiar stories I had known for so long. The names unfamiliar to me blended with well-known stories.

Each day bubbled over with surprises. My friendships with fellow students and locals grew deeper, and my passion for travel and connection with the timeless space in which I found myself present began to flame.

I discovered a certain comfort in the permanence of things. Still, at the same time, through every centuries-old pub or castle I ventured into, the richness I had heard in stories passed down for aeons, and the reverence I had for their long-lasting strengths stirred an undercurrent of uneasiness. Beneath my delight and wonder, I was constantly reminded that change is inevitable. We are here, and then we are gone. We hold a treasure in our hands, and then it slips through our fingers or is thrown; it's lost. We are alive, breathing the same air in one moment, and then we are ghosts haunting a memory. We are strong, fortified, safe, and then we are ruins where a cold wind blows over fields where a cavalry used to ride or over stones where ducklings used to waddle.

I couldn't yet focus my thoughts or emotions in any way that could make sense of what was swirling in my mind. The contrast of long-lastingness with the knowledge that all was fleeting just kept lapping up within me like the waves on the shores beneath those chalk-pebbled downs. We were all in motion. We *are* all in motion.

Moving past and over and beyond was a truth I was beginning to understand at a depth I hadn't before. It left me flushed with eagerness and an openness to learn and feel more of it all while I could.

Faith

As a kid, I remember Tennessee's green hills rolling up and away from our porch, and stormy clouds encroaching and darkening the sky while lightning bugs sparked up the heavy air. We lived in a ranch community sliced lightly in two by a single main road lined on both sides with small, red-brick family homes that divided the acres and gardens of my childhood. Down the road, the hillside curved into a small pond, where we would often bring our bread crusts to toss into the water, creating a feeding frenzy for a paddling of ducks.

Back then, we were a family of five, and we lived in a community where fundamental religious beliefs were served heavy-handed. Our tiny house was filled with the same routines and church-going activities that any Baptist family in the South would be familiar with: There were prayers of thankfulness before every meal; we attended church three times a week (Wednesday evenings, and twice on Sundays); my Mom regularly signed up my sister and me to play some chosen hymn on the piano for the churchgoers. I attended a Christian school all the way up until I was 12 years old.

I remember praying. *Praying.* There was so much praying in my childhood. As an adult, I believe in prayer and its power when offered from an honest place. But as a child, prayers were saddled with an immobilising fear of God. Harsh judgement was the consequence of sinful thoughts or actions and the endless guilt layered on my shoulders when I'd "sinned" in some way. I grew up understanding that there was a very long list of possible sins I could be punished for—some of which most religions would agree were wrong. Lying, for example.

With other sins, I didn't understand where the wrongness lay. Girls wearing pants, for example. Or why bullying was never good behaviour unless. the one being bullied was fatter than should be. Or their hair had gone too long without a cut. In this case, it was accepted that the overweight sinner or unshorn could be verbally brutalised and shamed. I also grew up confused about why shouting and screaming happened so much in my home, even though the hateful, daggered words often broke more than one of the commandments we had to memorise in Sunday School every week.

I grew up fearing a version of Jesus I no longer believe in. As a teenager, Jesus was to me a long-robed, bearded dude hanging out in the sky above us, no matter which State we lived in. He was always looking downward, watching, judging, devising punishments, and getting really pissed off, eyebrows arched and frown-faced, if we humans fucked up in some way.

Sure, we were also taught that God was a protector and answered our prayers. But for some reason, as I grew older in a Christian, on-the-path-to-divorce family, my doubt in this God grew to outweigh my faith and fear.

In the decade that shaped my teenage years, I would often sneak out the side door of our household religious beliefs. We were Baptists, damn it, and my dad rained fire if ever another religion swayed my interests or tempted my beliefs to shift. *Why shop if you're not going to buy?* I'd hear my dad ask when I expressed my curiosity in exploring other faiths, who their Gods were, and what rules they played by. *Why explore other religious beliefs when we all know Baptists believe in the true faith?*

The poor Catholics and Nazarenes. It was so sad for them; they came so close. The Mormons? How far-fetched their beliefs were. So many wives. The Jehovah's Witnesses or the Jewish? We didn't talk about them. I never knew a thing about those beliefs except that they were wrong and sometimes some of them showed up at our doorsteps with pamphlets. And the Buddhists? From the way my church community responded to them, they may as well be BFFs with the devil. There was so much worshipping of false Gods around me, I had to beware. This was what I was steered to believe as a teen, and not just from my parents. I came from a long line of Baptist preachers. Any transgression was a punishable sin.

But then, in my early teens, my parents enrolled me in a California public high school rather than one of the Christian schools that had so far been my foundation. I made friends with teenagers from different religious backgrounds. Some of my best friends were Mormons. We had backyard BBQs and took beach trips. Eventually, those friends would travel to other countries on missions, basically combining cultural exploration with doing good things, not unlike the companies I would start myself later in life.

Some of my friends were also Catholics who, once in a while, came to my church's Wednesday night youth group with me. We memorised verses, ate nachos, and talked about boys. I made a friend who was both Buddhist and African-American, and we'd talk for hours on the phone about Buddhism. I was intrigued. Buddha, I learned, was all about peace and love. There was no room for hate or judgement. He was so happy! There was no one God, and nothing was permanent. Change, in the Buddhist perspective, was inevitable. Its tenets were to be kind, be calm, and be at peace.

How refreshing.

My dad, in particular, was furious about my inquisitive nature surrounding other religions and beliefs. He was threatened by my innocent and curious exploration of other faiths and met my young questions with fear, anger, and warnings. God wouldn't love us, he'd threaten, we'd burn in hell if we dallied in Catholicism.

At about this same time, my parents' marriage began unravelling at a rapid pace. So while my dad was banging on about God's wrath, he was also enraged with my mother, storming through the house and slamming doors, red-faced and spitting mad about whatever injustice he perceived had been done to him this time.

Juxtaposing the rage, hypocrisy, judgement, and control evidenced by Christian preachers in a religious household against the seemingly bright offerings of my friends' religions (travel, family dinners, peace in the house), I eventually came to dismiss organised religion as a whole by the time I'd entered college.

Prayers lifted up in the way I'd been trained to pray growing up weren't a part of my daily habits throughout those years, nor were they when I began to travel overseas. I didn't morph into a wicked person; I just was never inspired to make attending a church service a necessary element of my weekly routines. To me, church, religion, the Jesus I grew up learning about—all that seemed, to me, a sham and a letdown.

So, instead, I set my sights on learning about real people— present-day heroes and icons from history. I explored new cultures with gusto and genuine interest, making long-lasting new friends no matter which deity they sang or danced to. I sought out peace, joy, and awe-inspiring adventures that could fill my heart in ways beyond what any Bible story ever could.

I had grown to be dismissive of paying homage to a holy dwelling of any sort. On the surface, I just wasn't interested and admired the architecture and aged stained glass windows instead. I realise now that just beneath the surface, I carried with me so many heavy stones.

I wasn't dismissive of religion because I didn't care. I was dismissive because I was so wounded and let down by the realities of my life not aligning with religious teachings. These stones I carried with roughened tension, ready to hurl them at the slightest suggestion of conversion, judgement, or invitation to pray to a form of God I had rejected.

And so, when I stepped foot in the UK, my head full of stories from the Medieval, Renaissance, and Victorian history, despite the brimming excitement to explore the grounds of castles and prisons and palaces, I held zero expectation that any sacred space—cathedral, church, or cross-filled graveyard—would touch my heart in any facet.

But they did anyway.

This long-held truth of what a God was or wasn't would fold in on itself, unfold, then fold in again as I ventured through naves and transepts and came face to stony face with saints and angels, crucifixes and tombs. Religion might not have a place in my heart, but faith?

Faith was a thing that perhaps could one day be revived.

The Climb

INITIALLY, I HAD FLOWN across the ocean to explore this island kingdom with great expectations of how I would feel being in the actual presence of medieval castles for the first time.

But in the end, even though I had consciously dismissed them from my personal hit list of all I wanted to experience in England, it was the immense cathedrals dotting the island that unexpectedly struck me with childlike wonder.

The first trip I took to St. Paul's Cathedral in London was unplanned, as many of my best trips tend to be—spontaneous, with or without a map, and several hours of freedom inviting me ahead. I ditched another trip I was scheduled to take to some countryside village in favour of a day on my own exploring London.

St. Paul's was one of the places I had wanted to see, but only because I felt obligated by the unspoken law of tourism: I wanted to obtain proof of my visit by taking some snapshots.

Turns out that at the time, I couldn't. It was dictated by the cathedral's written law that there were to be no snapshots inside the cathedral. It wouldn't have mattered anyway. St. Paul's was too amazingly vast for its impressions to be unjustly confined to the substandard film in my 35mm.

Built in 1675, St. Paul's famous dome ceiling looms high, its arching walls adorned with Biblical paintings of scenes from familiar fables and parables. Its walls are guarded by statues of saints and apostles intimidatingly larger than life in size, and most aged hundreds of years old.

During the excursions in my first couple of weeks, some of the local, rural churches and cathedrals I had visited had felt dark, cloaked, and damp. St. Paul's felt different. It was elaborately decorated with wine-coloured drapes, art depicting parables, and filled with candlelit columns and tombs. Gold framed the art-adorned walls and encircled the columns. The halls seemed to glitter and shine. Upon just walking in, chin lifting and gazing up, I experienced how the shimmering gold and magnitude of the splendour thundering down from the lofty galleries could bow and humble a person. This, I remember thinking, this is how people are moved to fear God. I felt so physically small, the coins in my pocket so meagre.

Whether we are describing living beings, landscapes, or structures, height and size are two primary elements that are essential to expressions of power, strength, and intimidation. From most any geographical point in London, the bulging dome of St. Paul's dominates the city skyline—a presence that can be seen for miles.

For that reason, anyone who makes the physical effort to climb to the highest gallery of the dome is rewarded with an incredible 360-degree view of the sprawling streets of London. From the ground floor, eyes and chin tilted up, I began my dizzying climb of the 528 spiralling steps up to the top of the dome through each of St. Paul's three famed galleries.

The first circular gallery rests above the open choir, where the nave and the transept intersect. This is named the Whispering Gallery, and it rings the inside of the dome just before the ceiling begins to arch inwards. From this level, above the ground floor but perched in the open air of the gallery, I could sit and see more closely the painted ceiling in all its glory, surrounding and cupping the prayers lifted up from kneelers below. I could look straight down into the nave below me, peopled with priests and tourists.

It is named the Whispering Gallery for a reason. Sitting on one side of the inner circle, at the base of the dome, you can whisper something secret, something no one else could hear, your lips pressed close to the wall as if you were telling your secret to the wall itself. Your whisper would not sit in place and hide but sneak slowly away and travel by quiet sound around the massive ring until it found someone on the opposite side of the dome where your secret would whisper into their listening ears. But I was by myself and didn't have anyone I knew to send my secret whispers to. So instead, I just sat still and quietly admired the paintings on the interior of the dome, listening to other people's whispers scurry along the walls.

Another 100 or so steps up from the Whispering Gallery,

accessed by a tighter spiral staircase, is the Stone Gallery. This staircase was made of iron, centred with a single black iron pole, and had black, triangle-shaped, gridiron stairs staggered steeply around it as it rose. As the steps carried me higher, the space expanded above me while also somehow seeming to drop beneath me so that I felt suspended in the open air. Secure but vulnerable, my heart pounded with both fear and excitement as I ascended.

The Stone Gallery stairs guided me from inside the dome to the outside, the walkway hugging the widest and most central part of the dome's exterior. I was no longer viewing the enclosed high and holy space of the cathedral but the vast openness of the air from great heights.

The view was incredible. Every landmark starred on my map was visible plain as day from the Stone Gallery. The view of the city below the horizon was jigsaw puzzled into place. The neighbourhoods of Whitehall, Westminster, Covent Garden, Trafalgar, and Soho, each district crowded with black taxis, double-decker busses, pedestrians, and peddlers pieced together in chaotic unison. I could see stoic Westminster Abbey, the inky Thames River, the turning London Eye, Shakespeare's Globe—all of London's streets wove in and out of themselves. The peek-a-boo spires of lesser churches, the meandering lanes hiding merchants and city rats, modern pubs, coffee houses, and underground stations. I could see all of the highlights of London that tourists line up to see and take snapshots of—everything except for St. Paul's.

It was cold that morning, and windy, and my nose was constantly running. This day, I would set the precedent for the first several months of my time travelling in this new country. I was too excited and too determined to explore more to worry about my physical health, and chose to just keep moving.

I climbed the narrow and final flight of steps up to the Golden Gallery to view the city from the highest point of the cathedral. As I walked along the outer rim of one of the tallest domes in the world, the corridor encircling the tip-top was so narrow that my backpack kept getting lodged between the walls. I breathed in the fresh, cold air.

I took in as much as I could. The details I could pick out before from the gallery below were more difficult to discern now. From on high, London displayed a bigger picture before me. Its inhabitants, numbering in the thousands, were no longer clearly visible.

I couldn't make out a single individual on the streets below, as I'm sure looking up, no one down there could make out my small head peeking over the Golden Gallery wall. That is the effect of St. Paul's. It reminds visitors that anyone within its vicinity, inside its cloisters, or out in the city is insignificant and tiny—at least on our own. I scanned the panoramic horizon line one last time, then made my way back down the 528 steps.

As I took careful step after careful step circling back into St. Paul's, I began to consider the emotions that had been stirring while I explored this place on my own. The Cathedral had caught me off guard, as would also come to be the case with the churches. I was captivated by their eminence and beauty, their thunderous choirs and reverential silence, the candle-lit spaciousness furnished with stern, stone angels and long, wooden pews numbering enough for the gathering masses.

I never expected to be so moved, so enthralled by these religious structures. Yoking the physical buildings themselves with the ideologies of organised religion, I had not initially given cathedrals a second thought. But time and time again, quietly standing solid in each quaint village or centred at the buzzing capitals of every European country I would eventually come to visit, I found myself drawn to these holy places.

When I walked through arched doorways or down stone corridors, I felt an embrace that could only be described as divine. The energy was still, but deep. The ages-old architecture and the sacred spaces within these cathedrals emanated a sanctity I hadn't felt in years.

My long-held truth surrounding God or a greater power or force was beginning to shift. For years I had coldly rejected any emotion connected to a higher power. At St. Paul's, I began turning over thoughts in my head. The cathedral reflected two things back to me: The first was power and the corruption that often accompanies so much glory—the kind of power that judges and excludes, hates and condemns. A power that I had turned away from.

But then, second, it reignited a long-forgotten surge of emotion. Walking along the nave, observing the other visitors and worshippers, I couldn't help but also acknowledge the palpable existence of faith, and our human longing for guidance, protection, beauty, and love from a higher power. I wasn't so moved to return to church or pick up a Bible, but I was moved by the power such grand places of worship could possess. How so humbly magnetised I could be once again, finding shelter and comfort within such walls and climbing the stairs to such heights.

Teachings from a Tomb

I SPENT THE REST of the day in awe of the city—in awe of the drippy streets and their perfectly suited names: Fleet Street, Pudding Lane, Cheapside. I was charmed by the narrow lanes and passageways of the hidden crypts and tombs, the old walls and aged books, the unfamiliar spellings of British English.

Through abbeys and churchyards, past memorials, and through poets' corners, I wandered. It gave me goosebumps to see carved into plaques and walls and monuments the names of Kings and Queens and writers and playwrights I had spent my undergrad years studying. Statue after statue, tomb after tomb, square after square. It was dizzying the way the names and people and places came to life right in front of my eyes. The huge stone statues of Queen Victoria, Oliver Cromwell, King Charles I. The tombs of King Henry V, Elizabeth I, and Mary Queen of Scots. Centuries of history on display in modern times. No longer figures in pages of my books, but touchable or climbable artefacts and monuments that I could be a part of.

But there was one particular moment amidst all the new-to-me sensations of this day that slowed down my starstruck response to the famous historical figures and gave me pause for deeper reflection.

The afternoon had arrived, and the sunlight came and went behind chilly clouds. The city wound down from the buzz of the morning frenzy, and my solo wander had led me to Westminster Abbey where, inside, one of many large tombs had been placed flat on the floor, centred prominently, and was encircled thickly with red poppies. Looking closer, I could see the tomb belonged to an unknown soldier from World War 2. We didn't know where he had come from. We didn't know what victories or challenges he might have had. We didn't know his name, yet the tomb was inscribed with powerful words that told a moving story about how he had served and died for his country. This tomb was meant to honour and represent all those soldiers who had died in the same way—without knowing exactly in what way they had contributed or who they were.

Most times, good or heroic deeds, if done quietly, remain unknown. It's not often that we come across unsung heroes of any description who receive the same accolades that kings, warriors, and rulers with names we all knew would receive for their heroism—the fame and glory rewarded for their victories. But here, with this tomb, the unknown soldier had been held up to the light.

I remember being struck by this patriotic gesture—by the human sensitivity of the British, the English legislature that would spend money and time to revere a common soldier alongside Kings and Queens. Back then, I hadn't yet spent time in the US Capital, Washington DC, and while I had soldiers in my family who had lost family to American wars in past generations, I had never come across anything honouring an unknown soldier. Seldom is public praise given to our silent heroes. All the soldiers I knew or had read about were named. We knew of their heroic feats. We watched movies about them and praised their efforts. But only if they were exceptional. We don't recognise the everyday, common warrior who died for his country without a notable victory beneath his or her belt.

As often happens, my mind shifted from the flux of excitement surrounding all that I had been able to see and do and understand. I slipped into a state of reflection and consideration and began to compare what I knew and had learned from my tiny pocket of the world in the US and what I had started to observe in Britain. Both countries spoke the same language but embraced a completely different culture infused with and comprised of additional differing cultures. Atop that, Britain had also been permeated with so much long-lasting history. As I ended my evening walking the darkening streets of London, I kept tumbling the stones within my mind. I was beginning to understand.

Later, I told my roommate Dee about the tomb of the unknown soldier at Westminster Abbey. I described it with optimism, joyful in having discovered that the nameless were honoured equally amongst the named here in England. I expressed what a novel and progressive gesture I thought it was. She then kindly informed me that Canada also has a tomb and memorial for an unknown soldier who also died in a war. It was only then that I remembered that the US also celebrates a tomb of the unknown soldier in Washington DC.

As this knowledge and memory sunk in, my understanding again began to shift. The tomb, the words, and the intent I had first responded emotionally to during my lone exploration of the Abbey in London still moved me in some way. Except now, in the space of one day, I had moved from unintentionally visiting the tomb of the unknown soldier in London to discovering that there are several such memorials in other countries. In fact, up to 50 countries remember their unknown deceased soldiers with such tombs—enshrined and honoured and memorialised.

Perhaps this eased the pain for families who had lost their loved ones who never returned from whichever war their country had sent them to. My trailing thoughts led me to the further reflection that while such memorials offered comfort and engendered a national bond of camaraderie, perhaps the tomb I had visited this day was part of a global political trend. A gesture that kept a country's honour intact when the real atrocities of any war might possibly drain away such honour.

While my day had been dedicated to a lone exploration of the city, as the evening began to rise, I had made plans to reunite for dinner with several of my Castle-kid friends (as we who were living at Herstmonceux were fond of calling ourselves). As I rounded the corner of the meeting point, it occurred to me that I had created and experienced a day that encompassed the past and the present with a cast of characters from many nationalities. All my life, I had been an American in America without such stark side-by-side comparisons of what truths I believed, had grown up learning, or even just thought I knew about the current world, its politics, people, and religions.

For the first time, I was an American who had travelled with my Canadian friends through England. Yes, this particular cocktail of nations was all English speaking, Western, and had a strong base of ties to the English monarchy; this was not an abrasive cultural clash. But as far as intermingling with other cultures and nations, these first few weeks in England for me would only serve to be the tip of the iceberg in what would become a lifetime of travel. But I didn't know that yet.

All I knew then was that it had been my first day wandering through a fascinating, new, and (in some places) ancient city.

In London, I had spun off on my own from our coach to fulfil my personal thirst to connect with history and visit the abodes of monarchs and popes from days gone by. Another friend studying political science had chosen to wander through Parliament and visited the home of the Prime Minister. His own career in the ebb and flow of politics and governance loomed ahead, and thus his interest was in the modern-day rulers of England. My roommate, destined for a future in medical school, had a passion for modern art and set off to consume what she could in as many museums as possible before she would become locked into her textbooks and exams. Between us, we had explored British history, religion, modern art, and current politics during our free day in the city of London. We had divided and pursued the knowledge of all the things we loved.

Reunited, we chose a Thai restaurant downtown and dined on pad thai and spring rolls and beer. Afterwards, we went for drinks at a Mexican restaurant called The Texas Embassy. Caught up in the exchange of stories and sharing of sights we had all taken in, we had a few too many beers and missed the last train back to Hersonmonceux. We ended the night by taking a cab with an Indian driver back to an Australian hostel to grab a bed and probably one more beer.

Had I been asked in these early days of my exploration to describe what a night out in London would entail, my stereotypical expectations would have been laughable. All I had known of England had been learned solely from history books and stories. I had yet to modernise my understanding of the power plays between nations or the cultural intertwining of all the nationalities I would eventually come to experience. With my growing knowledge of each war and treaty, and with each cab ride and bar chat, it became plain to see how people and nations tangled themselves amongst each other.

But on this night, these notions were only just beginning to make themselves known to me. I had neither an idea how much I was to learn about the world in my four-month visit to the UK nor that what I would come to learn would only teach me that there was so much still ahead for me to experience and take in.

It was naive, maybe, to believe that I would experience what I expected to experience. But inexperience helps us define our future not at all. Inexperience: the lack of learned knowledge; we all sit in this place at some point in time. It is in this space that we build our first truths. Without exposure, we begin to accept and fear the things that we accept and fear. That acceptance and those fears become beliefs, and our beliefs become our truths.

We live in this way—knowing how we think things are in our world—until something crosses our path to change our paradigm. Until then, we pad our floors and gate our borders and have faith in the personal world we create and believe in, whatever these truths may be for us.

Our personal worlds are usually comfortable, safe, predictable, and calm. But they are small. They are self-defined. They are limiting. They are facades on a small film lot in a big city, in the midst of an even bigger state, inside a country in the not-so-middle of the big, vast world.

These truths define our world as we create it to be, until one day we begin to question our truths. We seek validation of these truths, we seek proof of what we know. We wonder if there is more to understand beyond the truths we have tied together and hold fast to.

And so, we travel.

911

IT HASN'T PROVED POSSIBLE to tell the story of the first four months chronologically. I keep running ahead; the swing of excitement in the retelling of these stories spurs so many tangents. Each vivid, giddy memory grabs my hand and pulls me to the next joyful memory and then to the one after that. The feelings I had then are alive in me now, shaken awake from sharing, each feeling just as full and each thought just as deep as when they first were given life.

While most of my first-time travel experiences are remembered with a jovial spirit and the open, authentic, inexperienced narrative of my youth, there are vivid, painful memories that I can't jaunt past. No one gets through this life unscathed. Most of the lessons we learn in life are not acquired from joyful discoveries, but from unexpected realisations that leave us with a bruise or a scrape on our hearts from the shock of them. These sobering experiences reshape our character, rewrite our stories, and undo who we are as we've understood ourselves to be.

Travel has a way of pulling back our beliefs. We pack our bags and leave on jet planes with eyes and hearts cracked to the seeping in of exposure, learning, and enjoyment. But, if you travel for long enough, if your eyes and heart are more than cracked but fully open enough to truly see, then you begin to view things beyond the expected. You see more parts of a story unfold.

It happens slowly, in tandem with the rush of adventure and shiny discoveries. These lessons that shape and shake us, not always are they delivered with a sharp left hook. Sometimes, they drip slowly into our understanding, stain our ideas and perceptions, and teach us a thing we didn't realise we needed to learn.

On the rocking train rides home or the rolling bus trips through countrysides, looking out over passing pastures dotted with chimney-stacked homes, we learn. We look, and we feel, and we take it all in. Revelations grip our very core, and the rest of "us"—who we were or what we believed—unravels.

~

MY PLANE TOUCHED DOWN in Heathrow on September 6th, 2001. Still adjusting to Britain's Greenwich Mean Time, a solid eight hours ahead of the Pacific, I had been cheating myself of a swift jet lag recovery by succumbing to a nap in my room nearly every day. I'd also come down with a common cold, indulging in meds to ease me through to a place of better health. Consequently, my afternoon naps were the deep, heavy sleep of the ill, drugged and exhausted.

Only a few days after my arrival, I awoke to a severe pounding on my door accompanied by urgent shouting for me to come down to the TV Room. The pounding sent my heart pumping, and even in my jet-lagged, lethargic stupor, the clatter on my door spun me from a dozy sleep into a heightened panic. I heard shouting from the other side of my door...something about...an attack? A plane crash? The words my Canadian friend was shouting from behind the wooden barrier made no sense and became duller as I heard his steps flee from my door and echo down the hall. Still, I picked up my box of Kleenex, foggy, confused, and concerned. I pulled on a hoodie and followed him down the corridor.

The TV room was nothing like the common areas of my undergrad campus years. Instead, this gathering place more closely resembled a dim, stale dungeon. The entire student dormitory was bare and devoid of life, colour, or light to decorate the halls. Only the basics had been erected to house staff and students, leaving the castle itself to be the grand centre attraction and the place we spent most of our time when on the grounds. The TV Room in Bader Hall (the name given the dormitories) was a small, closed room that rested under-ground. The air smelled damp and was laced with the scent of expired cleaning products. It was here, huddled on the dirty, hard floor in a quiet and sombre circle of a dozen or so of my new Canadian friends, that I watched, in real-time, the 9/11 attack on the Twin Towers—on my homeland.

If I hadn't mentioned before, the University I had travelled to the UK with was Queens University, which was based in Kingston, Ontario. I, being an American, was a minority within my cohort. Of the hundred or so students attending a semester abroad at the Castle, I was one of eight or so US-based students. Our perception of the world, our depth of knowledge in global politics—even US politics—was embarrassingly shallow compared to our northern neighbours. We statistically didn't travel as often, and most of my fellow students had travelled a fair share abroad—not only to Europe or the US, but to countries in Africa, South America, Asia, and the Middle East.

My Canadian peers were far more diverse than I was accustomed to, and they hailed from Tanzania, Kenya, the Czech Republic and Malaysia. Their parents and generations before were from Sri Lanka, Romania, and Colombia. They were Muslim, Jewish, Catholic, Buddhist. They were rugby players, pot smokers, writers, athletes, and ambassadors. They had a broader knowledge base of how the world operated outside of a Christian America. I was blond, white, spoke one language, had been California-educated, and my first overseas flight had been to England with this same group of diverse Canadians. Only a few days in, I'd already formed a pattern of learning something new from my fellow students every day, at every meal, and on every bus trip.

Despite their well-rounded experience and our diverse collection of faces, beliefs, and backgrounds, we all sat together, eyes wide and bewildered at the tragedy and panic that played out across the small, crappy television set in the back corner of the room. What we were watching just wasn't fathomable, and it seemed to me—as it did to most who watched the events unfold that day—as if we were watching a drama flick. Chaos on the crowded streets; smoke, black and choking, puffing forcefully from the buildings; reporters stumbling over the heavy words they reported. None of it made any sense.

In those moments, I wasn't able to grasp the enormity of what was happening in New York, the rippling impact this attack would have on the nation's sense of security, or, for years to come, the unwavering trust in our leaders.

A plane? Crashing into the Twin Towers? On purpose?

From the moment I sat on that beaten, dusty floor, jet-lagged and sniffling from a cold, my perception of world politics, of power and money, of my own American government, and the extent of human greed and cruelty began to splinter.

In a room full of 20-something Canadian students, in a 15th-century castle in England, on a continent across the ocean from where I had learned all that I knew about world history, politics, culture, and war, my fundamental truth began to break apart, piece by piece.

Being raised in the South, it's fair to say framing our presidents, soldiers, and veterans as heroes was part of my upbringing. They were fighters in the war on drugs, warriors for a free world, brave leaders of patriots and the US military, comprised of our fathers and brothers (and sisters and mothers). They defended our freedoms and sacrificed themselves for the good of the nation—and everything else we were taught to memorise as children.

For nearly 23 years, I had been spoon-fed one-sided patriotic ideologies and historical events. I had been a student of meagrely taught economics and studied an abridged version of "America the Great." The Land of the Free. The Promised Land. A country we sang about at the start of every school day when I was a kid in the south, attending a Christian school.

I had yet to learn that significant, perspective-shifting facts had been left out or tidied away in US and World History textbooks, where the nitty-gritty truth of opposing forces was not openly displayed for readers to learn and choose sides. I was beginning to understand that what was studied in our history books, absorbed from our media, and memorised from our Bibles offered just one version of the story. What we listened to in our classrooms, learned from the news, or heard shouted down from the pulpit are versions either lacking in enough truth to be an honest whole, or worse, intentionally curated to mislead, divide, and manipulate.

On the 11th of September, as I watched New York's skyline go up in flames, there would also ignite a burning in my mind, a growing understanding, and realisation that would continue to spark embers of new thought from that day, and for the days, months, and years— even the decades to come.

I began to understand that some storytellers were sorrowfully misguided while others knowingly withheld significant plot twists in the story. I do not mean to accuse our teachers, reporters, or preachers of intentionally being sinister or insinuate that they knowingly perpetuate beliefs they understand to be false. Most would likely defend their own words as truth, with good intentions in their heart, and belief in the stories they have been told and are retelling—stories of the goodness in one, the sinfulness in the other; the righteousness of one, the criminality of the other.

Throughout history, our stories have been told to us in this way: from those we have come to respect as an authority. Every nation or people down the ages tells a version of their truth intended for absolute adherence to that belief. Such absolute belief in a story gives it life and power. As I watched the attacks on the Twin Towers, I began to realise the prominence of this behaviour, this blind faith, within my own nation. I began to understand that the stark division between good and evil was not impenetrable. That conflicts are riddled with complexities that are neither good nor evil—usually, they lie somewhere in between. This served to be one of the biggest lessons learned throughout my European travels. It diminished my naivete and continued to mould and shape me even years after the initial onset of this particular teaching.

Until I was 23, I had mostly believed that the US flag represented the good guys. As Americans, we were united in patriotism and Christianity; we honoured family values. But this wasn't necessarily the truth in every sense. With religion, I had questioned authority years ago. As for my place in the world as an American—a representative of a nation heralded as a leader of the free world—over the months following the 9/11 attacks, and eventually, after years of international travel, my conviction in those beliefs began to dissolve. Not in the sense that I abandoned my loyalty to the American people—not at all. But my knowledge broadened in the way that a veil I had been looking through lifted for a moment, and I began to see the vividity of things. Greed, hate, the desire for power, cruelty—the image sharpened, and all its details became crisper. Suddenly, and yet slowly at the same time, America was no different than its enemies and allies when it came to political rule.

I understand now, and did also to some extent then, that America is not the only country guilty of lunging for world power. It was only that I was just then beginning to realise the faults, the imperfections, and the chess-like strategies of nations—including my own. Most countries would, of course, prefer their own version of history and their political past to be written in a brighter light in the pages of textbooks and news articles. Admittedly, my own education reflects this lack of revealing the whole narrative of the US, our national crimes, our political mistakes, and our dastardly deeds.

As young American students, we often took the spoon that was offered to us. Sometimes trustingly and blindly, other times without choice. But the timing in which I first ventured away from the States proved to reframe my patriotism. I might never have woken up to my sheltered and slanted worldview had I not been jolted awake by the pounding on my door beckoning me to come to watch the Twin Towers fall during my first several days in this new and unfamiliar country.

As it turned out, the first four months post-9/11 were spent learning about current political and international events through the lens of British media. Journalism, rising from newsrooms in the UK and Europe, outlined political viewpoints discussed and analysed around the lunch table over fish and chips by my politically savvy Canadian friends whose knowledge of the American political system and its players was greater than that of most Americans. That is how I learned about the deeper and broader significance of 9/11—what we think really happened, and what it really meant for our local and global communities. I learned about the international ties, economic connections, and power-fueled choices in history that led to this tragedy.

Ironically, it was through an act of war against America that I began to understand the never-ending power play between nations. Was it planned? Conspiracy theories still abound. Immediately, the US launched its soldiers into the Iraq war and the fight for freedom (fuel), destroying terrorism and weapons of mass destruction (who were the terrorists?) began. I watched from afar as Americans became united more than ever before, suffering from PTSD, the trauma, the shock, and the loss.

I remember one particular bus trip to London soon after the attack. The line of British citizens who showed up to sign the Book of Condolences at the US Embassy in Grosvenor Square wrapped thickly around the block. Unending sympathy and compassion for the American people poured out warm-heartedly from the British. I might have judged and begun to doubt any altruistic nature of the US government during these months, but my faith in people, regardless of their nationality, grew.

It was then, at the sight of that line, that it occurred to me that living Americans had never experienced an attack on their own homeland. There had been Pearl Harbor sixty years prior, but somehow that felt different. Hawai'i, though one of the fifty states, is geographically removed. It's so far out into the ocean and so very far from the soil beneath the majority of Americans' feet.

The difference now was that on 9/11, New Yorkers were going about their normal day. They were getting coffee to go, rushing for the elevator, the hurried clicking of heels on the tile while doing business on their cell phones. It was a bright, blue-skied Tuesday. The planes hit then. There, on American soil—in Manhattan. And as if the tremble of an earthquake shook the entire country from coast to coast, Americans fell victim. We went to war.

On walking trips through London and excursions through Sussex and Kent, war dugouts for marksmen and cement pillboxes that had once hidden soldiers in past world wars dotted the hillsides. Town squares and main highways celebrate past victories with copper and bronze statues of soldiers, captains, and political heroes. All of these serve as reminders of a war fought on their land. Churches and cathedrals had been bombed during the Blitz. Homes had been destroyed, and families had been slain. War was not history but a recent memory in the UK. The US had flown our soldiers to another land, waving flags of red, white, and blue. We erected bandstands and hosted BBQs in memoriam. "We" fought a fight that only the soldiers saw up close—some of whom were fortunate enough to have returned to the safe haven of our unravaged, American soil.

There have been books written about 9/11 that will cover far greater depth and breadth than I intend to do in these pages. I mean only to be transparent with the sudden and permanent shift in my perspective of American identity, world politics, and calibre of a people—all of this triggered by four hijacked planes.

Months later, at the end of my first round of travels to the UK, I flew home just in time for the winter holidays. When I arrived "home," speeding down the 91 freeway and looking out the window at the passing commercial buildings, I found myself genuinely shocked at the patriotism being flaunted. Red, white, and blue flags flew unapologetically from the top of every building. They were pressed up into every window and stuck to every car bumper. *America the Great! War on Terrorism!*

I didn't understand. It felt to me that the US media had blind-folded its citizens and patted their heads in a calming manner. The headlines fueled the rage and injustice that 9/11 had ignited by whispering for fatherly vengeance on terrorists in the name (or under the guise) of freedom. And I could see it had worked. Family and friends' comments on terrorism reflected a menace I didn't align with. Their opinions seemed to lack a questioning or research for the truth that my British news journals proffered.

While 9/11 was a tragedy, whether a conspiracy or act of war, the movements of the US afterwards, and how this power play was exposed, analysed, discussed, and denounced in non-US media had ignited within me a new consideration of the role of American jour-nalism. I began to devour the media that positioned itself in a place of power to maturely and intelligently call out national leaders. I began to read the words of journalists who exposed and questioned author-ity, and urged the common people to look closer, think critically, ask questions, and rally against violent, inhumane actions. I learned then how the media can manipulate a story and tamper with the telling of facts to lead readers to adhere to specific political agendas.

Perhaps this is something many people come to understand when they reach a certain age or witness a horrific event. I sup-pose we all start off believing in the altruistic intentions of our own country until something unthinkable happens to spark doubt and plant questions.

Regardless, having experienced 9/11 while travelling in the UK sparked that doubt in me. Because I had not been subjected to the same version of news stories and discussions that most of my family, friends, and fellow Americans had, my understanding of good and evil, patriots and terrorists, heroes and villains had irreversably altered.

Pockets Filled With Rocks

MANY OF THE SITES in Sussex lured me in solely because my years of study had created a familiarity with them. Because my Bachelor's was in English Literature, travelling through England was a trip to the motherland—the homestead of Keats, Byron, Wordsworth. I had first been captivated by the beauty and truth in their written words and then by their personal histories. Their lives had been tragedies, or episodes of wild intrigue, or foundations of ageless wisdom. Their poetry and prose, their passions and purposes—their life stories drew me in. Writing essays in college and analysing their literary feats wasn't enough; I wanted to witness where their personal plotlines had meandered.

But there was something more than experiencing the physicality of it all. Something more than securing a snapshot of myself smiling next to a dated plaque on an old cottage.

On many occasions, visiting the preserved homes of historical figures or authors became moments when I stepped into another person's timeline and was able to get a glimpse of their story. Those were moments when I learned something about life or love or death that wasn't like anything I had encountered in my own young life. In a way, their learned lessons had something to teach me. Their experiences, victories, and losses had been preserved, studied, heralded, and pitied. When such a figure from the past has lived in a way that their stories outlast their own human lives, there is something there to take note of—a lesson we can watch unfold from a distance, and truths we can tuck away until our time comes to live these moments ourselves.

This is what happened for me on a simple afternoon visit to Virginia Woolf's house. The 20th Century author and feminist's fiction and poetry had woven their way into my studies. Her home, Monk's House, a 16th-century cottage cosied away in the heart of Sussex, had become a museum embraced by gardens, orchards, and hills.

Inside the cottage, I walked amongst her everyday things. I took notice of her small wooden chair, the turquoise walls, the shelves stacked with weathered books, and of course, her writing desk. It was all so movingly simple. The words that had been crafted by pen on paper, words that would earn her a reputation for centuries to come as a pioneer in English literature—so many of those words had come into existence on this simple desk. The realness and smallness of the space humanised her while still humbling me. I observed the tidiness of the rooms, the aged blemishes on the creamy green walls. Great works arose from such tiny spaces.

I peeked into her "room of one's own." I ate an apple off her tree in the garden and looked across the bright green lawns at the cement bust marking the place her ashes were buried. The hardened face was drawn, long and serious, cut off at the shoulders. Below was a plaque honouring her memory and engraved with words from one of her novels.

"Death is the enemy. [. . .] Against you I will fling myself
unvanquished and unyielding, O Death!"

While strolling through the gardens and appreciating fully the idyllic panorama of her hillside view and the bubbling river in the distance that twisted through the green landscape, the reality of Virginia Woolf's fate began to sink into my mind like a wave breaking on the shore.

It's one feeling to show up to a celebrity's house, bubbling with high spirits and eager to peer into their home-turned-museum. It's another experience entirely when the joyful flow of the visit quickly shifts, and the current picks up speed, spilling you from star-struck wonder into their harsh reality. You are pulled under, into the hidden depths of their life, the personal intricacies of their mind, their thoughts and emotions. It's the moment you realise the truth of their story—the story not read in their fictional pages or portrayed in tourist centres. It's a weighted feeling, a drop in your stomach when your energy merges with another's, and you enter the physical space that had once held the last pieces of their life.

In my mind, an empathetic struggle gradually emerged as confusion of what had gone wrong and a clearer understanding of what the writer suffered behind her words began to surface.

That she had chosen to end her own life was something I had learned from my studies. She hadn't been dead for all that long in 2001 when I visited; maybe 50 years. Of all my favourite British writers, she had lived the closest to my own timeline. I knew she had suffered all her life, and when personal tragedies weren't the cause, her depression played its part in creating daily strife and unhappiness. She had married, written, and rebelled against the confines of her era until it all became too much for her and she ended her suffering herself.

What I hadn't known before is that she did it by filling her pockets with rocks and stones. She walked across the tangled, grassy field, towards that same twisted river I had been admiring from her garden. She didn't set her rocks down. Instead, she threw herself into the river and drowned.

I'm not sure why this method of ending one's life jolted me so much. Perhaps it was because it seemed so uncommon a choice while also frighteningly easy for anyone to choose to do. Perhaps because such a tragedy existed in a place of tranquil beauty. Perhaps it was because any struggle would have gone on unseen beneath the surface, or because the place she had gazed upon often from her wooden desk, in the ebb and flow of her writing—a place of peace and inspiration where the river flowed with joy and calm—became her chosen place of death. These thoughts, like stones, piled high in my mind while looking over the breezy slopes.

The twist I found most saddening was discovering she was 59 years old when she made this choice. Fifty-nine years old.

She'd lived in London during World War I, and her family homes had been damaged and lost during the Blitz. She'd suffered great losses as her parents, protectors, and friends had died too young. She'd suffered years of sexual abuse at the hands of her half-brothers and was institutionalised many times when what was then deemed "madness" took over her mind either alongside or because of these traumas.

Still, she wrote and rebelled, suffered and recovered, sunk and swam until one day she couldn't anymore. As is the tragic ending of so many creatives, suicide was the only way she could end her pain.

Sixty years later, as I explored her home and items, I began to connect with her suffering on a different level than I had when I had merely read her books. She was intelligent and creative but shackled by her position as an affluent woman in the late 19th and early 20th centuries. She'd been immersed in the intellectual culture of high society but had a limited ability to garner respect, and of course, back then, women's rights were minimal, and support for them was virtually non-existent. How trapped she must have felt. How unseen and unheard, even with the success and fame she experienced during her lifetime. It seemed to me an uphill struggle with a heaviness that went unacknowledged.

At 23, my only knowledge of suicidal individuals was that they crossed these troubled waters in their turbulent teen years when we morph from childhood to adulthood, navigating our emotions, hormones, and relationships with very few tools. Some of us just don't make it. It had never occurred to me that those of us who get so far into adulthood—59 years in—would still struggle.

And yet there, standing quietly in a blooming garden, among roses and lilies in the pond and fruitful apple trees, there was her small writing lodge, a prettied-up shed with all her writing things carefully placed inside. It seemed like life should finally have been so peaceful for her. But she had chosen to die anyway.

I began to rethink how exactly it was I thought our human lives played out, and what human survival had meant to me up until that point. I guess I had figured that if a person could overcome hardships—if we could make it past adolescence and its physiological changes and gripping insecurities; if we could make it past college and the first years of adulting through the trail of "failures" we all leave behind; if we could make it through the midlife panic attacks and other crises that come to ride side-saddle to our joys—if we could reach an age where we made it past all of that, then we'd be set. We would have made it. We would have figured out how to manoeuvre through our life until the victorious end.

Giving up at 59, to me, seemed an age too close to finally finding peace. The 50s, to my twenty-something mind, should be the years when we finally achieve wisdom and inner calm. Where the slowing down of time is something appreciated and a way of living that delights. Fifty-nine seemed to me an age when the complexities of the world would finally untangle themselves and make sense, or when we'd be able to navigate through the confusing rapids using the skills and experience we'd learned along the way. It seemed to be that those who had reached 59 could be someone who teens and twenty-somethings would look up to for help and reassurance that our troubles would fade and that, eventually, everything would be all right.

I never realised that people could give up hope at 59—that suicide could be a fate you finally tired from outrunning.

It disturbed me so deeply as I walked away from the quaint, half-hidden cottage. I turned over in my mind the truths that had been revealed to me from this visit: the truths embedded in the sadness and fame of just one life, in the beauty and tragedy, and in the small and finite lives we all live.

Wild World

ONE OF THE THINGS a traveller can't help but do is wander. Our feet take us further, further, and then still further, little by little, until we either arrive where we intended or become lost beyond hope. Or until we are just done wandering.

For most trips, our destinations are pins on maps. But often, it's the accidental journey, the roads we didn't mean to go down, that wind up giving us more than we'd charted. These side alleyways, wrong turns, and detours challenge us with the unanticipated or reward us with unexpected delights far more enriching for the soul. Often, our wrong turns turn out to be the roads we were meant to take all along.

Each day of those first few months in England was packed so tightly with discoveries in quaint villages, spectacular city sights, and random hallway chats in the dormitory with the Canadians I seemed to bond with more tightly each passing day. We laughed while visiting Oxford, punting in unstable boats in the scenic university setting. We felt the same smallness in London museums displaying huge paintings and marble statues from centuries past. Our maps failed us as we happily lost ourselves in the vast, chaotic maze of local markets, the joy heightened by the bustling excitement of haggling, or the variety of seasoned curiosities that captivated our attention. Many of our days in the city were limited, giving us only a handful of hours to cram with as many sights and discoveries as possible. But just as much as the locations and events highlighted and crammed into our itineraries, I treasured the free-time wanders—the space in between our to-do's where we had no plan at all and were free to wander where we pleased.

One particular free evening exploring the city stands out

in my memory. The hour was nearing midnight, and most of the London pubs had closed. People were criss-crossing walkways and roving about in the streets, many singing drunkenly as they hailed taxis or stumbled underground to catch the Tube home.

I was somewhere near Covent Garden, wandering with my roommate, when I heard him. The husky, soft, and deep voice of a late-night street musician—a large, dark-skinned man wearing a wide-brimmed, black cowboy hat. He was strumming his guitar to a dwindling audience in the darkened square and singing a favourite Cat Stevens song—*Ooh baby, baby, it's a wild world*—with a slight smile on his face, looking only at his strings as he played.

I remember hearing the low, calming chords of his voice drifting through the chilly night air. My wine-infused breath quickened as the notes blew gently over the stones where I stood. The music filled the space and lingered in the air. In those moments where time ticked slower, the music was more than a sound in my ears, more than a passing beat or nod. Those chords as he strummed, the baritone of his voice, and the words of his song scooped up the magic of the evening. They enveloped the memories in the making, the deeper meaning of my own wandering that I was still just beginning to understand—not just the walk through Covent Garden, but the wandering that had led me to this midnight spot where the musician on the street played his songs. I was listening not from my ears but from my heart, and as each note was played, my soul felt more and more completely at home.

His song fit the mood just so perfectly. It was the kind of moment that, whenever I hear the song again, so many years later in life, my mind returns to that one specific moment when the musical bars in a line held the magic of that moment together. The crisp, cool lateness of night, the shared laughs and wine with new friends who already meant so much to me. The freedom in our agenda that evening created space for late-night wanders, and in that moment, "Wild World" became a song that will forever transport me back to that period in time—that specific moment.

Every once in a while, time slows down. It slows for those who slow down, too, and truly feel it—the present moment in all its stillness, all its beauty. Within the whirl of nighttime lights and clatter and blur, there exist these hovering moments of magic, of beauty, of calm where stillness completely fills even the busiest of spaces. These are moments that connect us by the heart.

Looking back, we were moving so fast through our days, seizing every opportunity to sign up for a tour or plan excursions every few days, or immersing ourselves as fully as we could in each different place: Dark nooks of old, ivy-cloaked churches or the vast, lordly cathedrals of each new English city, the museums and markets. We slept almost never but remained energised by the momentum and stimulated by every sight and sound. We moved with energy and curiosity as twenty-somethings set free and far from home tend to do. The return date for our flights seemed so carelessly far away.

However, as we moved collectively through the days, the calm and peace between the movements found me. During those evenings, I'd walk the warmly lit streets, straying a little behind my group to soak up the hum of passing taxis and double-decker buses ending their shift, eavesdrop on the passing British accents, and side-step beggar pigeons on the walk. I'd feel the light rain on my hair and the cool breeze on my ears and listen to the songs from the streets with my soul. With each street musician picking guitar strings or playing the saxophone, I would tip my head back to look up at the lights, the towering monuments on street corners—statues of monarchs, horses, or cherubs—and I would feel so incredibly full and happy to be where I was that I could just cry.

It was more joy and freedom than I ever thought I would experience.

While I had chosen to travel and take a sidetrack that wound me through British adventures across the pond, there was a life I had stepped aside from back in the States.

This life, including all of its players and carefully laid plans, had kept its momentum moving forward in my absence. The semester schedules, the American holidays, the family weekend BBQs, the future I had agreed to with my partner—moving in together and planning a wedding after I had travelled a bit and tired the travel bug "out of my system." The narrative I had started back in the States remained punctuated and expectant for my return. I was going to rejoin this carved-out path close to Christmas, packed with stories and gifts collected from my trip overseas, and kick off the New Year by settling comfortably into a life ready to unfold for me.

Looking back, I can see uncertainty rippling toward me like an unseen thing from the deep. The life I'd left behind in the States reached out for me, tried to touch base, to stay connected on the line.

The stories I retold through emails and calls to family and my partner were received with a blend of excitement for me and the new experiences I was having, and concern for the calls made when I was suffering through homesickness. There was also, from some, a growing uneasiness with the way I had delved in and worn this new life abroad so fittingly. It stirred up mild alarm in those who expected and wanted me back home.

My partner's future was clearly wrapped up tightly with where my future was headed, and the general vibe my US family was feeling from me generated the same unanswered question in their minds: Was I coming home? After one particularly lively and open-hearted email retelling one of my many joyous tales to my mother, I received the following email in return from her:

Again I can't emphasize what a fabulously gifted storyteller you are. You will be a phenomenal teacher and author one day. I am sure your vacation/educational experience will augment your life. Please keep everything in your heart—while all of this is wonderful, it isn't real life. I worry about you being so far away with the world in such a desperate situation.

Remember: What you are experiencing is great and life changing and horizon expanding, but it's not everyday. Life is lived in the everyday.

Her words rang true but at the same time were not true at all.

What I was experiencing was great and horizon-expanding and would prove to be life-changing in just about every way a life can be changed. And she was right; life is lived in the everyday.

But hadn't I been doing just that since I stepped off the plane?

I was living every single day even more fully than I ever had before. I had broken rules and routine, living for four months in a different country—in a castle, no less. I wasn't sleepwalking through those days, even if it did seem a dream at times. It was because I knew the clock was ticking on my own time there that I said yes to every possible adventure. I dug in deep to each opportunity, absorbed as much as I could from each historic landmark, each castle and cathedral, each pub crawl and conversation in different accents, believing it was the last time I'd ever have the chance to see these fantastic sights and do all I was doing with abandon. *Imagine if we lived our entire lives this way.*

No. Mom was right with her words, but what she missed—what anyone misses if they don't set out and explore for themselves—is how a different version of life can fit so much better than the life we've set out from. Mom didn't think my life in the UK was *real* because it didn't fit the pattern that anyone who knew me was used to. But the truth was this: I had never felt more alive in my life. Life felt more real to me than ever.

Dormant parts on my inside lit up in ways I had no idea were possible. I knew it was important to keep a firm grip on realistic expectations and on who mattered in the version of real-life I chose. But that didn't mean I couldn't make a new choice or that something else in my everyday couldn't feel and become more real than I ever imagined.

Back then, it was a struggle for my mom to understand, and I don't know that my partner waiting for me back in the States ever understood either. In addition to wedding plans, he and I had a dog, shared an almond-coloured fridge, had shopped for diamond rings, and a California condo awaiting more of my furniture. The ties I had kept to life in the States were still strung, but with each passing day, they were stretched tight and straining.

Mike flew out to spend a week with me at some point in October. My journals go quiet during the week he was there. It felt strange to stay with him in his room at the castle, instead of in my own room I shared with Dee. When he arrived, he either joined my new friends at the pub or the dining hall—a dynamic that was wedged in rather than comfortably buttoned—or, I sat with only him and felt the absence of joy that being in the company of my friends had been giving me.

I felt I was missing my life in the UK when my life from the States came to visit. I hadn't expected it, but his arrival—this import-ant person from the life across the Atlantic merging with the seedling life I was starting to grow across the pond—clashed with my life in the castle.

During his visit, we couldn't identify exactly why it felt so hard to be reunited. We couldn't properly talk about it. But we felt it. Our conversations were more often arguments. As I tried to share with him the joys and discoveries I found quaint and charming in the UK, he ridiculed me in the disdainful way Americans are often reputed for when travelling. I cried every day.

It was a strange collision of emotions. I had talked him up to my new friends, missed him terribly in the weeks I had been gone, but I was falling in love with this new life so rapidly and fully, it was hard to see where he or any love I had for him would fit. On the day of his arrival, I couldn't get to the airport fast enough. But when I saw his face emerge from the crowd in the terminal, somehow it was shocking to see him there as a part of this world. The out-of-placeness felt icy sharp. There was a weirdness about it, and even more strangeness in that being with him left me feeling off-centred.

His visit was only for a week, but it was a trying week. Rather than a joyous reunion, we realised with each day's miscommunication and disappointment that our relationship didn't connect the way we thought it had. In fact, each day's fights led us to believe we were breaking up. We could not align with each other as we seemingly had just a couple of months before.

During his visit, our entire group had planned to visit Canterbury Cathedral, about 90 minutes southeast of London. Rather than journey with everyone else on the bus, as per usual, Mike and I made our own way there by train, intending to stay the night and head back to the castle on our own the next day.

Our day in Canterbury was glum. Before his arrival, I had been excited to visit this particular cathedral for the first time and share this with him as part of my weekend excursions with my fellow students. However, I remember feeling apart from the group, which left my emotions disoriented and lost. Not because I couldn't navigate on my own, but because our experiences were not shared that day, which was an unusual feeling.

My studies in English Literature meant that Canterbury was an incredibly special Pilgrimage for me. As the site of historical events and the location of a favourite piece of literature that I had studied extensively and would eventually teach, I knew this would be a highlight on my trip. Visiting Canterbury was an experience I had looked forward to so much leading up to it—one that I had, at one time, been ecstatic to share with Mike since his visit coincided with this planned excursion.

We arrived at Canterbury Cathedral after dark. There is something magical about arriving at night to places. Somehow, things feel different shrouded in the night. A place is calmer, quieter. A place feels more strongly of itself when no one is around to crack the air with an intrusive shout or shatter the shadow with a camera flash.

Canterbury Cathedral struck me as ominous yet welcoming and warm. It was magnificent in its beauty. Its huge arches and pillars and stained-glass windows, carved with such intricate and endless detail, were so lovely in the lamplight. Dark and shadowy, but light and spacious all at once.

No one was around when we arrived. Of all the cathedrals I had seen in each English city and would come to see in all the countries I would eventually travel to throughout the world, Canterbury Cathedral struck me differently. It was less intimidating and glittery than St. Paul's, but no less impressive. Maybe it felt this way because I arrived in the night. Maybe because my first glance down the cloisters and corridors was when I was alone and the solitude, the quiet felt precious to me. Maybe because the only noise was my own footsteps on the stones. Maybe it was all these things. Canterbury just felt different. I was enthralled.

While exploring the cathedral was personally a peak experience when in England, Canterbury illuminated just how flattened my romantic relationship with Mike had become. His travel experience included him wanting to take photos of me posing by the gates of the Cathedral. I preferred to experience the cathedral by walking along the corridors in the shadows alone.

For him, he could see historical landmarks, think they were cool, and snap a photo. But for me, I was *in* them. I felt the energy and presence of these aged places in my bones—the ghosts of past lovers walking along the transepts and alleys, the wars fought outside the walls and murders bloodying the stones, the manuscripted verses telling tales that would repeat themselves throughout history, the vaulted cloisters and slabs of stone halls imprinted and dented into smooth hollows on the floor from centuries of hurried steps and solemn prayers.

After our fights, I spent time in my head trying to sift through what it was that was real. My relationship and plans in the States had been real—the homemaking, the wedding, the white picket fence life with a dog and kids, eventually. The organised containment of it all contrasted so starkly with the experiences I was having now.

After Mike left to return to the States and wait another seven or eight weeks for me, I thought it would all be okay. I thought we had just hit a speed bump too fast and that I had been caught up—like my mother warned—in a life that wouldn't shape-shift into the reality waiting for me back home. But deep down, I knew. My every day in England was real too, and I had trouble configuring all of those living and much-loved parts into the same life.

It was too much. There were too many pieces now that just couldn't fit into the current picture, and I knew I had to choose which pieces I would keep.

~

I HAD ONLY BEEN wandering for a couple of months on my travels. But that was enough. My feet or a plane could only take me so far.

Between my feet walking the streets of London, and the mechanical wings spanning across the wide salty pond, my heart had begun to wander wider than either feet or planes could ever hope to travel.

With each day that passed, my heart had begun to catch glimpses of an invitingly different future, where unseen labyrinths beckoned, hidden pleasures and spikey pains awaited. With each moment and each new experience during my travels overseas, the depths of my learning drilled deeper. My heart had begun to grow within my chest and beat with increased vivacity.

It mattered not at all if this experience was a pub lunch in the grassy downs, an afternoon dazzled by the glittering heights of St. Paul's, laughing and learning in a bubbling exchange with my Canadian expatriates, or a melodic, lone walk down the lanes. Each moment was vibrant in its shiny newness, hardening beautifully into precious stones and glossy pearls I knew were for me to keep.

And so, I exchanged my diamond for those pearls.

Cry on the Plane

THE STIRRING HAD GONE deeper than my bones; it went into my soul. The twinkly brightness of it all lit up places inside me that I never even knew were dimmed. In those four months, there had been an awakening. New folds of learning were endlessly piled before me as my former understanding became a thing outgrown with the undoing of long-held truths: Cathedrals still held holiness, even if religion did not; politics could be trendy; hope can be lost at any age; American governments are not always so great; I was not in love.

But in that unravelling, I'd come to see there was so much more beauty and life in the world for me to experience than I had ever imagined. Castles were real, I would find (and lose) Spanish Zebras, and time had revealed itself to be a beautiful blend of infinite impermanence.

It was as if I had peeked through a doorway I had always been curious about and was instantly welcomed into a room abundant with bright faces and beckoning possibilities. But the first door was just the beginning. Behind one door, I would find an open, vast, high-ceilinged room lined with even more elegantly carved doors of every colour and design, each bidding a turn of the handle and a promising venture within. I just couldn't wait.

The entire four-month trip had begun with weekend excursions and snapshots of monuments and castles. As I'd roamed and traipsed and wandered through the semester, the excursions took me farther from the castle, out past the pastures of moo-cows, into the city's medieval and modern mazes, and still farther beyond the country's borders. During those four short months, I also travelled to Ireland, to France, to Belgium. I flew to Scotland—twice. I dined on haggis, waffles, escargot and knocked back countless pints of Guinness.

My fellow students-turned-friends and I took the train, a plane, a bus and the chunnel. With every few passing days, I realised my photos would reveal more of the people I had grown to love than the places I had longed to see.

As the semester came to a close, I crammed every minute of every day with every possible experience. I shivered through my second trip to Scotland in December to view Loch Ness. I sat in the shuttle for one more visit to the seashores of Brighton, one more coach trip to London, one more pint in a pub, one more song on the street.

My roommate Dee and I had branded ourselves as two girls who were going to live life wide awake. We were going to do, see, taste, hear, touch and feel as much as we could while we were alive. "Sleep when we're dead" became our mantra and our daily vow. We nearly drove ourselves into an early grave, we did so much and slept so little.

By the final week of our trip, we were living not only by our original motto, but had added "cry on the plane" to round it off. We were so determined to spend every single moment awake and alive and feeling all the joy in the moments that we could. Yes, we decided; we could cry on the plane, alone in our seats, lifting into the clouds above Heathrow, hours after we had left our castle for good, grieving for all we had left behind. But we would not waste a single moment's joy while it was here to be had.

And so we did just that. We drank. We took long train journeys and danced in cosy pubs and wrote our stories furiously and messily into our journals and laughed until we cried and loved wholeheartedly every last bit of it. We hugged hard and long everyone we gave a goodbye to in those last days. On our final night, we had again stayed up all night, refusing to sleep through any of these final moments—moments of being with those who had come to mean so much to us, moments we wanted to always remember.

We wanted to grasp forever the eye-opening, life-changing experiences that would bond us and create lifelong friendships— the kind of friendships that cement when people have undergone a pivotal, personal transformation that each bore witness to for the others. The trajectory had changed for so many of us who had collectively experienced this together—the travel, the learning, the threading together of new truths.

At Heathrow, we were dropped off one by one in our terminals. It happened to work out that Dee and I were the last two standing after everyone else had been seen to their gates. Our separate gates were just next to each other, so we were able to walk with each other as close to the other's plane as was possible. Finally, we had to board those planes and say goodbye.

On the plane, in my seat, I wrote feverishly into my journal, thinking about the final laughs and tears and memories and songs I had shared with the inspiring people I had met in the most incredible places. I didn't want to forget a thing—not a place, not a face, not a chat, not a moment. It had all meant so much to me. The cathedrals and palaces and memorials and lanes and pubs and the stories were all so wondrous. The castle, the cows, the ducks, the village pubs, the Canadians, all the travel, in every kind of way—the sum of all of these small parts had created a new heartstring connection to a life I hadn't ever thought existed.

And so, on the plane, I cried. So. Many. Tears. I cried for all I was saying goodbye to, for all that I had learned. I cried for all the truths undone and for all that I had to return to, the life that didn't seem to fit me anymore. For the explanations I would have to try to give, the hollowness I already felt and the guilt that draped itself over every bit of reasoning I anticipated offering to others.

Not every conversation I planned to carry when I touched down in the States would be complicated. The joy I found in travel, in self-discovery, in learning so many of the ways that life can hand you treasures? That, I knew, would be effortless to explain. Those stories would dance off my tongue. The energy around them would be contagious and shining.

It was the inevitable cutting of cords I knew was coming that I dreaded. The hurt and disappointment my choices would cause others. I cried for this too.

I pulled my sleeping mask over my eyes in hopes that no other passengers or flight attendants would notice the fat, silent tears that began to fall. But the tears only wet the mask, soaking it through, and dripped in streams down across my cheeks anyway.

I was so sad to go.

It was only an eight-hour flight, but decisions were made in that short time that would change the course of my life. By the time the plane landed, I knew this would not be the end of my travels; rather, this was just the start.

I would return for more.

Queen's University newspaper of record since 1969   March 24, 2003   Vol. XXXIV No. 6

QUEEN'S GAZETTE

A jewel in the crown P8

Is this a just war? P5

FORUM

March 24, 2003   Queen's Gazette   Page 7

Learning comes to life outside castle walls

There is a castle that stands well guarded and enforced, pitted with narrow windows, allowing only room for an eye and an arrow, overlooking a murky moat. Perhaps long ago, knights galloped here, and wispy-haired maidens looked dreamily out its towers. Servants walked its candlelit corridors and dirty dogs dozed on the damp stone floors. Long ago, this castle was a manor, a fortress, and a smuggler's lair.

How the days have changed it. Fog rolls in from the surrounding moors, and as it retreats, it unveils the castle as something new.

The 15th-century brick castle no longer houses upper-class English families as it did in days of old. The vine-covered ramparts are the same, the drawbridge still spans the moat, but the lords and ladies that haunt the cloisters have changed faces. Today, it is home to a community of more than 200 people from more than 12 countries.

The International Study Centre now resides at Herstmonceux Castle and serves as a place where students from varied backgrounds can spend several months of their academic life. Here, students from countries including Canada, the United States, Mexico, Belgium, Trinidad, Kenya, Pakistan, Iran, Russia, Japan, and the Czech Republic can begin or continue their studies.

These students are whisked away almost every weekend on trips to London, Oxford or Cambridge. Day trips are offered to Stonehenge, Bath, Canterbury, and Portsmouth. Week-long trips to Edinburgh, Brussels, and Paris are carefully planned to enhance the stu-

CHRISTY NICHOLS

Notes From Herstmonceux

dents' education, and they are also given opportunities to visit Dublin and Cardiff.

They visit ancient monuments and historical landmarks, and can stand in the grass and smell the faint scent of battles fought ages ago. They can admire the brush strokes of Turner and Picasso, and read through glass the inky pages of Shakespeare's folios. Lessons are taught within the castle walls and brought to life outside of them.

Beyond studies, students mingle with locals in the small surrounding villages. Pubs within walking distance are frequented, and a minibus service provides a regular commute into the towns of Rye, Eastbourne, Lewis, and Battle.

Not only are students from a host of foreign backgrounds introduced to English living, they are introduced to Sussex. These students volunteer in neighbouring schools, borrow books from nearby university libraries, produce plays to raise money for local charities, and take part in darts competitions at cosy pubs.

At a castle concert, an elderly English woman sits beside a

young politics major, listening to the melody of operatic notes resounding through the ballroom and out the window into the shadowy courtyard.

Herstmonceux Castle does more than build bridges between English and foreign customs. The 153 students who make their home at the ISC not only experience what the lapping banks of the Thames, the windy London streets, and the sweeping English hills have to offer, they also have a chance to learn more about each other, and acquire a faint taste of the vast number of cultures that make up our world. At the ISC, Canadian and Czech citizens eat a lunch of curry and papadums with Belgium and Mexican students; Pakistani women stroll through the castle's rose gardens and chat with the English gardeners; Japanese students form study groups with African classmates, and Russian natives are introduced to Scottish whisky and highland dancing.

The clashing of cultures may still be as loud as the clashing of swords, but the coming together of peoples is peaceful at Herstmonceux Castle. The souls that now wander these corridors learn as much from each other as they do from their surroundings. Education here is enriching and exciting, and the exchange of knowledge and tradition proves invaluable not only in England, but also outside these castle walls.

Christy Nichols is a former student at the International Study Centre at Herstmonceux Castle in Herstmonceux, England, who returned to work this year as a don.

The Island Buffaloes

AS THE STORY GOES, a herd of wild buffaloes were once ferried across choppy ocean waters to be part of an island movie set back in the 1920s. They performed their duties as adornments to the landscape; and then afterward, they were all left behind by the film crew.

The buffalo is a creature of myth and abundance. They were the sacred life force of the Native American tribes and the symbols of survival and courage.

With shaggy, thick-horned manes, and towering up to 6 feet tall, the buffalo was built to travel wide and far. They thunder as they roam in mighty, mighty packs across the plains. And when the torrential summer thunderstorms descend across their valleys, they don't seek shelter, or patiently wait it out. The buffalo know there is only one quick way to get through a downpour.

They turn their heads towards the dark, howling sky and they run straight through the storm.

This particular pack who were left behind have been thriving in the Pacific for nearly 100 years. A herd of about 600 now, they freely graze and roam the hills of Catalina Island. An island laced with palm trees and circled by marinas and dockside bars is the least likely place to find these beasts, meandering lazily amongst the dry hills.

They live in warm weather and have never experienced snow or the kind of bone-deep cold their thick coarse fur is meant to protect them from.

They breathe in the salty breeze and yellow sunshine through their noses, tourists snapping selfies from the road.

I don't know if they feel an instinctual longing to stretch their muscular legs across a dusty grassland, without a scent of sea salt in the air. I don't know if they feel at all grateful to live without the threat of wolves, or hunters. I don't know if they miss the songs and dances that had praised them for centuries or the artwork of their likeness coloured upon cave walls.

I don't know if they grow tired of the sameness of their small population and yearn for new buffalo faces at all. Or if perhaps they feel smugly privileged living exotically with their ocean views.

The story of the island buffalo living out their days in tropical sunshine sticks with me because while it's not their natural habitat, they made it their home anyway. They were built to travel but found themselves vibing with the island life.

As any traveller knows, we can adapt to our surroundings with relative ease if we choose. Even if the new surroundings weren't what was anticipated at all, or if the weather is strikingly unfamiliar.

Even if the surroundings are absurd.

Buffaloes roaming a small island in the Pacific? Whoever heard of such a ridiculous notion? If there exists such a thing as island buffaloes, then there might as well be such things as foxes hunting along pebbled beaches and zebras living wildly in Spain.

Sometimes when two perfect panoramas are combined, such as an island bobbing in the ocean, or a pack of musty migrating land mammals, the result is something extraordinary. Something unusual and unexpected, but also curious and pleasing.

Thinking about the island buffalo incites in me a joyful eagerness to know what else this world has hidden in its pockets.

From their story comes the pleasure of discovering something unexpected.

As many of us travellers have discovered when finding ourselves in new places, unexpected relocation isn't always a bad or a hard thing, but a place where one can stay. A place where one can thrive.

Perhaps these buffalo thrived living a life unexpected. Perhaps they found a life where they no longer needed to run through storms.

PART TWO

Recharting the Map

The United Kingdom
2002

The Castle, the UK, & Beyond

HERSTMONCEUX HAD STOOD FOR over 500 years, so in the eight months I had been gone, the castle hadn't changed too much.

I arrived back to my red brick towers and duck-filled moat, this time for a year, in the guise of a student advisor.

With the incoming cohort of students I was in charge of, we created exciting itineraries for each weekend excursion and travelled to London, Ireland, and Scotland. Again. We climbed the Eiffel Tower, visited the Shakespeare & Co. bookstore, and wandered circular streets until we found ourselves lost in Paris. Again. We visited darkened pubs, became enamoured of musicians, stayed up all night laughing and then got up too early for coherent travel. Again.

I did it all again.

While packing for the move back to the UK, I knew it would be the next chapter—a new chapter. I reminded myself that I couldn't expect to relive and re-feel all the momentousness I had experienced or the exhilarating discoveries I'd made the year before. The year before had been saturated with so many eye-awakening "first times." But I didn't prepare quite well enough for the disorienting cocktail of emotions I would feel with this new-old adventure.

It was not the same experience. I was still in awe of these places, and living in the shadows of the castle only increased our chance of run-ins with rumoured residential ghosts. I rounded each corner of the castle half-expecting to encounter a familiar face from the year before, ready to share more laughs and carve new memories.

Yes, the halls echoed with the shouts of cheerful students, but they were not the same friends I knew and had grown to love. The ducks were still quacking and waddling their way into the court-yard. The chestnut trees and rose gardens still welcomed with their vibrant colours and leafy blooms.

But in some ways, returning to Herstmonceux Castle stirred up a slow sadness in me. My students were travelling, learning, and writing stories of their own. As a former castle kid, they relied on me to point them in the direction of the best pubs, revealing my innate ability to help them all get almost irretrievably lost just about every time. New faces shared new perspectives and unexpected shenanigans at every turn.

I felt privileged to be in an advisory role, planning, tour-guiding, supervising, and creating incredibly fun experiences and memories for my students during their year abroad. I was, after all, still exploring and living each day and feeling each moment as fully as I could.

But though I kept a busy schedule organising and attending events with the new students and found myself aboard a mini-bus or a coach to explore another interesting location every few days, I also felt a little lonely. I hadn't quite found my groove in my new role returning to the castle. I was an in-betweener—not quite a student, not quite a teacher; not Canadian, not British.

The castle, as lovely as it was with its ducks and its moat and its ghosts, could be an isolating place. The entire village had a population of about 60, and the nearest pub was a good 45-minute walk down a very narrow, shaded-over, one-lane road.

However, despite the absence of equals, I was still completely stoked to be living the new life I had chosen to veer into. Even though I carried a melancholic longing for the magic of the previous year, the responsibility I now carried for the 2002 student group, coupled with the biting cold weather and the bland food I never got used to, kept me genuinely happy. I loved living in England.

And so it was that in this second year, I decided to venture out beyond the castle, outside the parameters of weekend itineraries and excursions, and began my own adventurous exploring. Of course, I loved my castle companions, but it felt time to add to the collection of loveable characters in my narrative and see who the neighbours were.

A few elderly English ladies who lived in the village down the road had formed a book club, and I was invited to attend one evening. Following the banter of their conversation would prove to be an adventure, but so too was the commute.

You see, to get to the charming 250-year-old cottage where the book club met, I could only walk. The walk took about half an hour and led me down a winding, narrow path that trailed beyond the green, walled-in safety of my stony, impenetrable castle. Near the start, the path kept close to the 800-year-old, moss-cloaked stone church. Silent and cold, I could sense it watching me.

Beyond the church, I had to pass the graveyard. Rumours held that graves of children born out of wedlock had been found outside the graveyard walls, their desperate and grieved parents burying children as close to heaven's gates as they could.

Inside the graveyard walls, some stones stood erect, while others lay fallen and crumbled so loosely, the site of the original grave was a guess.

Alone and slightly terrified, I continued down the narrow path as it wound itself away from the castle, snaking between the tall chestnut trees that grew thick and dark along the road. Tangled branches arched up and reached over and across the road, tightening over the path like a smothering canopy. Eerie noises from forest creatures croaked from the brush.

The moonless night blackened my journey, and there weren't many houses along the road to offer comforting porchlight beams to guide my way. I carried a flashlight to feel somewhat confident, but the spaciousness and depth of the countryside expanding beyond the trees allowed for such a heavy darkness that my light was nearly useless.

Fright took over, and no amount of self-calming could ease my fear. Every single ghost story I had heard while living at Herstmonceux and every ghost I had retold stories about were now vividly and intently pursuing me in the icy night.

As I walked, my light bobbled ineffectively onto the trees and bushes, so I decided that rather than walk that terrifyingly long path, I would look straight ahead and run down the slippery path as fast as I could before the tendrils of creepy shadows could reach out their claws, open their jaws, and consume me. I kept to the very centre of the road to remain an equal distance from either of the dark roadsides.

Finally, heart pounding with equal parts exertion and adrenaline, I arrived at the 17th Century house. It was a warm village home, grand but not spacious. The inside glowed by the light of a fireplace, and as I entered, I was welcomed by the kind, wrinkly, and spectacled faces of my hostess and served hot, salty soup.

I was the youngest in attendance by about 40 years. I loved being a part of the book club. We chatted about the pathways of plots, the comedic characters and the excellent use of literary devices. By the end of the evening, I had relayed to them my terrifying trek and how fearful I had been of all manner of ghosts and spirits accompanying my walk in the dark, which amused them greatly.

We laughed and yapped the evening away, then sat down to a candlelit dinner with more serving utensils aside my plate than I could count. By the end of the evening, one of the women sympathised with my fear of returning by foot down the path in the cold and offered me a lift home so I wouldn't have to walk alone in the dark with my ghosts.

I accepted the ride, but I probably would have been okay on the return trip. While my head had been full of all kinds of haunting imaginings on the way to the book club, the stories from the book we'd discussed, the women who had read it, and the stories I was creating for myself to tell by joining their dinners and venturing further beyond the castle—this buzzing excitement would have overcome my fears.

My second year at the castle was steeped in fond memories and a more profound personal learning that only flamed the desire to keep learning more. My life in the UK was frothy rich with an ever-growing cast of characters and meaningful exchanges that continued to spike my curiosity and broaden my understanding of people, places, and myself.

Unfurling the US version of my life to consider how it could play out if I chose it revealed just how flat and pale that life seemed to be for me in comparison to the lure of treasure chest opportunities I found stretched out before me in a life here. I needed to rechart the map.

And so, I travelled more. And after another year living in the castle, I chose another path. I decided to stay even longer.

I just wish I'd been more of a rake when I was young. I wish I'd just followed my balls into battle, instead of sitting about, thinking of reasons not to take risks and make memorable mistakes. You can't make love to beautiful girls when you're dead. When I lie dying I ought to be mulling over my most dramatic and ecstatic memories...I've wasted my life being sensible when I should have been cavorting and gallivanting.

LOUIS DE BERNIÈRES,
The Partisan's Daughter

The Recharted Map

The United Kingdom & Europe
2001–2008

PART THREE

The Moments of Beauty We Keep

Greece & Crete
2007

TIME TRAVEL IS A THING of sci-fi and fantasy. It is taking a space-ship, a DeLorean, tapping sparkly ruby slippers, stepping into a Stonehenge-esque circle—some vessel or way of passage that serves as a conduit from the present and transports us immediately into someplace in the past or maybe even the future.

In that physical sense, time travel may or may not be real, at least not yet. But our ability to ignite our thoughts, our memories and emotions as a vehicle for time travel? That's as real as the nose on your face, as real as the heart beating in your chest.

When we travel, time fluctuates in ways that just aren't consistent with our day-to-day rhythms. We are used to the measured passing of minutes and hours; our daily routine creating a familiar, unchanging pace. But when our surroundings and experiences shift suddenly or drastically or excitably, the idea of regulated time goes out the window. A few days of travel can seem impossibly infinite. An entire sunshiny summer can pass in a flash.

There are moments that calcify themselves, heavy and unendurably long, and there are moments that float past and fast away.

Memories come alive when our emotions trigger them. Our thoughts traverse these mountains of memories and create our ability to travel through time, back to the moments long gone. It's how a song in our ears or a scent on our nose can conjure up a much-missed lover or long-loved place.

Sometimes, the past creeps and hangs on to our present like ivy embracing a wall. Beautiful, tangled, and choking. These past memories keep hidden the wall behind and obstruct our view of what is real in the present moment. Our inside thoughts shroud our outside world.

And other times, the present is so pleasantly perfumed, it arouses memories deeply rooted in our past. We can feel, years down the road, the untethered freedom, unimaginable joy, or deep love that was once so tangible. The present external moments take us the other way, and we travel inward, into our past memories, and we dwell inside those long-ago moments for a while.

These crystalline moments from our past never fade. Instead, they patiently wait in the deeper forests of our memory for our thoughts to creep-crawl back to them. As we unfurl each tendril, we reawaken the magic once lived in moments long gone, and sink into the light still found in those places.

Greece and Crete gifted me such moments.

Travelling to Greece and onward to Crete was intended to be enjoyed as a light-hearted vacation, but as each day played out with abandon, my heart was anything but light.

The ten days of travel placed me in a series of beautiful and ever-changing present moments, while the residue of memories and emotions from the past travelled right along beside me, challenging my outlook and my mood.

Those ten days, though whole-hearted and conflicting, courageous and calming, delivered more abundance of love, friendship, and adventure than was ever expected.

They were lush with experiences that taught me about myself through connection, hardship, or the attentions of flirtatious, Grecian men.

They are the moments and memories I still learn from, lean on, and yearn for, whenever I pick up the scent of ripening olive groves, whenever I hear the strings of a Cretan lute.

MONDAY, DAY 1
London

WITH JOYOUS ADVENTURE AND wide-open expectations for the days ahead, Tanja and I boarded the plane.

The trip that my dear friend and I had been anticipating and attempting to plan for six months was finally about to begin. We'd met for at least three different dinners at our homes in Brighton with the intention of booking flights and rooms in Athens and Chania. But each time Tanja opened her front door to let me in her home, we'd jump giddily into the "how are you's?" and each reply would bubble into hours of chatter that had been bottled up since the last visit.

This chatter could, of course, only be released with several glasses of our favourite red wine, which always resulted in an excellent evening of catching up on news about boys and relationships, struggles and victories with our careers, and updates on our parents and other mutual friends. Very little was ever accomplished in the way of confirming a travel itinerary.

Nevermind. We were finally on a late-night flight to Greece and on our way—I, having only just returned to London the evening before after spending the prior six weeks with family in California; Tanja having just returned from visiting her parents in Croatia.

We might have crammed our international excursions a little too tightly together, but summer was only so long. Besides, I'd continued living by the mantra I had forged living in my castle a few years prior; I never wanted to waste a moment. Just like travel buddies from trips gone by, Tanja and I would sleep when we were dead.

As has proved true with most of my adventures, our trek started off with joy, optimistic anticipation, and hilarity. We had packed flip-flops, pretty dresses, bikinis, and books. But we'd done so without acknowledging this: we had yet to unpack or decompress any experiences from the trips we had just finished with our families. Both of us expats, our life choices had denied us family time on demand. So these visits to our homes across the sea or an ocean meant trapping all the goodness of family reconnections and packing them into a cramped amount of time.

These visits home were high-speed events spent soaking up enough family reunion to last another eight or twelve months. Our family trips home to check in, reconnect, and catch up were important, and in some way, fueled our ability to step back into the lives we lived overseas.

As an expat, there would always be an element of newness or uniqueness to be found in my life in the UK. Even in the routine, day-to-day tasks, I found charm in what locals would consider mundane: the train journeys, the tea shops and quaint pubs, the colourful array of international friends I had made. It was always exciting to return home to Brighton after a summer visit home to California.

However, tethered to the newness and freshness of life abroad came the sacrifice of expat life living most of my days so far from my family. Each break home to California served up both a joyful reunion and a sorrowful departure. As per usual, this airport goodbye found me sobbing on the curb, snotting into tissues, as I bade farewell to whichever family member had been nominated to drop me at LAX.

Cry on the plane I would, but upon landing only hours later, I was fast to remove myself from the sorrow of this round of goodbyes and eager to fly fast into a light-hearted, buoyant, and fun-filled holiday. I would immerse myself again deep in the joy I found overseas—the kind of joy that made every tearful goodbye worth the flight.

It always took a while to sift through and settle my kindled emotions after shifting back and forth between lifestyles, cultures, and loved ones. But this summer, I left no space for such a transitional process. We planned to fly from London straight to Athens and spend one evening in the ancient city. The next day, we would ferry from the major port city of Piraeus and float smoothly south across the deep blue Aegean Sea for six hours before docking in the port at Chania, on the Mediterranean island of Crete. Tanja's close friend from her days studying at Cambridge was getting married that Friday, and we were arriving just in time for the bachelor party. I was travelling with Tanja as her date.

Somewhere over the Alps, we ordered drinks from the aeroplane bar and decided we would skip dinners all week to avoid fattening up from the decadent Greek cuisine. Family visits also meant little time for love life, and we were ambitious to seek any opportunity for a summer fling. After a silly, hushed, and clarifying conversation on what exactly *fellatio* meant, we cheered joyfully to ourselves and looked forward to an abundance of good vibes, gorgeous beaches, and the attentions of hot, sandy Grecian men.

TUESDAY, DAY 2
Athens

WE ARRIVED AT ABOUT 9 p.m. The city was stifling—bustling, even at that late evening hour. Glowing amber lights reflected off beat-up cars and warmed the walls of rough-sided, graffitied buildings.

My first impression of the capital was that it was not a very pretty city to look upon, but often that's the case for big cities, especially within the airport neighbourhoods. When anticipating Athens, our heads had been filled with ancient statues of gods and goddesses and columned temples crumbling but still dominating an epic landscape bedecked with twisting olive trees. We anticipated the streets lined with handsome men in togas and adorned in bronze breastplates and seasoned helmets.

That way of thinking is akin to flying into LA for the first time with the expectation of disembarking from the plane to be greeted by either an eruption of glitter and the flashing lights of the paparazzi or the cheery, Southern California sunshine—complete with warm sand at your feet.

Instead, you are herded from the plane into the traffic-jammed, smoggy, dirty outskirts of the actual metropolis, with very little fanfare and very little glam.

However, the crowded, dirty airport in Athens did not stain our spirits. Tanja and I found our public bus easy enough to catch and ride into the city centre. From the centre, in the stream of passing headlights and honking, we flagged ourselves a taxi for the final leg of our home-to-hostel trek.

We arrived at Dioskouros in a pedestrianised section of the city that was charmingly nestled just below the lit-up Acropolis. Here, the honking of taxis succumbed to the quiet laughter of nighttime walkers and late evening diners. Music from some nearby cafe added to the gentle cacophony of cicadas invisible to the eye but lining every branch of trees outlining the paths. Here, beyond breathing the recycled air of our aeroplane, traipsing through the dirty and pallid airport, and navigating the busy nocturnal traffic, here we could breathe deep and feel both comforted and revived upon our arrival.

The whiskered and smiling hostel owner greeted us with kind, sea blue eyes and, at his own Grecian pace, proceeded to provide us with four different paper maps that unfolded too-largely over his small counter space. Each map heralded a particular destination with the best route highlighted: The first map indicated how to locate his favourite restaurant, the second map guided us to the Acropolis, and the third and fourth maps directed us to a couple of something elses often sought by travellers. I don't remember what they were. I do remember that he was a very nice older man, speaking ever so slowly. In contrast, we were excited to have landed in Athens and were beyond ready to drop our bags in our room and explore the city with what remaining waking hours we had in us.

During one of our more successful trip-planning dinners prior to our flight, Tanja and I had managed to book a dorm in Athens, sharing with four other girls in a basement room of the hostel because, well, we were 20-somethings, and budget travel was how we could finance our never-ending insistence on exotic adventures back then.

For some reason, the hostel owner had decided to upgrade us to a two-person bedroom upstairs. *Perfect!* In this upgraded bedroom, the only window was above the head of the bed, and lacked both windowpane and screen. The green, beaten wooden shutters folded in half and were secured open with a latch. They didn't fold closed or lock, and we could lean right through and out the open window and peer into the alleyway below. However, I don't remember feeling that our security was threatened at all. Instead, we admired the quaintness and charm the room offered compared to our homes in England, which were screened, paned, closed, and grey.

Here, the house-turned-hostel felt safe in the way your own bedroom feels safe. Its hue felt sunny-warm even in the blanket of the night. In the corner stood a swivel fan, the second source of airflow besides the open window. Inside the room, the temperature felt about 400 degrees Fahrenheit. It was almost unbearably hot, but we were still grateful to have been given our private space. Shuffling the map of the Acropolis to the top of our stack, we left our room behind and headed into the city at night.

This had become my favourite way to enter a new city—arriving in the evening when the centuries-old monuments softly glow in the dim, golden lights. When I reflect on the places I've explored with any depth—England, Italy, Greece, and so many others—the impression of the city that makes its way to my mind is how the place feels as it appears in the dark.

It was in the dark after hours that I first stepped inside Canterbury Cathedral years ago, during my very first trip overseas. During the previous summer's travels, it had been in the night that I had arrived by train and foot to the seaside village of Manarola in Italy to hike Cinque Terre. I had to walk up the steep hill, bag on my back, hoping the hostel owner was still awake to greet me.

There is something magical about the way a place sits in its dignity without the throng of tourists or the harsh glare of a hot sun. Ancient sites seem more regally seated in their element and place in time without the bother of an awake, modern world bustling and shouting too close. To me, this is how such locations are meant to be seen—as they really are on their own, without crowds. Still here, still imperious in the dark and the quiet.

And so it was as we approached the Acropolis. Uncrowded. Dimly lit. Quietly breathing.

The Acropolis is an ancient citadel located on a rocky outcrop above the city of Athens. Within it is contained the remains of several ancient buildings of architectural and historical significance that I had probably read about in a history class at some point. The most famous of these ancient structures was the Parthenon. It stands high on a hill, and the walking areas surrounding it had been recently re-paved.

Not too long before our trip, there had been traffic-jammed streets elbowing in too close to the monument, but the Olympics held there some years back had changed all that with a respectful nod to the history of the place. Now, tree-lined promenades paved with large slick stones designed for modern needs of pedestrian commuters and tourists blanketed the ground. Branchy trees obscured romantic teenagers who'd snuck off the path to find dark places for a secret rendezvous. The walkways weren't too well lit, but I again didn't feel unsafe here, even though it was sometime around midnight when Tanja and I deciphered the map and found our way there.

We wandered around the site, eventually clambering up a slight hill, searching for a "Look-out Rock" the hostel owner had circled on one of our maps. We weren't sure what to expect of such a rock, but as we rounded a corner, a rock the size of a small house came into view. Stairs had been both carved into the side and nailed firmly to the massive rock. The wooden steps scaled up and around toward the rock's flat upper surface. Assuming we had found the "Look-out Rock" we were meant to find, we climbed our way up to the top.

We perched on the warm, stony flatness, in complete awe of the sights stretching before us. To our right, we were rewarded with a perfect view of the Acropolis, its white, crumbly pillars lit up like a flame in the vast night sky. Far-off landmarks sat atop distant hills that dotted below and beyond us, as did the vast expanses of blinking city lights. Scattered in shadowy clusters across the surface of the rock, tangles of youths talked quietly, laughing with their cigarettes lit in a smouldering glow, and clinking their glass-bottled beverages.

The moon was low and cut precisely in half as noise from the city below had become a hushed whisper. The hurried energy from our recent journey lifted, and calm settled over us as Tanja and I found our own cornerstone and took in the night lights of Athens. Above the din of nighttime revelries, we sat in peaceful quiet, Tanja with a cigarette softly glowing between her fingers.

It was almost 1:30 in the morning when we left the "Look-out Rock" and headed into the city to seek out some dinner. The path down the backside of the Acropolis was dark, slippery, and branches from trees overhung the path in some places.

Though I never saw a single cicada, I could hear hundreds of them singing in the trees, creaking their legs or wings together, and making such a clamour that it at times forced us to speak louder to overcome their racket. It seemed the trees must have been more full with these insects than leaves, but the cicadas remained camouflaged the entire time I was in Greece; I never once saw a single bug.

We walked down a stepped, narrow walkway paved for pedestrian diners, lined with different restaurants and decided on a rooftop bar that offered live Greek entertainment. Our first Greek meal consisted of red wine, cold beer, Kalamata olives, fish paste, bread, and the sweetest honeydew melon and watermelon I'd ever had—much to the amusement of our old waiter. I couldn't understand a word of Greek, but he made it very clear that our selection was the funniest combination of menu items he had ever been asked to serve.

Every culture has a proper way to order local cuisine and the appropriate time of day to eat it. Perhaps we were ordering a confusing combo of breakfast and appetisers, but we didn't speak Greek, and his English was minimal, so we ordered a selection of food we knew we'd enjoy. The waiter might have been amused by us, but he was kind and brought me an ice bucket for my red wine. Chilled red wine was surprisingly pleasant, and given the heat of the night, a delight I wouldn't have expected: and the first of many firsts on this trip I was about to find myself fully immersed in.

That first night, I'd learned to say a few words in Greek, including *hi, please, thank you, good morning, sea turtle, octopus,* and *crickets.* I spent days practising *please* and *thank you,* only to learn that the Greek don't actually use so many polite words in their friendly but direct manner of speaking, but I hope they appreciated me trying.

Our sleep that night was uncomfortably broken. Lying sweaty atop damp sheets in the stifling air was far from serene, and we were too jetlagged to sleep. Our quaint, street-side window let in heavy air and outside noise, so any small commotion from the street below frequently woke us.

When morning came (far too early given our late night and shallow sleep), we set out to explore the city surrounding the Acropolis and to take in the city in the daylight hours for the first time.

I discovered and purchased my first of many frappés—an amazing, foamy coffee drink served over blocks of ice. These would never fail to perk me right up. I'd come to drink a frappé almost every day of our trip. We realised it was too hot to eat in the day, so we mostly spooned down cool yoghurt while the sun was high, and ate larger, meatier meals in the evenings, despite the ground rules for dining we had set for ourselves en route on the plane the day before— to eat light and skip dinners.

We wandered through the suffocating city heat until about 2 p.m., then with our bags repacked and stuffed in a cab, we taxied to the port in Piraeus, where we boarded the ferry to Crete.

It was the largest ferry I had ever encountered. It felt like a 5-star hotel inside, complete with a dazzling chandelier sparkling up the main lobby and an escalator that took passengers up to the 3rd floor. It boasted three outside decks, and snooping around the First Class cabin section revealed luxurious beds and bathrooms enjoyed by those not travelling on a budget.

Dropping our bags in the hold, we then found some comfortable chairs on the back deck of the ferry and stretched out in recliners under the big, Greek-blue sky. We waved goodbye to the city as it slowly disappeared underneath its own smog-smeared air, and we gently motored off into the Aegean Sea.

During the six-hour sea voyage, we read and napped, indulged in frappés and checked out the surplus of tanned Greek men roaming the decks, and watched our first sunset settle over a Grecian horizon. The Aegean was surprisingly calm. The water was so still, without huge waves, jumping fish, or threatening fins circling. There were only gentle swells and a sticky, salty wind that tangled up my hair and slapped against my skin.

The good vibes we sought, we found from the start. We were travelling by boat away from the mainland, beneath a hot sun, enjoying icy drinks, soaking up beautiful views, laughing with a good friend, and excited for the unknown adventure awaiting us ahead. Breathing it in deep, it all smelled so good.

After a while, we could only see miles and miles of placid saltwater expanding from every side of our ferry. There was neither any visible land nor any other boat in sight as the sun deepened its red hue, dipped lower and fuller into the horizon, then vanished in a burning snap.

WEDNESDAY, DAY 3
Chania

THE HARBOUR CITY WAS nothing less than enchanting. It was nearing 11 p.m. when we wriggled through the crowds of people with
luggage departing the ferry, caught a cab in the frenzy of headlights
and honks, and made our way into the heart of the Old Harbor where
our rooms in the Pension Theresa awaited. Airbnb wasn't a thing then,
but discovering unique home rentals has always been an option for
savvy travellers.

Pension Theresa was an almost 700-year-old building of the
Venetian era with some Turkish touches added over the centuries.
Primarily, it was built to be an administration office used by Venetians
and Turks. Gradually, it became home to Greek and Turkish families,
each family taking a room and sharing the common kitchen.

Eventually, the building became a hippy commune before it
evolved into its current identity as a quiet kind of hostel, except this
hostel lacked any check-in desk or shelves full of fliers. Even though
rooms were rented out in hostel-like fashion, it still very much felt
as if we had rented someone's home. But even then, the atmosphere
offered hints of the blended cultures it had housed throughout time—
from the shelved antiques and art-filled walls to the vibrant, energetic
warmth emanating from each wall.

The rooms were tidy and quaint, feeling more like a small cottage sitting at the edge just west of the Old Venetian Harbor alongside
vine-covered 14th Century Venetian buildings. The stairway inside
the front entryway was narrow and wooden, cork-screwing its way
around once, then back again in an "S" shape before landing us on the
second floor.

Our room was decorated with well-loved books lined on shelves
and stacked in corners. Delicate antiques crowded into unlocked glass

cabinets, and above us rose a loft with rail-free wooden stairs boasting a small kitchen tucked away at the top. The room was furnished with an ornate wooden wardrobe, dulled mirrors, a clean shower, a double bed, with all the colours of soft blues and lamp light closed in with rustic brick walls.

The room had the character of centuries peeking out at us from every corner. You could still feel the essence of families who had once lived there. A round table and two rounded iron chairs stood in the middle of the room, and a wooden bench near the door welcomed us in. We slept there for almost a week, and when the time came to pack and leave, I found that I felt as if I were moving out of my own room. It felt so much like an embrace.

In reflection, this space was offering up the long hug I didn't know I needed, the embrace of goodbye I still clung to deep down after having bid farewell to my family, once again; after having chosen to live in another world, once again. There were no feelings of regret or second-guessing when I returned to live overseas. It is just a truth that it will always hurt my heart to leave my loved ones behind. Without realising it, this room had given me just the nurturing and love I must have been missing.

Dimitris picked us up half an hour later at almost midnight after we'd showered and changed from our long sea voyage to Crete. We were not weary. Like the evening before, we were ready. Tanja, ready to celebrate, meet Dimitris' family, and see her old friends from Cambridge, and I ready to make new ones.

Dimitris and Tanja hadn't seen each other for ages, and it was a sweet and long-awaited reunion. Shortly after arriving, however, Dimitris informed us of an unfortunate recent event; his uncle had died unexpectedly a few days before. It was traumatic, and his family were so saddened and shocked, they had considered cancelling the wedding. But rather than a last-minute cancellation, they decided that the events of the week would be toned down. Celebrated, yes, but hushed out of respect for the departed. Instead of a bachelor party and wild week-long shenanigans as had been planned, Dimitris' family planned to host a dinner for us and other foreign guests who had travelled from afar to attend the wedding.

His family was warm. Little English was spoken around the table, but we were welcomed to a meal of boiled goat, lamb, Greek salad, homemade bread, and homemade wine direct from the family's vineyards. The wine both looked and tasted much like mild whiskey and was excellent as it tingled across the top of the tongue and sent fiery vibes down the throat. The family was so hospitable and kind considering their sad situation, serving guests they hadn't yet met, and the lateness of the hour. Dinners are often served between about 10 p.m. and midnight in Crete, so it was normal for us to arrive so late and eat. A plate full of vine-ripened figs and grapes was presented for dessert, again, fresh from the vineyard. Perfect.

After dinner, Dimitris drove us into town for late-night drinks. We wandered along the harbour, and I dipped my feet in the warm water. The harbour was fairly small but lined with restaurants and bars promoting a lively but not rowdy ambience. The soundwaves of the live music bounced across the water and danced with each other, scurrying from one wall to the next.

Jutting out from the east side of the Old Harbour was a fourth century lighthouse that blinked throughout the night. Locals told stories that it had been built by the Egyptians as a guide for one of their Sultans. Moored sailboats and speedboats rocked gently on one side, and the clip-clop of heels and laughter of passers-by on the wooden dock added to the sweet cacophony of the evening. The language I could hear was incomprehensible to me, but the atmosphere was not. I enjoyed the vibe, the easy new friendships, the familial gestures, the ancient landscape nudged by the bustle and lights of a modern age. While Chania was a little touristy, it had managed to not feel tacky, and for how busy it seemed, it didn't propagate an overwhelming frenzy.

Inside a hearty tavern, we ordered drinks at a small table with some of Dimitris' friends and were introduced to new people—mostly other wedding guests from Cambridge and PhD friends from England, where Dimitris had spent time studying.

I remember sitting at the table, listening to their chatter, and looking out at the harbour lights. It was only the first night, and I was enjoying myself, but I felt a little left out. Likely, I was mostly tired. After all, it had only been 24 hours since we arrived from the UK to Greece. But looking back, I understand what my younger self was feeling. I was still reeling and recovering from having spent the six weeks before our trip home in California.

All those family goodbyes, the emotions and tears from leaving home again—they had been swept to the side when excitement for the adventure with Tanja had intercepted them. But the sadness and missing my family had not dissipated—especially now that I was present amongst the closeness of Dimitris' family. The nostalgia resurfaced, and I was reminded of my sad, rushed goodbyes. The goodbyes are always the hardest part.

I believe I was also finally tuckered out after two days of travel and endless stimulating newness, so my mood was a little lower, and I actually had a moment to notice my energy beginning to drain. But I still felt good and optimistic about what experiences were to come.

Of the new faces sitting around our table, two were from the UK. The first was a short, bellied Indian guy from Manchester named Sasha. Sitting at the table that first evening with him, I was not attracted and less than impressed. The men Tanja and I had hoped to meet were golden-skinned Grecians, and this he was not. However, he was kind and harmlessly talkative. And unbeknownst to me, he would turn out to be a lovely addition to the ensemble of foreign guests—friendly and polite and an amusingly organised trip planner with simple but specific expectations.

His travelling partner was Adrian. He had a stunningly gorgeous face, dark hair and thick lashes softening over sharp, large, deep green eyes. He stood over six feet tall, his broad shoulders becoming of him. Unfortunately, his personality seemed to be a blend of overbearing masculinity and pushiness. He was so obtrusive in his conversation, assuming points and gesturing beyond the borders of his personal space so much that I mainly avoided him and barely offered him any of my remaining energy that night. It took me a while to warm up to him.

Tanja and I, throughout the three years we had been neighbours, roommates, and friends, shared one constant commonality: we were always desperately in love with someone. This trip was no exception.

While I wasn't immediately fond of Adrian at all, Tanja fell for him completely. Part of our agenda for our 10-day trip to Crete was to meet handsome, suave, swoon-worthy men. Tanja succeeded the first night. For the next three days, she couldn't stop talking about Adrian. He had been educated in French schools, and so though he was Italian, he spoke with the thickest French accent I had ever heard. My initial feelings toward him wavered back and forth, and so when I found him charming, his French accent came across as amusing and funny. When I found him exasperating, his accent was annoying and grating on the ear. The topics he chose to talk about and the opinions he tactlessly threw down onto our tables were likely presented harmlessly enough, with good conversation as his intention, but my first impression was that he was an asshole of the most polished type.

Tanja is a Croatian beauty, olive-skinned with dark eyes and darker, silky hair. Her smile and bubbly laughter could light up a room. Her attention to Adrian was returned with unabashed flirtation. How she could be infatuated with him was apparent, despite my cynicism.

At the end of our table, there also sat a friendly German/Danish couple. The wife was quiet and sweet, and her tall husband was kind as well, except he displayed a nervous twitch that made one of his eyes blink rapidly for a while behind his thick glasses until his friendly eyes crossed for a moment and he then blinked himself back to normal to carry on eye contact with whomever he was conversing. It was disconcerting and made for a challenging conversation. As a result, I can't remember a thing we had talked about; I only remember his twitching eyes.

I also can't remember how our night ended or how late—although it must have been. The long day of journeying, arriving, and voyaging had taken its toll. Apart from the dinner table with Dimitris' parents, I had socialised but felt more distance than closeness. It's likely I needed connection—the thing that I had, at that point, been unable to feel—a little more than usual to fill the void I was still feeling from my visit home, but I didn't realise it just then.

Just then, I was only feeling "tired."

THURSDAY, DAY 4
Chania

BEFORE RETIRING ON OUR first night in Chania, the other UK guests had agreed on a time to meet for breakfast the next day. I was growing ever more weary, so I asked Tanja if she wouldn't mind bailing on them so we could hit the beach on our own time.

It was now Thursday. I had slept so well during our first night in Chania but had woken up feeling tense for some reason and couldn't shake it. Tanja sent the boys a "thanks, but no thanks" text, and we wandered down the cobbled lanes to find a café on our own instead.

Greek coffee, dark and rich, poured into delicate antique porcelain. Each hot swallow perked us awake into the warming sunshine of morning. Before us were plates laden and sticky with generous spoonfuls of honey decadently dripped over fresh, cold fruit and chilled yoghurt. Satiated, we finished our breakfast and set out in search of a beach.

We wandered through a bustling street market lined with local vendors selling an array of pastries, meats and soaps, then carried on down to the sand. We sauntered past cheerful families set up with their umbrellas and colourful towels. We stepped past topless older women with leathery, deeply tanned skin without a speck of self-consciousness. We snickered past speedo-clad boys running back and forth, tossing a ball in the air and shouting in Greek at each other. We carried on down the stretch of sand until we found a spot that was less crowded and was accented with dark, jutting rocks that emerged from the sea, past the waves, and onto the shore.

For hours we laid immersed in summer vibes underneath the warm sun. I drank a cold Mythos beer while Tanja read aloud to me poignant love scenes from her book *Shantaram*. We dipped in the warm, salty sea whenever the Cretan heat on our sweaty bodies demanded we take a break to cool.

I shamelessly smiled at hot, olive-skinned Greek men when they passed by, laughed at pale young men who were likely office geeks on holiday and who mostly seemed to walk stiffly in pairs, suffering a bit in the harsh climate. How harmlessly amusing it is to witness discomfort worn so obviously by those who find themselves out of their element. But lying under the hot sun, so near the crashing ocean, and below the wide blue sky, a book and a beer and a friend nearby, I was completely enveloped in mine.

Sometime later, I immersed myself in the ocean for a solo dip. There had been another beach-goer sunning near us for some time, who I now saw enter the water and swim easily toward me. From a distance, he had seemed somewhat attractive, but as he came closer, his horrible seediness was grossly apparent. He treaded water my way, and in a thick Greek accent asked me, "You want to swim together?"

What?

He seemed to be at least 20 years older than me.

No. I don't want to swim together. Not at all. Swim that way, away from me, you creepy old man.

I declined and paddled off back to shore, irritated. He didn't at all fit the profile of the Greek man I was ready to meet. The afternoon hours had passed, so Tanja and I decided to go back to our room and shower.

However, on our walk back to our charming Pension Teresa, we became distracted by an unusual sight. Behind one of the restaurants overlooking the beach was a clothing line strung with octopi, recently dead and hanging out to dry in the sun.

There were about a dozen of these cat-sized creatures pinned to the line—no flies or bugs buzzing around. They were drying in the sun, each suction-cupped tentacle dangling into stiff, pink curly cues.

My lifetime of travel has taught me a greater awareness of the importance of knowing exactly where my food comes from. An understanding of the journey a meal can make from the sea to the table has since impacted my dining choices. This moment would prove to be one of the moments that, in time, would lead me to this decision about mindful food choices. It was a bit of a shock back then to see what a grilled octopus looked like before it became an entree marinated in olive oil and garlic. In the same way, I suppose, it would still be a shock for most meat-eaters to see the fresh corpse of a baby cow just before ordering veal parmigiana.

But that afternoon, after casually meandering past the octopi hanging on a line, we decided to sit down at an outdoor table and eat one.

The dining area was set up on a rocky jetty extending away from shore and along the water into the bay as the light waves slapped at the rocks. A branchy, tree-covered canopy created shade, buzzing with the racket of overheated cicadas. Again, as in Athens, the cicadas' song overpowered our voices, and we had to speak up just to hear each other over the din of the raucous things. Even though we looked hard at the leafy overhang, we *still* couldn't see a single cicada hiding just a few feet above our heads.

From our table, we watched local young kids diving off a stone wall into the still water of the harbour, the sun shimmering down on the sea behind them. Angry little ducks added to the cacophony of the bugs and local Greek chatter from other diners. In the distant sky, two helicopters circled out and returned again over the sea to scoop huge buckets of water to help douse a nearby fire.

We ordered one sun-dried octopus each, flavoured with local pressed olive oil and accompanied by homemade bread spread thick with garlicky butter. As a side, we ordered fresh Greek salad served with sweet red summer tomatoes, crisp green cucumbers, and a generous slice of chunky feta cheese. A plate of Kalamata olives rounded out our order.

The *ohtapodi* was exceptional. We ate every last bit on our plate—although I didn't have the heart to eat the head (the beginnings of my present-day refusal to eat them would emerge more and more on this trip). I permitted Tanja to eat the head off both of ours. *Poor little ohtapodi.* These days, while I'm not a steadfast vegetarian, I have stopped eating octopus. I know now that that hot day in Crete was most definitely a moment where I began to connect the creatures I felt affection for or was in awe of with the creatures I could order off a menu. It was the effect of seeing what happens to animals when we choose to eat them. For those who grow up on a farm or a fishing village, you know. I did not grow up in any such environment, and the rawness of the quick transformation of living creatures to lunch items struck me. Even though seafood in Crete was likely as sustainable as it gets, bearing witness to the behind-the-scenes struck a chord with me. Something about it just seemed unfair.

Tanja and I had only meant to stop for a quick 20 minutes, but it turned into a lengthy afternoon meal that readied me for a nap.

Back at our Pension, we crashed for an indulgent three-hour nap, which meant I was acclimatising to Greek culture just fine. Sleep during the day and remain awake late into the hours of each night.

Tanja and I freshened up and made our way back into the charming harbour town, which also seemed to be waking up, ready for whatever the evening revellers might bring. Rejuvenated, we revived our mission to meet gorgeous Greek men and displayed zero qualms in flirtatiously making eyes at handsome men who also appeared to have freshened up for their evening.

Down by the bar-lined section of the harbour, we admired the abundance of tanned, masculine perfection and were admired and winked at in return. But, alas, no hellos jubilantly ensued to lead to any of the fiery entanglements we were interested in.

We found ourselves down an attractive side street where the clientele seemed to be more local college-aged people, filling each section of tables checkering outward to fill the street with lively chatter and music.

Tanja and I settled in. One Greek god strolled by us. Another Greek god sauntered past. Another. Nothing. No conversations were struck—not even a friendly passing wink down this alley. After years of living in England—and we both loved the English—Tanja and I were seeking men flaunting more exotic shades. Tanja was hoping the ever-annoying Adrian would meet up with us and focused her attention on sending him text invitations to join us. Me? I was eyeing strangers. The men were incredibly beautiful. My Adonis was here somewhere, damn it. *Keep your pretty eyes open, girl.*

Chania was small, and its nightlife neighbourhood adequately just as small, and I had noticed one of Dimitris' friends who we had met the day before meandering nearby. I pointed him out to Tanja. "Isn't that Nicolas?" She presumed this would mean that our acquaintance Adrian was near, and even though I didn't see Adrian in the vicinity, Tanja sprung out of her seat and chased Nicolas down to find out if he was alone or if there was a chance her Adrian was about.

The grouchiness and tension I had woken up with that morning began to creep its way back in. I must have still been tired and still recovering from my internal stress from the previous few days. The commotion from heavy travel, hormones, and tiredness were pulling me down with their heavy weight.

Tanja led Nicolas back to our table, who also had his brother with him. Another hot-from-a-distance-but-not kind of man, similar to the older Grecian treading water near me earlier in the day.

Nicolas's brother was named Georgios or possibly Dimitri, as that seemed to be the only names men were given in those parts. Georgios, Nicolas, or Dimitri. Most men I met were called one of these names. Georgios (or Dimitri) seemed shy and didn't speak English or Greek the entire time we were all there. After they sat down at our table, I noticed the guy sitting at a table behind us was also someone we had met earlier (the owner of a bookshop we'd stopped into), and so I waved a friendly hello. He was also not hot but was very kind. Before I knew what was happening, Tanja had noticed him as well and invited him over too.

And just like that, we'd created a situation that would fail to send a beacon to any gorgeous single Grecian or Cretan strangers enticing them to sit and have drinks with us. She had hopes of meeting Adrian, I had hopes of meeting a hot stranger, but there I was, having an intellectual conversation with a shopkeeper, our new acquaintance Nicolas, and Nicolas's shy, introverted brother sitting quietly in the seat beside me.

Perhaps my inside voice was being a tad bitchy and shallow, but our goal was to meet one of the hot Cretan or Greek men that Tanja and I had been hoping would populate our itinerary. None of these men was flirty or young or hot, and so I became increasingly annoyed with the way the evening was shaping up with rapidly dimming chances for hot summer love. A few minutes later, Adrian and Sasha also showed up so that now Tanja and I were completely encircled by men I wasn't attracted to. Even if a hot Cretan man had wanted to flirt with me, he would have had a human barrier of English-speaking older men to elbow through, and I doubted that would happen on this night.

Fine, I decided. A submissive "whatever" was the best attitude to wear as the night was a lost cause for romantic pursuits, and I decided to just enjoy eye contact and non-suggestive conversation with nice people at my table. Besides, there was still the wedding to look forward to soon anyway. So I ordered another margarita.

FRIDAY, DAY 5
Chania

THE WEDDING DAY HAD arrived. The morning of, Tanja and I discovered that the small church Dimitris and his wife had chosen for
their ceremony was booked every weekend for the next seven years.
Yes—the next *seven* years. And so, the wedding was held on a Friday
evening.

Here I was, about to attend a wedding in Crete, amongst lovely
people in a spectacular setting, dining on the most delicious food
and wine next to a stunning sea, on a lovely and much-anticipated
holiday with my dear friend. But somehow, the ingredients of our trip
didn't add up to explain my mental state. For the second day in a row,
despite having enjoyed our lone beach excursion the day before, my
mood upon rising was low.

I couldn't place it then, but knowing myself as I do now, I
can recall the series of events that had bound me up so tightly: the
emotional wreckage that exists the week after leaving my family for
another year abroad; the exhaustion of travelling across time
and a great distance to live where I lived; the intense heat of the
Mediterranean despite the never-ending orders of frappés or cold
beers; and the luckless encounters we'd had with men failing to salve
any emotional need for connection. It was all wearing me down.
Try as I may, I couldn't escape from my internal mental and emotional
churning.

Plus, I hadn't felt any quick attachment with the other guests
as I often do when meeting strangers on the road. Other than all of
us wedding guests living and travelling from the UK, we had little in
common and hadn't quite bonded with that unnamed vibe that often
gels me to a new friend for life within an instant during a journey.
Or over a beer.

I realise now that when my energy is low and drained, mustering new energy to connect with strangers—nonetheless during such momentous and personal occasions as family weddings—leads to over-exhaustion and mood swings that I'm just terrible at hiding.

To exacerbate the moodiness, we encountered a somewhat frustrating morning in an attempt to manage our travel from Chania to the wedding site. Having run several errands in town, we found it challenging to get the help we needed from tourist agencies whose English was limited. Lines were long and confusing, directions to the bus station were given in the friendly, local manner—which is to say, directions were given by gesturing and pointing, so the need to repeatedly stop and ask for clearer directions added to my irritability. Perhaps if we had learned more Greek, our experience would have improved.

Our mission the day of the wedding was to find our way by bus to another village 40 kilometres away and stay for the night. We had needed to repack our belongings and side-step pedestrians and motorbikes in the narrow, commuter-trafficked street as we hustled down the city centre of Chania towards the run-down bus station.

Buying the tickets, it turned out, was easy enough. But actually boarding the bus and claiming a seat turned into a fiasco.

It seemed to be perfectly normal for ticket sellers to sell hundreds of tickets for a 30-passenger bus. Our 3:30 bus pulled into the parking lot and exhaled its fumes next to the cracked and crumbling cement curb. Loads of locals lined up between the buses and pushed through with their bags, boxes, and suitcases, all waving their tickets in the air and shouting over the idling bus engines.

Confusion was rife, and the crowds of people shouted with agitation in the heat. Those who were forceful enough to elbow onto the bus did so, and the unlucky who didn't fit on the bus had no choice but to wait in a cracked plastic chair in the shade to board the next bus, which wouldn't come for another hour.

We were packed amongst the unlucky. After a morning of rushing around in the heat, sorting out our travel details for the next two days, and carrying our heavy bags hurriedly through foot traffic, we found ourselves stuck waiting outside in this dumpy bus station, on twisted metal benches decorated with graffiti, grime, and chewed gum. It sucked so much.

I know we are each responsible for the energy we bring into a space, and I was genuinely trying not to be pissed off. Honestly, I've learned to expect that some things will just go wrong every time I travel—you have to expect this. Arrivals will be late, journeys will take longer, and expenses will be higher than anticipated or even needed. It's just the nature of things when travelling to a new country. But that morning, I just didn't want to deal. I was dripping sweat just by standing still in the heat, so far from the breeze of the ocean. Travellers around me were grumbling in several different languages. I didn't understand the words, but I understood the misery on their faces and the drooped surrender of their shoulders.

Of course, the extended wait meant a bathroom visit was unavoidable. To describe the toilets at the public bus station as less than inviting is an understatement. I have yet to visit a bus station bathroom that is appealing in any country, actually, but as usual, I was dying to go.

The toilet paper was not kept inside each stall, but rather a ream of toilet paper was spooled by the main door as you walked in. The stalls (if you could call them that) contained flat "urinals" with ridged footpads, pee-stained and grimy. The footpads were hip-width apart and framed a tennis ball-sized hole in the ground I was meant to half-stand above or hover over. There were no actual toilet bowls in the stalls, and I thought for sure that I had entered the men's room by mistake. I checked the outside signage no less than three times before committing. Yup, there was a stick person in a dress painted on the sign outside the bathroom door, and I watched as a little boy hopped out of the men's room next to me. I was in the right place, unfortunately. Up to that point, it was possibly the filthiest toilet experience I've ever had in my life—and that includes times I've accidentally peed on myself.

Afterwards, I noticed the sink I was washing up in was positioned right next to the open, blue metal door, which had been propped wide open with a large broken brick on the cement floor. This meant that in the bathroom mirror, the entire lounge was reflected back to me, and of course, me to them. Everyone who looked could see without trying into the women's room, at least in the sink area, as I stood there soaping up my hands—all the sweaty men with dirty bags and overtired women and bored children—they could all see right in. *Yup*, I thought to them, *I just peed standing.*

At that stage, my mood still grumpy, I decided the situation sucked for everyone and that it would be better to just chill out while we waited. I bought Tanja and me some frappés to cheer us up while waiting to catch the next damned 3:30 bus that we hoped would come by 4:30.

The 4:30 bus showed up at 4:27. An announcer over the intercom told us which bus it was, first in Greek and then in English. Almost instantly, there was a stampede of sweaty, cranky people making a move for the bus before it had even come to a stop, throwing their luggage in the narrow door and pushing past each other three at a time to claim a seat.

We almost missed this one again. People were crowding around and trying to force themselves in the bus, many whose overheated bodies were too wide to do anything but wedge themselves inside and up the two or three steps into the bus. But Tanja slid in from the side and squeezed herself in. As the bus driver took her ticket, some woman elbowed her way in front of me, but this time I had learned local bus-station etiquette and pushed back with my forearm saying, "I'm with her," and climbed in behind Tanja. And that was it! We had made it on board.

I think maybe some people who missed the 3:30 also missed the 4:30, but not us. The bus doors creaked closed, and the old bus lurched forward, leaving the crowd of disappointed travellers behind in a bellow of blackened smoke.

Next stop, Georgioupolis!

FRIDAY, DAY 5 (LATER)
Georgioupolis

THE BUS RIDE TOOK about 40 minutes and wasn't bad at all. Once we were on our way, my mood seemed to lift with every bumpy lurch. The rural road climbed over scenic hills, boasting tangled vineyards and olive trees to my right and sloped green grasslands to my left, sinking low until the land met the deep blue sea far off in the distance. Every few kilometres, a small white chapel brightened up the landscape. The curvy coast was an absolute delight to follow from our cracked leather window seats.

Georgioupolis, we discovered, was tucked into a small cove. As we departed from the bus, we carried our bags to the first tourist office we spotted to find directions to our accommodation. I had proven myself useless in remembering how to pronounce any Greek. I couldn't seem to recall any words that I had practised when I actually needed them. It didn't help that Greek uses a Cyrillic alphabet, with each letter appearing to me as a foreign geometric shape that I couldn't decipher. Every upside-down V and sharp cornered S was a struggle. As has often been the case, I depended a lot on the kindness of strangers on this trip—especially when I was alone.

On this afternoon, a kind stranger sat behind the desk inside the car rental place, and we told him we were looking for a hotel by the name of "Kikidopus", "Kikidodus", or "Koladious," but was, in reality, a place called (probably) Kokoladis. The stout man behind the desk laughed and responded (probably), "Kokoladis? Which one? They are all called this!"

Great. We were rounding on less than an hour before the wedding, and we had no idea the name of the place we were meant to check into. Luckily, the ever-so-organised Sasha had texted me the number of the accommodation—the *katályma* we all had booked.

Our call was answered by a chatty old woman who, moments later, came hobbling over from a couple of blocks away. She was about four feet tall, chubby in her long skirt, and incredibly happy to see that we had arrived. She showed us the way down the road to our simple but welcoming rooms.

Everything got better immediately.

This room was cute and practical. Not as charming as the Pension in Chania, but we were happy enough to stay there. It was a second-floor room, and it offered a balcony with a wide view of all the other guests' balconies. A fig tree grew in the yard behind, and the treetop was just level with our white wooden railing. The ripened fruit tempted us from just barely beyond our reach. I could hear the comforting sounds of the ocean mildly roaring in the near distance.

The balcony next to ours was separated only by a very low wooden partition, and we could have easily stepped over into our neighbour's rooms or they into ours. We didn't, though. It was too hot to leave the doors closed to trap heated air, but security didn't feel like it should be a worry on this day. We felt safe there, and the sound of the waves was a sound we craved.

The room came with two beds, one with a stained sheet (mine, but I didn't care) and a bathroom with a shower. The shower was basic, consisting only of a hose hanging out of the tiled wall. The floor was cement, with a drain next to the worn-out toilet. It would do. We had 45 minutes to get ready, and a kind lady who Tanja had met outside the hotel offered to give us a lift to the church. Our day continued to turn around.

We had been informed (warned?) of just how conservative the people of Crete were and how women in strappy tops wouldn't be allowed to enter churches. Respectfully, I had tucked away any cleavage I would normally attempt to proudly display and made sure my shoulders were covered. We would acquiesce to the expectations of the local culture on such an important day.

Wouldn't you know that when we arrived at the wedding, the women seemed to all be wearing strappy, sleeveless dresses? In my conservative top and skirt, I felt prudish and uncomfortably hot. Turns out, while it is customary to dress conservatively inside the church, the chapel where the ceremony was taking place was extremely small—as in perhaps only standing room for seven or eight people at the most. The only space inside was for the soon-to-be-wedded couple and their parents. The guests were free to dress as they wished, standing in the wispy grass and stone roads ribboning out from the entrance of the chapel.

I felt like a nun. This was the wedding night—our chance to meet the seductively charming strangers we had firmly pencilled into our travel plans. We had both wanted to feel sexy and mingle as we flirted with single male wedding guests. Tanja said we were still sexy in our chosen attire and not to worry, and she was probably right. But I would have chosen to wear something that didn't have a "buttoned up all the way" feel to it.

The ceremony began soon after, and it was absolutely beautiful. The small chapel was identical to one of the few I'd seen dotting the hillsides from the bus earlier. Perched on a sloped green hill, the humming of the cicadas fell in tune with the strings of a lute and mandolin strung love song. The charming white church bathed in golden afternoon light as the sun began to dip behind us.

More than 850 guests were in attendance at this wedding, half of which came to the ceremony while the remainder waited at the reception hall down the hill.

A stone path with wide steps led to the small white chapel through the trees lined with light green and white ribbons and softly burning candles.

When the bride arrived, she was tenderly led along these steps to the church, her white dress billowing gently behind her. In front of her, two men played the lute and bouzouki (a long-necked stringed instrument) and sang traditional Greek songs as she slowly but purposefully approached the chapel.

Then the ceremony began, and the guests closed in a little more tightly around them, all standing and watching in respectful silence. The priest had long, decorative robes, and even though I didn't understand a word they were saying, the matrimonial recitations were intimate and sweet. The love between the groom and the bride, their families, their guests, the setting—it was so magically palpable. I remember feeling overwhelmed with emotion and ever grateful to have been present as an invited guest on this green-golden hillside, attending a Cretan wedding amongst the warm smiles and teary strangers.

And then, *he* arrived. The Greek God I had been waiting for. He arrived in the form of Manos, a tall, broad-shouldered, dark-haired man with a chiselled jaw, wearing a crisp white shirt, dazzling with his penetrating, sapphire eyes and a smile that could have easily undone every one of my buttoned-up buttons. He was everything I had hoped to meet. Any grouchy residue I might have had melted away as he turned his smile towards me and said hello. *Hello.*

Hellos turned into the friendly, flirty chatter I had been waiting for. He had an MA in physics, taught physics to high school students, doubled as a tango instructor, and held my gaze with blue eyes deeper than the cosmos. He asked me all the right questions and flattered me at every turn. *Why wasn't I married? Where was my boyfriend?* He showed me how to throw rice at the happy couple at the right moment they emerged from the chapel. I just smiled, flirted back, and casually mentioned I was in Chania for a few days, even going to be alone the last night, *wink, wink, nudge, nudge.* For the next two hours, we talked and laughed and teased. I had no idea where Tanja had gone but I was not worried one bit.

As the guests began to make their way to dinner, Manos told me he was leaving the reception early to go tango dancing and asked if I would like to come? *Yes! Yes, I would like! Take me and tango me and dip me and speak to me in honeyed Greek language that I don't need to understand.* This was exactly the side dish of fun we had been looking for.

But...I said no, regretfully. Double emphasis on the *regretfully.* As much as I wanted to go, I felt it would be too impolite to abandon my friend on this particular night of all nights. I hoped Manos would ask for my number, maybe ask me out on a different night, or at least dance with me at the wedding.

Unfortunately, as we arrived at the reception, I was expected to sit at a table reserved for "Guests from England," directly under the bridal party table. He was seated about 14 miles away, on the other side of the massive hall accommodating 850 party guests, and I didn't see him for some time. The wedding celebration was toned down due to the groom's uncle's recent passing, so there wasn't as much mingling amongst other guests as there might have otherwise been.

The feasting began, and so did the dancing. A little while later, I finally spotted him. I noticed him and his friend rise from their table and extend their affectionate polite goodbyes to the bride. I saw those deep, mesmerising eyes search me out in the crowd and then lock in on mine. I waved a friendly goodbye, he blew me a kiss, and then he was gone.

Fuck.

The grouchiness and irritability quickly returned. I glanced over at my friend. Tanja seemed so happy and overwhelmed with emotion from the beautiful wedding and having watched her longtime friend get married. She was also, fair enough, too enchanted for conversation. It seemed I was on my own for conversation amongst the other foreigners sitting at the table demarcated with a sign labelling us all as "Guests from England".

Tanja has an enviable ability to just let go and float away when she needs to. She's ever so present in the moment. It's good, so good, for the soul, I realise, not to harbour stresses and just enjoy mountain-peaked moments in life like this one was for her. But for me, I couldn't join her at her level on this one, so I took a look around to see where else I could focus my attention.

Honestly, I was disappointed with my options. At my table was Tanja, in her own world and happily smoking a cigarette, but the rest of the guests I sat with made me feel like I was at the wrong table. That's where I was in the rollercoaster of moods I had been riding on thus far in my trip.

Next to Tanja was Jessie, an English lesbian who said inappropriate and dirty things too loudly, knocked over two drinks in the course of the night (breaking one) and threw up in the ladies' room. Her companion, Ron, was next to me, an obese English gay guy who, when earlier we had danced the Greek circle dances (the Sirtaki?), was so drunk, his heavy arm on my neck weighed me down like I was propping him up rather than joining the circle of friends. Down the table loomed Adrian, who I still hadn't really warmed up to and whose comments managed to alienate me even more during the course of the night. Sasha, who seemed genuinely cool, sat too far away for conversation. Magda was there too, a young Greek woman, but who was someone I hadn't met yet and unfortunately sat just out of my line of sight with no opportunity to swap seats. Finally, at the end of our table, sat the German or maybe Dutch guy with the twitchy blinking eyes. I sighed. *Thank god for the endless supply of homemade wine.*

The festivities carried on like this for several hours. As it was nearing 4 a.m., things were beginning to slowly wind down, although most people seemed happy to stay and mingle even if the dancing was slowing.

I was wearing out and ready to call it a night. Tanja, however, wasn't quite ready to leave, so I decided to make my own way home. I asked Adrian, who had rented a car, when he was planning on leaving the reception. He didn't give me a simple "not for a while." Instead, he launched into one of his asshole-ish, long-winded, French-accented replies I wasn't yet accustomed to: "Ven I leeve, I 'ave to take zee car with zee luggage to zee 'otel'. Zen, I 'ave to come back, pick up zee pee-pole, take zem to zee 'otel. Zen I 'ave to come back and pick up zee othya pee-pole..." and on and on he went. Apparently, the other guests hadn't checked into their hotel yet, so Adrian's car was full of suitcases. Fine. I found Tanya's bookshop owner friend, who was sitting quietly by himself, and asked if he knew about options for calling a taxi. He didn't.

Finally, I looked around the hall until I spotted the hottest looking waiter working the tables. I walked up to *him* and very politely and helplessly asked him how I could get a taxi home. There was an exchange of Greek between him and another couple of waiters, and then he explained to me in fractured bits of English that there was no taxi at this late hour in this small village, but he would gladly take me back to my hotel. *Great!*

I probably should have stayed at the wedding until the end of the night, but I had completely depleted my energy and had tired. I was still carrying this persistent feeling of not quite connecting with the others, and Manos was long gone (as was probably most of our table wine). So, I said goodbye to everyone, hugged Tanja, and followed the tall, dark-headed waiter out the door.

He drove a dirty pickup truck, to my delight, and wrenched open my door. I hopped right in. *Fantastic.* The night was so warm, and there were a billion stars twinkling so brightly up above us in the summer nighttime sky. He knew where the village where I was staying was, and while I had neither an idea of how to give him directions to my hotel, nor a memory of the name, I assured him I would know it when I saw it. (Sure I would).

We drove off into the night, talking and talking in simple English (he wasn't as articulate as Manos the Tango God) and was more dishevelled looking and sweaty from serving platters of food and decanters of wine all night—but he'd do. He drove me to the village, and we cruised up and down a few dark streets until I spotted the Kokodopolous or whatever the word was for the hotel we had checked into earlier that day.

Pausing for a moment in front of my hotel, he looked at me and said, "You want drink?"

Yep!! I sure do! Not even attempting to exit the car, we kept driving past the hotel towards this thatched-roof bar that was still open and serving drinks on the beach. I took a seat next to the water, and he ordered two glasses of red wine as we began to talk about sea turtles.

Why sea turtles? Because we were next to the water, and between our hilariously limited knowledge of the other's language, I thought this was as good a topic as any.

"Thelássies chelónes." That is how you say *sea turtles* in Greek. But he said he had never seen any here. We couldn't talk about much in-depth, but I didn't care. I was finally talking with someone not from the UK. A good-looking Cretan man was taking me out for a drink by the sea, and that was fine with me. It was a hot night, the red wine was chilled, and the crashy dark sea felicitously joined alongside us.

Suddenly, his cell phone rang. He answered it and rattled off in Greek, then hung up and smiled convincingly at me. He told me it was his boss. I think perhaps he was supposed to be working still, as the wedding reception was still carrying on. I asked if he was in trouble, and he said no, waved his hand, no problem. We continued talking.

A few minutes later, his phone rang again. He answered, talked frantically in Greek, then hung up and looked at me and very calmly said, "My boss is screaming."

What? Screaming?

"Yes. My boss is, ah, screaming."

I guess his little jaunt to the bar with the American wedding guest didn't go over well with his boss as they were trying to end a wedding reception hosting over 850 people.

So we had to abandon our half-drunk drinks. He drove me back to my hotel. I said goodbye in the cab. While there hadn't been enough sparks for a passionate goodbye make out session in the cab of his truck, he did take my number and asked me to meet him the next day. He would keep his promise and call a few times the next day, but in the end, I wouldn't answer. There were other plans to hatch, and I didn't know that I was up for more wine-infused sea turtle talk.

As he dropped me off, he stopped his truck in the middle of the road, which soon began to hold up a line of cars that had suddenly appeared. I said goodbye and jumped out. When I did, I noticed that the line of cars waiting for us belonged to the rest of the wedding guests from England, and we had been blocking their way.

I just smiled and waved at their faces through the window, in a happier mood now, having run off with the Greek waiter. Driving the second car in line was a cheerful Tanja, with a very exhausted Sasha in the passenger seat. It turns out that the tired and drunk wedding guests in each of the cars were a little pissed off because, as no one had bothered checking in before the wedding, the hotels had given away their rooms.

It was past five in the morning, and about eight people had nowhere to stay. Adrian was drunk and irate because no one would let him drive the car he rented, but Tanja and I were ecstatic and giggly; she because she was driving, and I because I'd had my date after all.

SATURDAY, DAY 6

Georgioupolis

THE MORNING AFTER THE wedding, at 6 a.m., Tanja and I finally abandoned the revelled-out wedding guests and tucked away into our own
room. I crawled into my clean but stained sheets and listened to the
sea. It crashed and rolled away again and again, gentle and strong and
loud in the early morning stillness when the light in the sky takes on
a bluish hue before dawn. The waves roared and rolled forward with
grace and might and crashed and splayed and pulled back, calm and
then fierce. My gaze shifted to the dark branches of the just-out-of-
reach fig tree.

A few feet to my left, Tanja had tucked into her bed, a little restless, turning in her sheets. I could tell she was listening to the sea, too.
After not too many moments had passed at all, she sat up, suddenly
excited, and shared one of her many spontaneous ideas that have
endeared us as forever friends. She said, "The sun's going to rise. Want
to watch it?"

And I said, "Let's take our bikinis."

So at about 6:15 a.m., with zero sleep all night, wine in our
heads, and joy in our hearts, we bounded down the broken stone roads
to the beach in the last moments of the lifting dark.

The coastline in Georgioupolis was shaped like a small crescent,
and in these blurry morning moments, was without a single other soul
on the sand.

At the northern tip of the coast, perched on the craggy rocks
was a small chapel, with foamy waves crashing behind it. The white
spray of the sea accentuated the white, weathered wood. The southern
tip of the beach was shadowed with hills, and behind us, rising high,
were the first peaks of island mountains that staggered and towered
in rows, stretching back to the west. A hint of golden daylight just

barely glinted on the horizon, but the hills cupping the small cove twinkled mostly with the porch lights of aged homes while the indigo skies still glittered with a million bright stars.

The sea was calm enough, and the tide was high. We jumped right in.

There are not words perfect enough to describe how good this all felt. The water was salty warm, and the sand on the ocean floor slipped through our toes like silk. We swam way, way out, kicking past where the waves broke and just rode the swells for an eternity. Or maybe an hour.

The sea kept moving always away, away, and back toward the eastern sky. And as the earliest light began to wake up the morning, it was impossible to be sure where the horizon lay, as the colours from the sea and the sky spilt rosy ink into each other, and so evenly blended air and water in the pink daffodil dawn.

One by one, the stars snuck away over and behind the darkened mountains in the west behind us. The water chameleoned from deep black to a shimmery silver to iridescent sunlight, and we swam and laughed, slipping in and out of our bikinis, the warm water rinsing over our shoulders, our hair like seaweed on our salty skin. Never before had I experienced an Aegean sunrise such as this. I don't know if I ever will again.

Two hours passed like there was no time at all. It was a little chilly when we dripped out of the sea to sit on the sand and gaze out as the sun made its full, grand entrance and warmed us just a little. Spectacular. We'd been so spoiled by having the entire beach and morning to ourselves that when a lone man with a camera showed up to snap pictures of the serene morning light, we were slightly annoyed. *Go on home, please. Leave us to our sleepy, golden beach.*

We made our way back to our *katályma*, climbed up the cement stairs, and crawled into our bed sheets. Only three hours later, Tanja awoke, declaring that she was starving. I had no fewer than 16 bug bites on my legs between my knee and my toes, including one on the bottom of my foot. That was my payment for sleeping with the balcony door open so I could fall asleep to the sound of the sea, my eyes drinking in the fig tree, its branches twisting away and up into the sky.

That entire day was spent breakfasting, swimming in the sea and lounging with Dimitris' other Greek friends who we'd not yet had a chance to meet. One of his friends was tall with a lovely smile, pale blue eyes that seemed endlessly light, and wavy, wild, soft brown hair. His name was Polykarpus. We sat on sandy towels, drinking frappés, and talking to him about a book he was reading by the Cretan author Nikos Kazantzakis, the same author of *Zorba the Greek*.

A hung-over Adrian and Sasha arrived at the beach, and Adrian joined me in the water for a refreshing swim. Though his company always seemed to trigger annoyance in me, when talking to him one on one out in the water, it dawned on me that perhaps he didn't realise how he came across to some people. Maybe he was an ego-driven conversationalist, but with the intention to be jovial and interesting. This was far more forgivable, and it was that morning that I decided not to be so hard on him in my head. Then, I could try and understand him a little more; I could just shrug off anything mildly offensive and enjoy the moment of chatter instead.

The sunny, post-wedding day on the beach eventually came to an end. We packed up and took a bus—much less of an ordeal this time—back to our sweet little room in Pension Theresa in Chania.

I so often get caught in the momentum of a place or in wonderful chats with friendly faces—the collective newness combined with the joy of being with old friends. The sun, the salt, the sea, the wine. The energy lifts us up so high that eventually, we realise how spent we have become. Depleted, we slide down into an emotional space where quiet and aloneness are a welcomed reprieve.

In one of these slides, after the events of the previous few days in Chania and Georgioupolis, the evening took a strange turn. Tanja was tired and chose to go to bed for a while, but I was a mix of energy and emotions. I was still buzzing from the day but also a bit restless and irritable. I decided to walk around the Old Harbor in the evening by myself.

It was good. I need this sometimes—more often than I realise—walking around mildly lost for a while, without a map or a destination or concern. It gives me a chance to take a closer look around at the place where I am: the people walking by, the shop owners busy with customers, the old buildings and cafés and small twisty roads with centuries of stories breathed into them. I just walk and take in the night air. It's when I truly feel I can see a place and just walk within it, amongst it, watching, listening, admiring, and soaking in each vibe. I walked past the boats on the harbour just opposite the humming nightlife that was just beginning to raise its frequency. The harbour collected the echo of the music, the laughter, the night, and I could walk, part in that world, but very much in my own. Thinking, not thinking, walking, watching, and taking a few breaths to myself.

This is when I saw the sea turtle.

She was swimming on her own among the small speed boats moored and knocking in the harbour. She floated at the surface for a minute taking in a few breaths herself before turning to duck down under the murky water.

It was incredible. I had never seen a sea turtle in the wild before. She was so calm and so big. I fumbled for my camera, but by the time I had dug it out of my bag and flicked it on, the creature had glided up and over and off between and then under the boats. The picture I snapped showed only the dirty harbour water, disturbed with bubbles and foam.

But what an amazing sight I had seen for just a moment. That waiter who'd driven me home from the wedding the night before (I might as well just call him Georgios, too) told me he had never before seen one, but here, just a few coves down, here she was. Maybe he had never looked long enough at the water. The sea turtle was huge and didn't seem to have been hiding. She had only come up for a peek and a breath.

After that, I decided I didn't want to be around crowds or a part of any rising revelry, so I headed back to the Pension to be on my own and chose to take the small iron staircase that led to the rooftop of our charming building. From there, I knew there would be a view of the harbour, even if it was a night view. I could feel the energy of the village and still remain in my own cocoon and just let all I was thinking flow freely.

On the roof, the outdoor area had been set up with a few tables and chairs under overhanging leafy plants and vines. It was so lush, this cosy, tiny rooftop orchard. Against the wall stood a small cupboard, complete with packages of uncooked pasta, a bottle of liquor, a fruit bowl, and Greek sweets, all apparently there for guests to help themselves to. The building opposite the street was almost completely shrouded in darkness, with tangled ivy encircling large, rectangle windows with neither glass nor screens, but only wide-open shutters that invited in the night.

The rooftop nook itself was very dark, but I kept the lights off so that I could watch from high the chatty harbour below. I could see the historical lighthouse blinking in the distance, and I listened to the water's gentle slap against the stones.

Glancing over at the ivy building once more, I saw something that hadn't been there a moment before. Standing, alert and taut in the window, was the silhouette of a naked man. From his strong legs to his broad shoulders, his masculine figure filled up the frame. A dim light was behind him, and he seemed to be staring across the space above our street and over at me. His posture was leaning forward a little, and I think he might have been trying to see if I was there or not because I was sitting in so much darkness.

I took a good measure of him. *Oh my god.* I looked away. *Be polite.* Then I thought, "Is he really naked?" I looked again for a little longer this time. He seemed strong, muscular, solid. And naked. Very naked. His hand on the window frame, he assumed a casual but investigative posture.

He was definitely looking my way. *Oh my god.* I looked away again, somewhat embarrassed. Then I thought, *what's he doing? Does he want me to look? Maybe.*

So I looked a third time, but this time the window frame was empty except for the light that took back the space where his masculine outline had been. *Damn. And, oh my god.* That night was gifting me with incredible, unexpected natural delights—a sea turtle and a naked man.

Moments later, Tanja joined me after waking from her rest, and I told her all about it. If he was still up there, it was likely he could hear us whispering and giggling, but he didn't return to the window. He had been a presence for me just like the sea turtle had been—gone before I could get a good look.

The entire trip to Crete so far had been a series of peaks and troughs, excitement and adventure, love and nostalgia, energy and exhaustion. As Tanja joined me, we started to retrace everything the past few days had given us. There was something about finally sitting still, watching, letting the encounters of the day and night and what they meant sift and sink into ourselves. The beaches, the wedding, the old friends, the new acquaintances, the sun, the frappés, the bustle of travel. I loved it all, but I was unrested, without the timing or space to release sorrow or worry. The truth was, I hadn't yet recovered or caught up with the tumultuous ripple of moments before landing in Chania. I just couldn't find my groove. The upswings and downward slides were finally taking their toll.

And up there, on the darkened roof, watching and thinking and talking openly, what I had balled up inside finally began to come undone: the thoughts I hadn't given space to; the emotions I'd fed frappés and beer and olives to instead of having given them room to breathe out; the sad goodbyes I hadn't shed enough tears for after having flown away from California (once again) and travelled so quickly to the Mediterranean; the anticipation of work and the teaching I would soon return to; the new school year set to begin a day after our return. I hadn't yet processed all of that. I definitely hadn't yet processed having travelled through three countries in only four days, all the hormone-fueled emotions and energy I'd spent without care, the love and loss our friend Dimitris had shared with us this week alongside his family, the wedding and the funeral, the strange fusion of being in my own element and completely out of place all at once. All of it had been swimming inside my heart as I swam in the sun and looked up and away. I hadn't wanted to look within at the well of tears when I had so much around to revel in.

The lone walk had helped settle my thoughts. Sitting in the dark just watching the night go by had helped too. Throughout my life, I've come to realise that this is a pattern I follow—that I close down so tightly too many of those thoughts and emotions that suffocate for too long. So often, I hope it'll be alright, that these feelings will dissipate, and I won't have to give them their moment or look at them too closely and ruin a day, a memory, or even an entire trip doing so. I tell myself I can just move effortlessly from joy to joy to joy—that I can keep going. That the tension I ball and weave so tightly will disappear into itself and be gone. But tightly woven balls always seem to find a way of unravelling anyway.

The nighttime orchard on the cosy roof hugged me close, and I finally had the space to put into words all that had been swirling inside. And then it broke free. I had a good long cry on that roof and let my frustrations and sorrows cascade out of my heart, and onto the shoulders of my friend, who listened, was comforting, sweet, and sorry for me.

It seems no matter where you go, no matter how much joy you find around you, how much excitement or sunshine, when your insides need to spill, they will spill. And so I did. Solitude had been needed. The dark had helped me feel safe. The view had been so comforting. The long cry and the still, lone moment with a kind friend turned out to be just what I had been in need of.

And then, things started to get better. Things started to get way better.

By now, it was nearly 1 a.m., and neither Tanja nor I had eaten dinner. Released from my watery emotions and Tanja now rested, we decided to return to the harbour below and sit at a seaside table.

The waiter at the cafe we chose explained he had practically nothing on the menu at this hour, so we ordered what he had, which was mainly salad and bread, but Tanja managed to order some *moussaka,* a type of Greek lasagna. Two orders of wine later, a hearty and much-needed laugh, Magda the Greek, who was also a wedding guest from England, happened to walk by. After inviting her over with a friendly wave, she joined us.

She, too, had been wandering the harbour, looking for others to join. She found us. The ambience of the late-night hours at the seaside café was waning, so the three of us returned to the rooftop of the Pension once again, where we raided what I thought was a complimentary bottle of red wine. I couldn't read the Greek labels of any food or drink, so I didn't bother with this one. I emptied the red bottle generously between three glasses, and we chatted away laughing, and cheers-ing into the late hours.

Turns out, I should have at least read the label. The wine was very thick and robust and tasted different from the wine I had become used to enjoying in Crete. I looked closer and read the label out loud: "Vin de Liqueur." The two girls burst into laughter. I thought I had mispronounced, but it turned out I had mispoured. It was a bottle of port I had emptied, not wine, and was meant to be enjoyed in much smaller portions than what we now had before us. Comfortably nosing through the cabinet of complimentary delights, I discovered a package of honey-sweetened pastries, and we dined on those as well.

It was a perfect way to end a day that cradled sea turtles, a naked Greek man, hot tears, a hot sun, and had begun with a sunrise swim.

~

THE DAYS THAT FOLLOWED the release on the rooftop were the most enchanting.

Time turned in on itself. It curled into a tight cat-like ball, so small and barely noticeable in those moments that time seemed not to exist at all. It was as if I had been fully released of any weighty worry or fracturing fears my mind would create and could finally just float through the days lightly and without measure.

These final three days, I became more myself and ever so present.

I allowed myself to completely, simply be.

Any attempt to chart the moments that filled the following days and bound them into the hours and minutes they possessed would be ridiculous. When my mind returns to those final days in Crete, all of the feelings champagne bubble from my heart: the lightness of joy and the magic of love and untethered freedom. Such moments were created in a morning or a week but stretched out far beyond that time frame, alive and surpassing the boundaries of time so that now, with just a flicker of thought, years having passed, these moments and their emotions return in full, spilling from the far reaches of my mind, filling again all of the space in my heart as if I were back on that island, back in that place, present, connected, and loved.

Time and love seemed endless and infinite there.

These were not moments to photograph to keep them close. No. I can only close my eyes, drift back in my mind, and breathe them in.

SUNDAY, DAY 7

Chania

WHILE SUNNING ON THE beach in Georgioupolis the day before, we had made plans with Dimitris to meet at his parents' house at noon this day for a three-hour tour of the family land.

Even though Tanja and I had again eaten late into the night—moussaka and honey pastries and wine and port—we awoke famished. Perhaps it was the rush of emotions we had washed up and over and out only hours before.

And so we indulged. Our late breakfast this morning was served up as chilled, fresh melon cubes, homemade crunchy granola, creamy Greek yoghurt, local sweet honey, and more soft, flaky pastries baked just that morning. And, of course, two cups of rich, dark coffee in dainty porcelain cups.

An hour later, we ventured to Dimitris' family home, where his parents had prepared us a traditional, generous lunch offering of fresh Greek salads, home-baked bread, local cheeses, roasted goat, baked chicken, rosemary lamb, and bowls of aromatic rice. The table was laden with every traditional dish, ready for us to dine. Even with full bellies from a late breakfast, we still happily sat around his parents' table, grateful again for the family-style hospitality we were shown.

By now, we had wised up as to how time flows amongst the locals in Crete. The hours pass by slowly, and events run late. The mid-day meal began at 2 p.m. We dined until three. Ever so full of every kind of delightful dish, we headed off on a trek through orchards, sumptuous hills, and bountiful farmland.

Our group consisted of myself and Tanja, Dimitris, Polykarpos (who I later found out was Dimitris' best man and the godfather of his child), Adrian, Sasha, Marina (another friend from Cambridge I hadn't yet met), and Dimitris' father.

I've long forgotten Dimitris' father's name, but he was warmly weathered in all the ways that men who raise children and crops, curate vineyards and orchards, and work hard in the fields all their life grow old to be. He was kind. He spoke no English, but his smiling eyes and calm demeanour were enough. He grinned proudly under the brim of his flat cap as he drove us in his old rickety truck through mountain roads, chatting in Greek to his son along the way.

A second car was needed to carry us all, and so we caravanned to the outskirts of his village, led by Dimitris' father up into the White Mountains through an area called Drakona.

Passing through acres of picturesque hills, we seemed to move through time, back to how the old country must have felt decades or centuries ago. The roads wound higher and higher, rising above dry valleys sketched and carved by borders of olive grove after olive grove and vineyard after vineyard. The sky was one of the bluest I'd ever seen, and the day was again blazing hot, but the sparkling sea was just in sight, peek-a-boo-ing between the hills from the east as we drove further inland.

Around each bend, old, crumbling houses peeked out from the woody and dusty hillside. Some were abandoned, and some decorated with laundry hanging on lines in the yard to dry. Some featured a broom or a truck in the drive or some other telltale sign that the house was thriving with life and bustling.

Dimitris' dad would pull over every now and then at unmarked viewpoints along the road, overlooking the small but vast views. We'd climb out of the vehicles to breathe in the hot air lightly fragrant with mountain tea that grew so wildly beyond the roads.

His dad was short and tanned, and his balding, white head of hair was complemented with a thick white moustache. He'd wave his muscled arm over the scenery that opened wide before us and speak rapidly in Greek. Dimitris would translate:

His family owned all of this land. All of the land you can see to the sea. Up that road, he gestured, is his wife's village. Her family still lives there. Down below, he waved, were his vineyards. Vineyards and orchards. More was to come.

We city-dwellers snapped photos as we drove, impressed by how much land his father had worked all his life. We inhaled it deeply, then climbed back in the car and carried on up the mountain.

The old road wound up and around, and the sea became a more distant blue-sparkling dot as the landscape became more pervasive. The hillside we hugged was cliffed high by stone walls that rose straight up toward the sky.

Around about the third wide bend, the landscape turned wilder with the addition of mountain goats surprising us as much as we surprised them. These mountain goats were perched and balanced on the thinnest, most uneven ledges of the cliffside. They gazed down at us with bugged eyes, rudely chewing grass with their mouths open as we passed. Delighted—and startled—we stared right back.

Dimitris' father drove along a little farther, then slowed down as we approached another drive that quietly veered off the main road. We had arrived at Dimitris' grandmother's house. She had passed 10 or 11 years prior, but her small home, built seemingly only with stones, still sat alone amongst the Cypress trees, not quite a ruin, but kindly inviting in its semi-crumbling state.

The house hadn't been lived in for all this time. The two-story, white-walled house was now overgrown with branchy trees and bushes shamelessly crowding the paths, grappling into doorways, and reclaiming the space. The herbs—thyme or rosemary and mountain tea—bloomed with abandon, blending fragrantly as they scented the air, abundant with vines and dusty perfumed leaves.

We climbed single file through the low, scratchy branches, legs scraped by dry bushes as we walked towards the house. In the yard stood a large, old-fashioned cement tub that had once been used for winemaking. It was purple-stained and dusty but could still be re-employed if desired. It was propped up so that the drain at one end could freely pour into a bucket or a barrel.

Dimitris explained that the cement tub would be filled with grapes from their nearby vineyard, then a few of the older kids would squash the grapes with their bare feet until the juice flowed down and out of the pipe at the end of the tub.

Exploring her homestead more, we discovered wild blackberries growing along the side of the house and road, and so we freely picked a few handfuls. They were thick and bitter and sweet and juicy and wild on our tongues.

The wooden door leading inside the house was unlocked, and I remember only one main front room, bare but still cosy with dusty wooden furniture sparsely scattered about. In the far corner was a rickety wooden staircase. Dimitris' father momentarily disappeared and scared down a small black bat that flapped around frantically before flying out an open window.

The house was so old that it was falling apart in places, worn by time and the wear of growing families and changing seasons. But something about it still emanated a cosiness. The air felt heady and wonderfully dense from all the love and life that had once breathed here. The rubble on the stone floors seemed to me to be more like cake crumbs, the wide, white walls like a snug blanket as the windows on each side filtered in bright, enchanting light. It was as if the house had seen so much life in past years that it was doing just fine on its own for a while—a brief repose. Dimitris shared with us his plans to renovate it and move in with his own family after a few years. How beautifully perfect.

I'm not sure why—perhaps it was the aroma of the wild berry bushes and the twinkling of dust we'd kicked up in the sunlight, the bitter wine in the ageing, disused house, and sharing all these warm memories with these old and new friends—but my heart in those moments felt so full, I could almost have cried. I think it was one of the most loved-in places I'd ever been.

As we started to leave, we discovered two old and dusty barrels parked in the corner of an adjoining room. They were still sealed and filled with homemade wine.

Was the wine still good? Could we taste it? Sure we could.

Dimitris syphoned wine out with his mouth by using a hose. A few dusty glasses were set up on a cobwebbed wooden table in the middle of the room, so we rinsed them off and poured ourselves a few sips of 40-year-old homemade wine.

What did it taste like? It tasted like summer in Crete.

STILL SUNDAY, DAY 7
Somewhere in Crete

LEAVING DIMITRIS' GRANDMOTHER'S HOUSE with a fond look back, we continued on. Driving still higher up the mountain, rounding even more scenic views of hillsides and far-off seas, we drove until we pulled off into a cleared area near an old church.

From there, those in the second car could only continue along a dirt road by foot; it was unsuitable for regular rental cars. Only vehicles equipped with 4 x4 could handle the rough roads.

Dimitris' dad drove his truck, which was dusty and dirty and perfectly suited for farm life in the hills. In Greek, his father apologised to us and kindly explained that the pickup could only hold three people inside the cab, and only two of the three girls would be able to fit inside. One of us nice girls would have to ride in the open bed in the back of the truck with the boys.

It was a chivalrous gesture, but wasted on girls like Tanja, Marina, and me. All my life, I've been the first one to volunteer for a bumpy ride in the back of a dirty pickup, and Tanja and Marina were kindred spirits. Happily, the three of us girls hopped into the rusty, ridge-lined bed of the pickup, holding on to the sides. So, even though Dimitris and his dad had attempted to be gentlemen and considerate hosts, in the end, it was Sasha and Adrian who were assigned to the comfort of the cab. Dark-eyed Dimitris and light-eyed Polykarpos stretched their long legs out next to us girls for the rackety ride in the rusty and dirty bed of the pickup truck.

And it was great! Grinning from ear to ear, we bumped and bounced even higher up the mountain and past more bug-eyed goats. The truck careened and loomed over more valleys, stirring up so much dust it seemed more like fog; it was so thick.

Dimitris' father drove us directly to their family's own vineyard.

There, we piled out of the truck and wandered through the rows of grapevines and fig trees, picking the fresh fruits—both of which were carefully fenced in with wire so that the wild mountain goats didn't break through to feast on the delights Dimitris' dad had worked so hard to grow.

A herd of goats scampered away fearfully upon our arrival, some of their collars fixed with bells that jingled as they hoofed off into the brambles. The boys set to picking, and we filled a cloth bag with as many fruits as we could, laughing and enjoying small mouthfuls of the sweet, sun-warmed fruit.

The afternoon had begun to turn late, and Dimitris' dad needed to drive Marina back to his village to catch her flight. He could drive us all, or we could easily walk. Tanja opted for the lift back down the mountain; the rest of us decided it would be pleasant enough to walk down the path carrying our sacks full of nature's bounty.

This is when I fell in love.

The sun, though slanting, was still a few hours away from setting. It settled less high in the sky to cast ambient shadows through the trees. It was just me and the boys: Dimitris, Adrian, Sasha, and Polykarpos.

For a few moments, the Greeks talked in Greek and picked the choicest figs, the Cambridge boys sat in the shade, and I climbed up the nearby rocks on my own and took in the stunning scenery of Crete's wild mountains outstretched before me. I absorbed the beauty of the craggy valleys, the blue beyond—both sky and sea—and listened for the tinkering of not-so-far-away goat bells.

A few minutes later, we all set off to walk down the mountain. Dimitris was lovely and commented how the entire afternoon had felt so wonderful: having his best friend Polykarpos there, and then his close school friends from Cambridge present, and even me, who even though he'd just met me, said that I felt like a part of his clan. He said it seemed like we'd all known each other for ages. The day felt so seamless.

It's a magic I often feel in places of unexpected beauty and serendipitous connection. When the unforeseen plays out with such charm and the experiences feel so perfectly planned, my heart beat a little more excitedly to hear this sentiment reflected right back.

As Dimitris pointed out caves tunnelling into the sides of mountains as he walked down the path, Polykarpos and I walked ahead of the others, kicking up so much clean dust our bare feet and legs were completely covered in a silky powder. My teal toenail polish didn't even punch through; the dust was so thick. It was such a full feeling. The energy vibrated so high from walking through the wilderness along these old, timeless roads with these men. Even though we were a little sun-blistered, bug-bitten, and filthy.

I talked and walked with Polykarpos, the tall, messy-haired, unshaven Greek, who listened with soft, sincere blue eyes. He was quiet but laughed easily and had a way of gently touching my back when he was listening to something I was saying, or putting his hand softly on my shoulder so that I knew his every attention was completely mine.

I don't know what it was exactly. Perhaps it was the ripe figs he picked and handed me, or the salty, sea-blown air arousing our senses, or the scent of the mountain tea that permeated our every breath, or the thrill of being out in the wild hillsides with these boys, but I was wholly untethered and drawn in by the essence of him. He could have grinned or winked or laughed with me just one second more, and I would have set free every pure, joyful laugh inside, thrust my dusty arms around his neck, and I would have been all his. I'm not sure if he even knew it.

The five of us traipsed back down the mountain where Tanja was waiting, relaxing on the stones of a fountain next to another old church, overlooking yet another stunning view. We washed off our dirty hands, faces, and feet in a fountain and ate more of the fruit we had collected.

After the views, the vineyards, the churches, the small homes, we stopped for a coffee at a village café, then headed back down the mountain, no longer in pickup truck beds, but back inside the cars.

On our way down the mountain, we stopped twice more. It was dusk, and the view of Chania was simply beautiful. Fading sunlight filtered its last bits of light over the valley. Beyond, the city lights closer to the sea began to blink on, and the stars above started twinkling awake. In the Old Harbor, we could make out the lights on the large ferry preparing to depart across the Aegean and return Tanja to Athens in just a couple of hours.

As we dropped her off, she hugged goodbye her old friend Dimtris and hugged a goodbye to me. She climbed the ramp, blew us one last farewell kiss, and boarded the boat.

I wasn't sure why, but in those moments I felt the tears well up again—even though I was going to see her in two days back in London after I took my own ferry and flight home to the UK. Even though now I felt I had finally bonded with others and didn't feel alone or apart anymore or anywhere near what I had been feeling leading up to the wedding.

And even though I'd already cried fully on this trip, I still felt the emotion swelling inside. I was truly sad to see her leave and for this day and this part of our trip together to end. It had been such a beautiful, seemingly endless 24 hours, beginning with the good long cry on our balcony the evening before, the magical day we had had, and now the storybook goodbye as she boarded a ship in the warm, starry night. It was just the end of the day, not the end of our trip, but I still felt an ending all the same. It was strange to leave without the one you came with.

The remainder of our group piled back in the car with Polykarpos and then headed into town. We met up for dinner at a restaurant Dimitris was fond of, and we listened to beautiful live Greek music with guitars and bouzoukis. I could understand not a word. I didn't even know where one word ended and another began, but somehow that seemed to be just perfect too.

Dimitris, Sasha and Adrian discussed the next day's plans. This embodied their whole night's conversation. They seemed to love to organise and ponder over details I would never worry about. But this arrangement suited me just fine because it allowed me to sit back and chat alone with Polykarpos, trying not to be too obvious about how intrigued I was by him.

He lived in London and was returning the next night to Athens—the same night I was. Except he was taking a different boat from a different port. He planned to head to his parent's home first and offered to drive me somewhere in Athens and asked for my number.

We talked a little about sea turtles again, and I told him the hilarious story about the naked man we had seen in the window the night before. We talked of music, and he kept placing his hand gently on my back so that I kept losing track of what I was saying. His touch and kind words affected me in dizzying ways. It seemed like he had no hidden intentions in them and that this was merely his nature. But my heart skipped every time he did, just the same.

We ended the night early—about 1 a.m. The Greeks went home, Sasha and Adrian went to bed. I wanted to wander along the harbour again on my own, so I did. I watched the late-night diners and listened to their merry chatter, but my mind continued to linger on the day's dusty feet, mountain tea air, warm, ripe figs on my lips, and Polykarpus' smiling blue eyes.

I realised even then that I would never be able to stay inside these moments—moments in which I was unmissably present, and yet also in a breath, light-years away. I could only close my eyes and breathe them deeply in.

And just like that, in the length of one day, all I had struggled with was no more. I had spent the first days of this trip feeling disconnected and lonely. But one rooftop cry and a dusty road trip later, everything my heart had been missing had been delivered: love, connection, and moments I would always treasure.

I wandered back to my room in the Pension Teresa at about 3 a.m., a little lonelier now without Tanja, but with my heart full, and slept my last night in Chania.

MONDAY, DAY 8
Beyond Chania

Despite the late-night dinners that we'd quickly become accustomed to, we awoke early. It was another sweltering day. Sasha, Adrian, Polykarpos, and I were to embark on a full day of exploration and adventure on our own. Without the groom, without Tanja; just a crew of newly formed friends setting out into the Cretan hills.

That was the plan anyway—seeking out a hill to hike and a sea in which to swim.

Sasha and Adrian, true to their character, fussed between themselves over directions and details as they leaned against their rental car. Polykarpos was driving his car separately, as his boat was departing from a city a little farther away from Chania later that night.

It wasn't difficult for me to choose whose car I'd rather travel in. Polykarpos' car was dishevelled, but clean, and smelled like freshly picked mountain tea.

For all the boys' planning the night before, they hadn't managed to determine the best road leading out into the country, so, being no stranger to Crete's back roads, Polykarpos said he'd lead the way.

I let myself into the passenger side, and as I shut the door, I asked Polykarpos if he knew how to get wherever we were headed. He grinned over at me. "No," he smiled, then started his car.

We drove through the curving scenic hillsides talking and laughing and flirting as the warm wind blew inside the car, ruffled any loose bits of leaves, and tousled our hair. We stopped for directions then continued on, only to stop again a while later, be corrected by a kind stranger on the road, and then turn our car around and try again.

I suggested just following the coastline East, and that seemed good enough for Polykarpos; the boys following in their car behind us didn't protest. The view was as gorgeous as it had been during our bus ride to the wedding in Georgioupolis, and during Dimitris' dad's tour throughout his orchards.

The hiking trip quickly became a directionless road trip, but we did stumble across a warm lagoon at Stavros Beach. Fittingly, this might have been the hill where *Zorba the Greek* was filmed—the film version of the book that Polykarpos and I had discussed in our easy conversations.

Polykarpos stepped from the car, his tall frame rising above into the shimmering heat. He was looking for "shadows" for us to sit in, but there were no trees or rocks or shade to be found. This little beach only offered hot, soft sand, a beverage stand, and shady umbrellas for those who wanted to splurge.

The lagoon's turquoise waters invited us closer on a hot, dry day such as this. Eager to cool off, I decided to leave the boys for a minute and swim all the way across to the other side of the bay. The bay appeared small, but the other side was a lot farther than it looked— about 250 metres or 800 feet.

As I first set out, I felt the relief the cold, blue water offered up, as I reached arm over arm, swimming away from the shore. The relief turned to a pocket-sized thrill as I could no longer touch the ground. I swam a few more strokes, well past any other swimmers. About half-way across, once any other swimmers were just tiny anonymous heads in the distance, I felt the nervousness creep in.

Was this fear? I didn't believe that fear belonged anywhere inside of this day.

There were no waves to be frightened of in the bay. Biting fish circling my kicking toes, maybe. But any such fish would see me as the predator. Right?

Or did I fear swampy dead corpses from the deep, mud-heavy, seaweed sagging bodies reaching bony, clawed hands toward my legs, now that I was so far away, and a decently lengthy swim from my friends?

Yes. All of these things took their turn playing across the stage in my mind. Why do I imagine terrifying thoughts such as these? Because I'm a child. But still, I continued to swim. I swam to the other side of the lagoon, inhaled and exhaled an exalted victory breath— the breath of survivors and champions—and took in the view from the other side of the lagoon, towards the people-dotted beach I had swimmed away from. Then I swam back.

When I returned, the Cambridge boys decided they would go for it too. They immersed themselves into the lagoon and swam athletically away. I don't doubt that any fear they might have had was drowned in their friendly conversations shouted back and forth to each other between the strokes. Their competitive departure meant I could spend the remaining minutes of Polykarpos' time swimming with just him before he had to leave to catch his boat.

Accidentally on purpose, I had left a book in his car, and so as he set out to go, I walked with him back to retrieve it. We hugged a long goodbye, and promised to reach out again when we were both back in the UK. He'd never been to Brighton, so I told him he should come visit. Soon.

And off he drove. Taking his infinite blue eyes, his inviting smile, and his wispy, mountain tea-scented hair with him.

Alone, and with my spirits soaring, I walked across the hot sand back to the lapping, turquoise water.

Adrian had rented an umbrella and was applying sunscreen in the shade. Sasha was securely goggled and splashing around as he explored what treasures lay beneath the water, so I swam off on my own.

My thoughts floated along with me. For a moment, they drifted to Polykarpos—how charming and tall he was. They twirled and swirled around the beauty of the crystal- clear blue salty sea as it floated me with ease. They glided down my body as I soaked in the sensation of how hot and tanned and wholesome my body felt. And then, too, my mind returned to the cosy villages we'd driven through while lost—the aged, grapevine-covered houses we'd passed, and the light, tiny little things Polykarpos and I had laughed about that morning and the evening before. I floated on my back and closed my eyes to the sun.

I felt completely in love.

Love leaves a powerful imprint on your heart. I'm not referring to the forever kind of love, the love that spans decades, the kind that is held sacred between lovers, or the unbreakable affection between parents and their children—no. Some love can be lived in just a moment. It's the type of deep, pure, love that catches a breath in your throat. The kind of love that takes up all the space in the room. It lives heartily and fully in the present, and then is gone. It doesn't stay.

This true, but momentary love is a love only accessed by transcending the depths of memory, sinking you gently back to the place where the deep but fleeting essence of love felt like magic and was so tenderly consuming.

A nudging feeling poked softly at my spirit—a feeling reminding me that this moment was the height of all the love I would be able to feel on this trip. This was the pinnacle moment, floating in the sea. All of the romance filtering in and out of the week was only glowing soft and strong now because each piece had aligned in all the right ways: The tango dancer at the wedding, the waiter sneaking out to give me a ride home, the dusty walk alongside fig orchards, and a sideways grin from Polykarpos, the reunion of long-time friends and close-knit families offering platters of home-cooked food, the warm sun and salty sea, and the homemade wine alongside rooftop tears and laughter that filled our quaint harbourside rooms and bloomed within our hearts.

Somehow, I knew that a phone call or a text or an email may never come, and if it did, that precious, truest of moments I was feeling just then in Stavros Beach would have lifted away. The dusty particles of so much magic would still be hovering over the hot orchards in Crete, blending with the wild fragrance of the rugged hills. This moment could not exist in its fullness back in my routine world, where things are spoken and hurried, instead of felt and drawn out slowly. Grins and glances were exchanged that permeated time, and while in some ways I could return to this moment in my mind, this moment could not return to me.

And that is the very heartbreak of it all. A moment of love surged and bubbled and burst through my heart like a geyser as I floated in the warm, salty water. Then it sank right back through me.

It was a beautiful moment, even if I knew then that I wasn't living out a romance novel that ended with a rush of passion, or the kind of love people talk about when they marry someone, or the eternal kind of love mothers and fathers feel when they hold their children.

These were just slivers of time that pierced me right through— right through my heart, right through my soul. It's a lifelong love I will always feel because the pieces of these moments pierce my heart still when my thoughts return to them. I can travel back to that afternoon under the sun and remember moments that I never want to lose: the wine in the old house; the dusty, dirty toes on a downhill walk, hot wind in my hair; the salty warm water. I want to pocket those days away in my heart. Keep them safe and treasured. And every now and then, cup them in my palms, close my eyes and breathe them deeply in.

~

MY LAST DAY IN CRETE found me enjoying the afternoon heat with only Sasha and Adrian. Just the three of us, and without my mood, wedding events, road trips, or gorgeous Polykarpos to distract me, I was able to spend a little more time getting to know the Sasha and Adrian contingent.

I discovered just how likeable Sasha was. An organised and clean chap, he preferred the day's details to be figured out and enjoyed doing the figuring. It was refreshing to be around someone who didn't stress at all about the figuring and was thrilled to be travelling to Crete. Where I would bound barefoot and without supplies, he would have appropriate footwear, sustaining food products, and would make comments about his sugar level. I found all this quietly funny, but he was so taken in by the beauty of the mountains and the warm rolling sea and spoke with a politeness that was truly British. I found him to be a sweet and amicable travel companion.

Adrian. I still found him to be overbearing, but he was showing more redeemable characteristics. He bought me a frappé while I was still sunning by the lagoon and sent a tanned, foreign, muscly Greek hunk to deliver it to me. My crushes on Greek waiters were adding up.

A little later, we decided to leave our hot beach to search for some nearby monasteries. I laughed at their seemingly coordinated outfits: floppy, white hats, necks adorned with cameras, and Lonely Planet guides in hand. We three piled into the rental car, and Adrian drove, reading and complaining in French about the unhelpful Greek signs while perky Sasha navigated from the passenger seat, helpfully giving directions. I sat in the back seat watching grove after grove of olive trees roll by and observed pick-ups full of watermelons parked along the road every few miles.

The first monastery we came to was built sometime in the 17th Century. Plenty of stray cats mewed and lounged on reddish clay stones. Giant oil terracotta jugs dotted the stones while bees buzzed over lazy lizards soaking up the sun. You could see for miles from the roof—flat land and row upon row of golden groves as the sun began to retreat.

Beyond us stretched a deep gorge that sharply narrowed and dropped into the turquoise and sapphire ocean as it splashed roughly into a jagged crevasse.

Daylight was still with us, but somewhere between our exploring of the monastery, and the enamoured gazes we exchanged with the sea, the sun had sunk out of sight.

Starving and parched and almost deliriously happy with our surprising discovery of the sea-view gorge, we finished off the water that had been warming in the rental car.

Looking to the guidebook again, we couldn't place where we were exactly or which monastery we had discovered.

It was almost 8 p.m., and I watched the remains of the sunlight recede behind the olive trees. We drove on roads pummelled by rockslides, drove past a checkerboard farm of honey bee boxes, and made our way back to Chania. The boys took me back to the hotel where I'd left my luggage in the reception. I hugged them each a sincerely warm goodbye, and off they drove. I had met them only five days before.

The moon was full that night, and the nightlife on the harbour was beginning to perk up. I freshened up in a restaurant bathroom and chose a table outside, listened to far-off music, deafening cicadas, and ordered a final meal of calamari, Greek salad, and chilled red wine. The waiters saw I was by myself and brought me complimentary Raki and fresh, crisp watermelon. I was so delighted.

About 10:30 p.m., it was time to make my way through the harbour and board my overnight ship back to Athens.

Sitting on the top deck under the fullest, brightest moon, I watched the people boarding below, the sea crashing around the hull, the Cretan village lights winking at me across the water from the harbour, and the dark mountains.

I wrote and wrote in my journal. The boat departed just before midnight, and as it pulled away, people who had been waiting in their cars or on their motorcycles on the island honked and honked their goodbyes to other voyagers as the voyagers waved and waved back.

And then we were gone.

I was in a dreamy mood, induced partly by sweet red wine, partly by salty sea and hot wind, and partly by Polykarpus's eyes still clear in my mind—and then also partly by the memory of the hills and sunset and sea that had saturated my entire day.

I wrote until the early hours of the morning, still looking up at the island we were ferrying away from, trying to remember all that had been seen and felt as I stared off into the dark water. I didn't want to try to sleep just yet—not until the sea mist blanketed over every last drop of light in Chania.

I wrote feverishly. My bag was full of bits of scraps of paper, even a napkin that I had used to scribble little details on throughout the week so that I didn't forget to write every single memory down later. I dug every scrap of paper out and transcribed them into my journal in whatever order I had found them. I wrote them down, mixed in with writing what I was watching on the boat.

My journey was to be a 6-hour overnight cruise, and many people who hadn't paid for chairs inside or for beds were sleeping on the ground outside on the deck. As I was writing, a middle-aged man laid down a plastic sheet right at my feet, which troubled me at first. It turned out to be a place for his young daughter, who then laid down and slept, so I guess it wasn't too bad. Or perhaps it was worse.

My thoughts wandered to where my people were now. Tanja was on a plane somewhere over Spain probably. Polykarpos was in another boat, on the same black sea, sailing to the same mainland as I. Dimtris and Sasha and Adrian were all in a house in a village on the dark island I had just left. All the Georgioses and waiters I'd met were left behind on the island too.

Before I boarded the ferry, I had bought a copy of *Zorba the Greek*. If Polykarpos had read it, then I would too. It was a philosophic, poetic tale that read vividly and passionately about Crete, its stoic people, its fertile hills, its sapphire, salty seas, its wild heart.

I burned through it.

~

4 A.M. FOUND ME CURLED up in an impossibly uncomfortable plastic chair amongst dim ferry lights and sleeping passengers. I half slept until the boat docked at 6 a.m. on the mainland of Greece. I was back in Piraeus.

The sun seemed too sleepy to rise and shine just yet, so it was a dark and sketchy port I arrived in, the safe charm of Chania's old port now more than 150 nautical miles away.

Piraeus is one of the largest ports in Europe, and even though dawn was yet to come, and despite the romantic dreams of Chania still flitting in my head, here it was business as usual. The early morning commotion of honking taxis, hurried motorcycles, and squawking seagulls echoed within the docklands.

I found the first English-ish-speaking taxi I could and paid far too much for a cab ride to the other side of the port. Sleepy and disenchanted with my surroundings, I had zero desire to spend my last day in Greece in the hot, polluted city of Athens—ruins or no ruins—so I sought out a friendly English-speaking travel agent.

He very kindly pointed out and wrote down (in English) a place where I could lock up the bulk of my luggage, showed me where the bus station was located, and which bus number I should board to get to the airport later that day. I then purchased a ticket for the 8 a.m. ferry to Aegina Island, part of the Saronic Gulf Islands, a 40-minute speedboat ride away. Forget the city. For my last day in Greece, I'd return back to the sea from which I had just emerged.

I'm not sure what I was looking for. I had 12 hours or so in Greece before my flight to the UK. And even though I had just returned from Crete, an island itself, the full-hearted experiences there left me wanting more. I wasn't ready to return to my working life in London, and I wasn't at all prepared to shift into the busy, smoggy, metro life of Athens.

My soul still craved the hot sand and salty shores.

TUESDAY, DAY 9
Aegina Island

HAVING SECURED MY LUGGAGE, I bought myself a bottle of water and walked the 15 minutes to the boat dock that would speed me away to another island. Smaller than Crete, and much closer, sure, but an island just the same. I boarded a 50-person ferry and fell immediately into a deep sleep, completely wasting my privileged view from a window seat.

Aegina Town was a small harbour with quaint shops and post-card appeal. For the second time in less than 24 hours, I cleaned up in another restaurant restroom. Fresh enough, I went about exploring the small village.

I was too tired to be motivated to do much of anything. My thoughts were a blend of nostalgia and sleepy murk. What I really craved was a beach to myself. So, I chose to keep going. I travelled even more local, taking a rusty unplanned bus ride south to an even smaller fishing village called Perdika, 9 km south from the port I had just arrived in. From there, I could seek out a smaller, local fishing boat without a schedule. Perhaps I would find a kind fisherman to take me to an even smaller island called Moni—an island that was sparse, its beaches quiet, its sea warm and clear. What was I searching for?

For all that I had felt in Chania to last.

Once I arrived in Perdika, I enjoyed a much-needed caffeine hit in the form of an icy frappé at a very local café—one where grey-whiskered Greek patrons squabbled amongst themselves good-naturedly, sitting on wooden benches in front of the small coffee shop. No tourists here!

The guidebook I carried had informed me there were boats to take me to Moni Island, but I didn't see any boats carrying passengers like myself—this is to say, solo, foreign travellers carrying beach gear.

The departing boats I saw commuted fishermen carrying fresh catch and fishing nets in the morning sunlight.

Breathing in, I practised over and over in a quiet voice the words, "excuse me, good morning, what time does the boat leave?" in Greek. Which probably did not sound at all like Greek to the Greek. Nearby, I noticed a 60-ish-year-old woman and her daughter (or maybe her granddaughter) standing patiently on the dock, about to board the smallest fishing boat I'd ever seen. In return, they noticed me standing patiently on the dock as well, and through a series of hand gestures and basic words that neither they nor I could fully understand, they offered me a boat ride to Moni.

The fragile-looking boat that I was welcomed to board was only about as long as your average kayak and about as wide as two average kayaks tied together. Peeling white paint boasted its seasons, and the well-sailed ship boasted a captain to match: wrinkly and withered, with liver spots betraying his years and too-big sunglasses propped upon his face underneath his worn captain's cap. The elderly captain was skinny and knobbly-kneed as he smiled a toothy grin and reached out his soft but weathered hands to help me jump down into his fishing boat.

As I did, the entire boat rocked dramatically, and I almost lost my balance and fell over and out the other side into the water. The Greek women were all ready in the boat and paid no mind to me as they cheerfully rambled to themselves.

I was told by way of pointing fingers and incomprehensible chatter to sit on the one wooden bench secured across the middle of the boat. The great-grandad of a captain was at the rudder, the old woman sat on one side, and her daughter sat cross-legged at the front, holding on to the mast. The whole boat tilted and sunk down to one side, but because of how small the boat was, it was impossible for us to sit so that our weight balanced it all out. It might as well have been made of paper. The daughter kicked the boat away from the dock with her foot, and we were off!

And it was fantastic! And absolutely crazy.

The distance from Perdika to Moni Island was only measured in time, and even with that, I can't promise accuracy. Surrounded by the ocean, the waves were huge and not at all generous in comfort like the bay in Georgioupolis had offered. The bay in Georgioupolis where Tanja and I indulged in a sunrise swim had been silky smooth, calm and glossy. Here, the open ocean swells between these two islands were large and intimidating. This rolling ocean seemed to swell so much bigger than what I had witnessed when I had crossed a larger sea in a larger boat only the week before.

This time, the rickety boat slammed into swell after massive swell. The boat seemed as if it would splinter into the water at any moment. However, this undersized boat showed as much heart as did its captain.

The blueberry sea and dry summer wind pushed at us, around us, over us, and under us as the little boat motored as fast as it could take us. Waves were impossible to outrun that day, and they crashed over and over onto our heads and into the boat, thoroughly drenching all four of us and any belongings we carried with us.

It was adventurous and a little ludicrous, but at that very moment, all I could do was laugh whole-heartedly out loud. Here I was, already changed into my airport clothes, ready to walk straight onto the plane in the next 8 hours or so. But I was now drenched through, my carry-on bag was soaking wet, inside my passport was saturated through every page. My only ID, my phone, though the battery was dead, held the only access to any number I might have called for help. My camera was jostling along inside the bag as we hauled ass across the sea in a fishing boat that barely was.

My companions were three strangers—two of whom were senior citizens, none of whom could speak English—and I couldn't speak Greek. There were no life jackets, and I had told no one where I was headed that day. In those moments, I remember momentarily thinking, "If this boat capsizes, and we all roll under, no one will ever know what became of me." Polykarpos or my new friends in Chania only knew I had taken a ferry to Athens, but no one knew I had chosen to visit an island rather than stay in the city for my last day. Besides, should I go missing, who would think to ask any of them? No one, likely. But there was no denying the spirit of adventure that sped through the air and eliminated any possibility of fear. The women laughing, the old guy captaining, each of us all soaked to the bone from such a thrill. Fifteen harrowing minutes later, we crash-landed abruptly, but safely, on Moni Island.

I tried to pay them, but they laughed and waved me off. The cheerful old lady fell as she climbed out of the boat, despite the captain helping her out, but each of them laughed and talked with such glee and seemed to have enjoyed the adventure as much as I had. The Greeks worry about nothing until they need to.

Moni Island was just what I had craved. I had surely made the best choice as to how to make the most of my final day until my plane left that evening. The small island was dry and rocky on one side but completely forested on the other. On the rocky side of the beach roamed wild deer and peacocks, just as the two, almost miss-able sentences in the small paragraph in my travel guidebook had promised.

The deer and peacocks dotted the tiny cove, as comfortably in place as seagulls and seashells should have been. The deer only turned their antlered heads my way as I walked by and didn't scamper off; they were without fear and seemed to be embracing the sunny island vibe.

It wasn't long before I found a lounge chair and umbrella set up on a cosy beach. There was a simple snack shack nearby, and only two small families enjoying the space along with me.

The water was impossibly beautiful. Green and blue and clear with rocks and sea, plants and fish lounging in the calm lagoon. I sunned and read *Zorba the Greek* and fell asleep and swam to cool off and drank a cold beer and just spent my last afternoon in Greece in complete relaxation and utter happiness.

Regretfully, 3 p.m.-ish spun slowly my way, so I packed up my damp things. As this wasn't too touristy of an area, I needed to wait for the next fisherman to depart so that I could jump on his boat for the ride back. By this time, I had adjusted to the logistics of island travel and had managed to time my departure with that of another local fisherman. He took me back to Perdika on his tiny boat, with less adventure than my first fishing boat trip had delivered. I arrived timely enough back in Perdika, only to discover that there was no bus anytime soon that would take me to the dock where the ferry to the mainland was waiting.

I hadn't thought this far ahead. Where was Sasha and his planning when I would appreciate it? I scanned for taxis, but this was a one-horse village, and there was no traffic at all. This town barely boasted a dirt road out.

A tranquil group of men were still sitting on wooden benches outside the nearby café, and I tried to explain my plight to a helpful waiter. The waiters in Greece hadn't let me down yet, so I figured asking one of them would be my best bet. It was now 3:25 p.m., and my ferry was meant to leave at 4 p.m. from Aegina Town, 9 kilometres away. I needed to be there to catch my plane on time. He kindly called a cab for me. Hanging up, he told me, "15 minutes."

Okay. Fifteen minutes for the taxi to make its way here, and then another 15 minutes to return to the port. This would leave me only five minutes to board the ferry before its departure back to Athens. I tried not to worry about the Greek perception of time at that moment. So I sat there, somewhat apprehensive, making broken-English small talk with the old local men. They had nowhere to be.

A few minutes later, within 15 minutes, my cab arrived. I thanked every one of the old Greek men who'd kept me company and jumped in the cab. I expressed as best I could my urgency to the driver, and off we raced. We raced around every curve of every dusty afternoon road, past motorcyclists and lone pedestrians and ambling goats. We sped towards the port and slowed down not at all. We sped past scenic fields and more trucks with beds full of water-melon. I took minimal notice of anything but the minute hand on the taxi's dashboard. If there were a speed law, we most definitely would have broken it.

We arrived just in time. Passengers were boarding, and I was the last one to hurry myself up the ramp smiling, apologetic, and grateful. This time, I enjoyed every moment taking in the close-up views of the choppy sea from my window seat on the ferry one last time. I didn't want to go.

A luggage pick-up and a bus ride later, I had made my way through the dirty streets of the city of Athens, falling asleep and jerking awake every time the bumpy transportation stopped for a local pick up.

All week, I hadn't slept much and had taken in a lot of sun; the last day, I had taken my sleep in snatches. Despite every chance of some leg of this day's travel going wrong, I'd managed to arrive at the airport on time. I tried to call Tanja, but I couldn't get the payphone to take my credit card. She'd had to leave a day early to interview for a job, and I wanted to see how it went. After only one day, I missed her.

An hour later, I boarded the plane. Under my clothes, I was still wearing my bikini from the Moni Island beach excursion. My journey from Chania to Brighton had looked like this: Taxi. Big ferry. Taxi. Little ferry. Bus. Fishing boat. Swim in the sea. Fishing boat. Speedy Taxi. Little ferry. Bus. Plane. Train. Walk home.

I hadn't showered since Sunday night after my dusty walk with Polykarpos from the vineyard. Monday, I had sweated through my clothes when exploring the monasteries and then swam in the sea with the boys. I had been blown by salty wind on the big ferry and gone island hopping and indulged in more salty swimming on Moni Island. I had returned with a cracked toenail, 16 bug bites, 3 blistered toes, and sand still in my ear.

I was back in Brighton, and it was time to re-acclimatise, but I just didn't want to wash Crete out of my hair. Not yet. So, when I finally turned my key in the door of my home at 1 a.m. in the morning on Wednesday, my bikini still under my clothes, I crawled immediately into bed and slept deeply, dreaming I was still in Crete.

WEDNESDAY, DAY 10

Brighton

WAKING LATER THAT WEDNESDAY morning, I didn't even look at the to-do list I had so responsibly left for myself the week before Tanja and I had set off.

Instead, I left my house and walked to the beach in Brighton. Pebbly and chilly, with grey, calm, opaque waters, the beach was still something I needed. I sat near the shore and read more of *Zorba the Greek*, bought feta cheese, Greek yoghurt and honey, and bought a few pieces of jewellery. I allowed time to let every momentous feeling from every rich experience of the past week just settle into my bones—to vine itself into my heart.

Tanja met me for a coffee. She was also still floating with her head and heart in Greece and Crete and had brought me some dried figs. We reminisced about our last week of adventures, and she admitted that in the final days, her crush had switched from Adrian to Polykarpos. We laughed and hugged and talked and I cried a little. She had bought *Zorba the Greek*, too.

After my day on the beach with Tanja, I went home and I began to write down this story. I started just a little before 7 p.m; I didn't stop until almost 3 a.m. I just wanted to remember as much as I could before any of the beautiful details were lost into the ether, or rather I lost them to the routine I found myself sliding towards. A seven-to-five life punctuated with alarm clocks, traffic, and cold weather. For sure, some sunlit moments in my mind would have disappeared into shadows.

As much as we try to tuck every little morsel of memory inside, there are always crumbs that fall beyond our grasp—the memories and moments that get away.

Still, I hope I've captured most of it.

Many times I've taken trips such as this one to Crete—travels where time elongates, and stretches out, long and full and reaching; travels where friends become closer and tighter, even though just as many tears as laughs are shared along the way. Travels where the small, unexpected, and almost indescribable moments swell with so much love and the purest joy; moments where I might have only a few pictures, and maybe a journal entry or two, but the experience has left an imprint on my heart and in my mind; moments left out of record-ed memory unintentionally; moments that, when recalled by others, only elicit a nostalgic grin and an, "Oh yeah..." whispered from your breath.

I have irrepressibly fond memories of other travels that are forever etched in my mind: holidays to Amsterdam, wild excursions to Sicily, weekend city getaways to Barcelona. But the lustre of those details are just faded glimmers now. I should have written more fully about them.

I didn't want to lose a moment of Crete. Ever.

I immersed myself in it all for as long as I could. I managed to stay on an island until my sandy self could be seated on a plane, sleepy and saddened to go. I kept alive in my mind the perpetual warmth of a charming Chania, the hot salty beach, the icy frappé coffees, the paperback books based in Greece.

So, back in my tiny, dark flat in Brighton, I wrote. I wrote all night until my back and knees ached and my feet turned cold. Dirty, as I *still* hadn't properly showered since the dusty walk with Polykarpos, I wrote until I could write no more, and headed to bed. I'm sure I reached some kind of personal record for both typing nonstop and not bathing. I walked, swam in seas, travelled far, and refused to wash any of it away in those final days.

The next morning, I would start work again and throw my energy into teaching, my students, and my responsibilities. I would show up. I would shower thoroughly, and dress in warmer clothes. I hoped I'd sealed as much of Crete as I could with my mind and my heart. Closing my eyes, I finally tucked away the prior 10 days, know-ing I had done all I could to remember every moment.

The wedding songs played on stringed instruments from the sunset hills; the daffodil sunrise swim; the drippy cold and crisp water-melons; the sweet homemade wine; the perfect, sun-warmed figs and grapes and hilarious goats; the salty sea and my endearing old friend;

my chatty new pals; all of the untethered laughs and undammed tears and the grinning, sideways glances; and the Grecian songs that played in my head, their melodies riding over the sapphire waves.

I wanted so much for all of these tiny, magical strings to be woven so tight inside my heart that I would never lose them. Each would be a moment of beauty I could keep.

The Thames River Whale

I WAS LIVING IN the Brighton Lanes when the sensational news story broke, and hundreds of corporate suits and skirts abandoned their desks mid-afternoon to lean out windows of riverside skyrises and over bridge railings.

They each clamboured for a glimpse of a young lost whale.

Hers is a sad story, though, of having lost her way in the dirty London river, and unable to find her way back to her pod. Or to be rescued and redirected back to the cold Atlantic in time for ocean waters and freedom to save her.

The river must have felt like an early grave to her. Accustomed to swimming in at least 19 metres of water, the murky Thames could only cuddle her with a shallow 5 metres. The crowded shipping boats and the rusty littered river bottom carved up her belly and the cameras flashed as, breathless, she was beached again and again. Eventually, firemen hoisted her onto a barge in the hopes of transporting her and releasing her back to the sea.

The human effort here, unfortunately, was in vain, and the poor thing suffocated before she could be helped, crushed by her own weight above the water, and suffered from convulsions.

The panic she must have felt. And how alone.

Lost travellers who find themselves in the uncertain care of strangers will have felt this crushing panic as well.

When we find ourselves desperately needing aid from others, and in a circumstance when plans we made have failed. When our hopes fill the air above our head, and dissipate into nothing. Which sometimes happens.

I remember connecting with this darling young whale, resonating with her fear, her failure, her loss. Her disorienting confusion as strangers scrambled, pulling at her belly and slapping dorsal fin.

How many wrong turns had I made? Not just in my travels, but in my choices? How many lessons were painfully learned, leaving me with puncturing loss and regret?

Many.

This panicked whale surfaced in me a heavy dread of the inescapable pain my wrong turns had always burdened me with. The mistakes I had made that I couldn't take back.

Months later, I visited her bones on display in the Museum of Natural History in London with my friend Luke. I think it had snowed that day, a freak cold snap in what I think was the month of April, but all the snow had melted by the time we disembarked from the train on our journey into the city.

Luke had heard that the bones ended up in this particular museum because of some long-ago law that decreed the contents of the river were deemed property of the Crown. (I also believe that this law came about because of a dolphin spotted in the Thames that the current king wanted to claim for himself). I can't be certain about the truthful base of this, but it wouldn't surprise me. One way or another, the whale had become the property of the museum.

The bones were still a little oily and arranged neatly behind a glass case. Her skeleton was much smaller than I imagined it would be.

It struck me even then, this notion about becoming lost and in desperate need of help.

How sometimes being in the wrong place can turn out to be the most fortuitous thing that one could hope for. Times when the kindness of strangers not only saves us but reinvigorates faith in human kindness and compassion.

But other times, an accidental turn can short-live even the most gentle existence, despite valiant efforts.

One moment, we can be in flow, exploring and adventuring, guided by our strengthening intuition.

The next moment, the flow comes to a shocking and tragic end, and all we are left with is sadness and oily bones.

PART FOUR

Things We Couldn't See Coming

Bulgaria
2007

MY FIRST EXPERIENCE TRAVELLING to Eastern Europe was a solo flight to Sofia, the capital of Bulgaria. I knew very little about Bulgaria, but my intention for the trip had been to visit my dear friend and former Brighton roommate, Lenny.

As the plane began to descend into the Balkan nation, jerking and rocking, the turbulence caused some nervousness for me—a nervousness which heightened as I didn't understand the language of those around me. The announcements from the pilot calmed me not at all, and most of the other passengers' reactions were also spoken in Bulgarian. There was no comfort to be had from their words. The plane seemed to circle and tilt quite a lot, and when it finally touched down safely on the tarmac, nearly everyone on the plane broke out clapping and whooping.

A man in the back row shouted something in Bulgarian, and everyone else laughed heartily. I was very confused, but the plane had landed safely on the ground. Seeing as the other passengers were in good spirits or relieved, whatever danger we'd recovered from in the air was enough of an ordeal to merit applause. It must not have been too threatening to elicit joy instead of tears of relief, I guessed.

There is something so special about seeing a good friend's face after a long time has passed. As I gathered my suitcases and walked through the sea of strangers also searching for their anticipated family members and friends, I caught sight of Lenny. He had caught sight of me too and was pacing behind the rows of Bulgarians, a grin on his face as we made our way through the crowded terminal and towards each other. My heart was light and a big grin on my face no doubt beamed back at him as we embraced and burst into rapid, excited English amidst the din of Bulgarians.

As my former roommate, Lenny had contributed a sharp mind, a warm sense of humour, an adventurous spirit, and a big heart to our flat on Over Street. He was on his way to completing a doctorate in quantitative physics and was easily one of the most likeable and personable physicists-in-the-making I'd ever met.

In our dingy living room in Brighton, we'd drink milky Earl Grey tea while watching documentaries on red dwarfs in the Milky Way, he with excitement, and I with a mixture of interest and confusion. Or we'd indulge in red wine at local pubs with other friends and roommates, watching favourite bands play and staying out too late.

Those years had been spent talking, laughing, learning, and moving through life with a healthy dose of curiosity, humour, and ambition as we reunited from our days or weekends and overseas adventures, reconnecting and sharing whatever was going on in our lives and where we were headed next. One day, his "next" turned out to be Bulgaria. So here I was for a good, solid visit and to once again, like the old times, share with each other what life had delivered to us now.

Outside the airport, the Sofia sky was bleak and grey and reminded me of the London sky I had left behind. Unlike London, however, there was a pack of about six or seven big, black, grisly dogs just beyond the sliding glass doors of the terminal, growling and fighting over food on the cracked cement. I was a little alarmed, but Len said not to worry; Bulgaria has plenty of big, wild dogs that wander the city, and they wouldn't bother us. *Unless, of course, it was the dead of winter, and they hadn't eaten much,* I thought just before he finished his sentence, explaining that if they did bother, we would just shake our keys at them. Good advice to know upon arrival.

Speaking of the dead of winter, that night, we saw the first signs of the change in season. As we set out from Lenny's flat on foot to search for a place for dinner at a traditional Bulgarian restaurant, the first winter's snow started to fall in fat, fluffy flakes. We walked down the main street, breathing in the crisp air in the evening lamplight. The cold filled our nostrils, and our hands dug deeper into our warm pockets as we filled the night air with our chatter.

Lenny's Bulgarian was coming along, having only been in the country for a couple of months. He claimed not to be too fluent, but he could navigate a menu just fine. This turned out to be helpful that first night, because the traditional restaurant we chose served "calf brains" and "innkeeper's bits." Calf brains with sauce. And I can't remember which bits of the innkeeper were offered, but I wasn't feeling too culturally adventurous on my first night, so I ordered the chicken.

It was freezing cold in Sofia that weekend. Even though it was mid-October, a cold snap had layered the slate city in soft, crunchy snow that night.

In anticipation of my visit, Len had taken a few days off work, and we'd decided to spend our time on a hiking trip in the mountains. It sounded good to me. I had perused a travel guide that talked about how scenic the Bulgarian mountain range was, and after city living in Brighton and London, I was looking forward to being out in unculti-vated nature again. Especially the mountains. Tropical destinations were often pinned on the map of the world I had taped to my bedroom wall, but the rise and fall of mountain slopes, the evergreen scents, the tall, tall trees, the timid and furry wildlife, the hours of hiking and talking and connecting with a more rugged version of nature—these were all things I craved to breathe in.

In the years we had been friends, Len had proven himself to be a pretty keen adventurer. He had climbed and camped in the mountain ranges of more countries than I can remember. He had swum between Croatian islands in the Adriatic, crossed rivers at night with candles as his only light in Brazil, and bought a camel to cross the Sahara desert. He had survived being hit by a bus, stalked by a predator in the jungle, and dared to go night swimming through stormy waters in the Pacific. We wouldn't be doing much more than hiking and sleeping in cabins, but should we encounter any danger, he kept a proven track record that all would be well. I would be in good hands trekking through the wild mountains of Bulgaria with him.

THREE DAYS LATER
The Mountain

WE WERE RESCUED BY a mountain of a man—a self-proclaimed champion of the 100-mile barefoot race in Japan back in '92. Or maybe it was South Korea. His English was bad; my Bulgarian was worse. But he was strong and eager and drove a car that could outrun the bears.

By the time we'd met him, I'd been reduced to a tear-stained, soggy human being. Everything ached. Finally sheltered from the brutal winter storm in a small cantina which the British would have called a canteen, I held the hot tea in my pink and clammy fingers. I had pulled my unsteady metal stool as close as was possible to the warmth of the cracking fire licking the inside of the stove. Len did the same, and we watched as steam rose from our soaked-through jeans. We still had over 13 kilometres to walk toward the only village that we hoped would offer a bus ride home. We hoped that Kostas, boisterous and big, would be our saviour from the many unexpected challenges we'd experienced so far on our hike through the Rila range.

He was the second Bulgarian—the second human, in fact—that we'd seen in days.

Both Len and I had kept our spirits up throughout the freezing trek down the mountain with the memory of the canteen we'd just left that morning. A corner stove had warmed the aroma of spices and roasted dried fruits. The scent infused the air, and cloves and apples had settled over us like a warm blanket.

Half a day later, bloodied and thirsty, we were desperate. The elements had been unforgiving, and I found myself trying to re-member basic survival instincts: Keeping my chest dry, wiggling my fingers and toes despite reopening wounds, keeping our path close to the slopes and steep rise of the hills when the trees were too sparse for shelter, eating frozen snow to keep hydrated. Reminding myself of these simple survival skills kept my mind from despair. My nose was red and numb and could smell only the bitter cold.

Somewhere on the mountain between the clove-scented cantina and Kostas' "chay", we had frozen and become soaked to the bone, wandering without a clue as to when we'd reach the next hut and uncertain whether it would be open or abandoned for the winter.

But I digress. The memory of overwhelming helplessness I felt keeps overtaking my story. It wasn't this bad from the beginning. The trip began with high spirits and lots of enthusiasm, if not with lots of supplies.

The Trek

TYPICAL FOR MOST SERIOUS hiking trips, we had planned for a very early start. Waking at 6 a.m. the next morning, Lenny and I made ham and tomato sandwiches, packed apples, chocolate cookies, and enough cashews to last us for two days.

I kept thinking that we needed to pack bottles of water, but somehow this slipped both our minds. I was wearing a long-sleeved shirt, another sweater over that, a sweatshirt, a fleece jacket, a scarf, and a waterproof coat I had borrowed from one of my other house-mates, two pairs of socks, and hiking boots.

My pack included a sleeping bag, thermal underwear, and three layers of pyjamas. Len had packed much the same.

What we *didn't* have: flashlights, a first aid kit, a Leatherman tool or pocket knife, water, and confident knowledge of the Bulgarian language. Len was wearing trainers.

Both of us carried this happy-go-lucky outlook on life, choosing to chase adventure with boisterous and blissful reck-less abandon. Neither of us really worried about anything because our "It'll be okay" attitude seemed to get us through most perilous scuffles. So despite being only half-prepared, there were zero worries at all about the expedition ahead. All would be well.

And all was well. The first day was truly spectacular. Bundled up, we took a cab to the bus station, which drove us a couple of hours through damp hillsides bathed in the clammy, early morning light. About 3,000 feet up the Rila Mountain range, the landscape gleamed with freshly fallen snow, and the windows of the short, white bus were drippy and cold and wet to lean against. It was good when we finally reached our destination, as I was getting a little carsick from the curvy roads.

The bus pulled into a stop in the middle of—somewhere. Neither of us was sure of the signs posted in Bulgarian, and there was some confusion between us as to where we needed to begin our hike.

Len had a Bulgarian map of the area, hiking trails, and the roads, but travelling on a Sunday in winter meant that normal bus times weren't necessarily in operation, and we needed to find our starting point.

I stood by in the cold, icy parking lot, while Lenny tried to confirm with the bus driver where we were on his map. It was quite amusing to watch. The Bulgarians, in their puffy coats and leathered, reddened faces under knitted hats, were gesturing and rapidly explaining *something*, and Len would reply with slow, spaced-out words and hold out his map.

This exchange was repeated several times, with passengers on the bus contributing in Bulgarian to the conversation between Len and the bus driver. Len stammered away in his freshly new, book-learned Bulgarian while I bounced up and down with my arms crossed in the snow nearby, blowing foggy breath into the air and trying to keep warm while waiting for a decision to be made and to be told where to go.

Although Len had managed to live amongst Bulgarians for some time, parts of the language continued to perplex him—and fair enough. Bulgaria uses a Cyrillic alphabet, much like Greek, so some shapes of letters are unfamiliar, and any familiar shapes have different sounds to them. Len would often get simple words confused, like directions (left and right), and his yeses and nos. He couldn't yet speak in the past tense, and to ask for help, could only say, "Can I...?"

But he understood with his ears a lot more than he could say with his voice, so when the bus driver told him how to get to our starting point, Len wanted to ask things like, "Is there a bus arriving later in the day?" or "Is this trail the best route?" or "About how far is it?", he could only hold out his map and ask, "Can I... ?"

More rapid Bulgarian and gestures ensued. Then Len's "Can I," which really got us nowhere, except deciding he had understood as much as he ever would. Nevermind. Off we went.

The first day of hiking was an amazing experience. The first hitch, though, was that I managed to get the zipper stuck on the waterproof coat I had borrowed—before we'd even started. It had gotten stuck at the bottom of the zipper, where you begin to connect the teeth and zip it up.

I pulled and pulled, Len pulled and pulled. We tried to pry it free using keys, but the damn thing wasn't going anywhere. I figured as long as it didn't rain, I'd still be warm with an open coat. And I was.

The mountains were stunningly beautiful. The woods we walked through were something out of Narnia. The trail was thickly dusted with white snow; frozen rocks and frozen puddles dotted the uphill climb. An icy trickling stream splashed down to our right, and lining both sides of the trail and reaching high into the frosty sky were icicled pines, the green branches peeking out here and there as they slowly thawed into the shiny blue morning.

The forest was quiet. Rarely a songbird was heard. Our pleasant conversation and armfuls of snow crashing down from tree branches every now and then were the only sounds. It was an unreal and magical sight. Two days before, I had been teaching in a chaotic classroom in London, and in one flight and one bus ride, I had completely transformed my surroundings.

We climbed for nearly 5 hours that day. It wasn't long before we realised we'd left without bringing water, but just grabbing a handful of snow off tree branches along the way and letting it melt in our mouths sufficed and kept us hydrated. Except for one occasion when I grabbed a handful of soft snow that had dry pine needles in it. The snow melted instantly in my mouth, leaving me with horrible dry spines sticking into my tongue and gums. It wasn't pleasant, but at the time, it was the *only* thing that wasn't pleasant.

Our plan had been to climb to the top of this mountain peak to an area on the mountain known as the Seven Lakes. This cluster of lakes could only be reached by foot. There were no roads, but there were a few huts dotted here and there for hikers to take refuge in.

The trail we followed was marked with coloured paint on rocks, tree trunks, and when we reached above the tree line, we followed yellow poles that served as trail markers every hundred feet or so. We would hike all that first day and stay overnight in one of the huts alongside one of the seven lakes. We would then climb over the peak the next morning, into the Rila Monastery a few hours of a hike down, and probably stay another night there before hiking down to a village where a bus trip would take us back to Sofia.

We had a brilliant time, climbing and talking and catching up on each other's lives and stopping to dig into our ham sandwiches.

The views were spectacular. In no time, it seemed, we were way above the clouds that lay thickly below us. The trail we followed through the trees was rocky and wild. It wasn't too much of a trail, overrun with tree roots and steep and closed-in in places, but we were loving the adventure of it all.

In some places, we needed to use our hands to continue walking up the trail, it became so steep. Sometimes part of our trail had transformed into a stream from the melting snow, so trudging uphill through running ice water, stopping to cup our hands and drink from the running water happened fairly often. The water was absolutely freezing. At this point, the temperature was just above zero, but our layers and constant movement kept us from feeling the chill too much.

When we came to the first lake, I stopped to pose for a picture. I was tired of looking frumpy in my oversized jacket, so I climbed out of it and its stuck zipper and let my hair down to smile for the camera. This was a mistake. In those few moments of being less layered, I nearly gave myself hypothermia. My fingers became stiff and began to ache so quickly. It was afternoon by now, and we had climbed to about 7,000 feet where the temperature had dropped significantly. It was so cold, it hurt.

After the poorly timed photoshoot, I climbed back into my broken coat, and we wandered as best we could up the rest of the peak. We couldn't tell where the trail was for sure but could see our destination. We were above the tree line by now, and a few of the lakes dotted with inviting huts came into view.

The seven lakes are cradled at different levels on the mountain, and some lakes were a few hundred metres above the others. We could see our hut perched at the top of a steep incline, with a backdrop of sweeping snow-crusted rocks—nothing less than majestic. The wind whipped around us as we climbed another half an hour or so towards the hut.

As we approached the arrangement of lakeside huts tucked in a tiny valley, we took in our surroundings. There was only a picnic table, a pile of chopped logs, and a large, heavy axe, which we carelessly played around with before sitting down to eat a little. Then we wandered over the next hill towards another more inviting hut down the way. It seemed inviting because we'd seen people there moments ago—the first people we had seen since departing from the bus hours earlier. It was here, at the populated hut, that we decided to stay for the night. We dropped our bags in the room and climbed up to the highest peak to take in the views while there was still daylight.

The view from the top of the mountain peak was breathtaking. We could see nothing but frozen, rocky slopes around us, and cottony white clouds below, stretching as far as we could see. The white sky bore down heavy and close above us.

The wind picked up, and I took a few more pictures, but the cold got the best of my 35 mm camera battery, and I was unable to take too many photos of the rest of my trip.

Len and I did our best Vinyasa Sun Salutations on what seemed like flat, ceremonial rocks at the summit. We shouted and whooped, echoing into the sky. Likely, our excited shouts scared or annoyed any animal that hadn't yet gone into hibernation up there in the chilly wild.

We could not see all seven of the lakes from our angle; three or four were staggered below and above us. The lake that our hut huddled against was directly below us, swampy, with reeds gently swaying just under the surface.

Pausing our howling, we took a moment of silence to breathe in the epic views. In those still moments, we watched as the glassy surface of the lake started to ripple, and tightly curled waves began to slap slap slap on the shore. Then, as we sat stiff and still in the rising wind, the mirrored surface of the lake shattered upwards with a loud rush, and a huge, red-scaled dragon with catfish whiskers and terrifying claws burst snarling from the placid lake and breathed fire over the snow caps as it swooped its leathery wings!

Or so we thought might happen if we waited and watched the impossible scenic panorama below us for long enough.

We imagined all kinds of things on that peak. I don't know if it was the altitude or the giddiness of reaching the top after our day of upward hiking, but the environment around us lent itself to our imaginations. The scenery was something out of a storybook. Even with the presence of the hut, and the marker poles, the Rila Mountains were very much untouched by human presence, and from up there on those cold rocks and grassy mounds, any reality seemed possible.

Returning to our hut, we found it chilly inside. The structure was wooden and built about three stories high. When we checked in, the Bulgarian woman handed us room keys, firewood, and matches. There was no heater in our room—only the one plugged in downstairs in the canteen area. Our room could only be heated by using a stove in which we had to build ourselves a fire. It was absolutely frigid in our room.

The toilets were outhouses and were set about 100 feet or so from the hut. As one could guess, they were *also* beyond freezing, and smelled like, well, shit. They smelled like frozen shit.

The elderly woman managed the hut. She greeted us with wrinkly smiles almost entirely covered by rounded glasses too big for her tiny face. Her thin white hair was held back with a child's plastic barrette, and she somewhat resembled a kindly Gollum. She lived there alone, isolated in the frozen fold of a mountain through the winter months, with no heating and a souring outhouse. Babbling pleasantly in Bulgarian, she welcomed weary hikers and offered them "chay"—hot herbal tea to defrost their fingers.

I couldn't understand why she would do this—live alone, use an outhouse, converse with strangers. But she spoke no English, so I couldn't ask her very much. I couldn't ask her anything, actually. But Len managed to communicate a little with her. Whatever she said, she seemed very happy.

Sitting in the heated canteen, Len and I paused for a moment with our chay to contemplate the problem of my busted zipper. I had managed to stay warm enough through the day with an open coat, but I didn't want to keep it that way.

As we sat there, perplexed, this tiny Gollum-shaped Bulgarian woman did an incredible thing. She saw me struggling with the damn stuck zipper, and approached. Muttering a few soft things in Bulgarian, she leaned over and took my coat from me.

She then reached for a sharp, jagged knife and, sitting next to Len and I on this wooden bench, she began to aggressively saw the knife back and forth against the fabric stuck in the zipper. We watched in horror as her thin, wrinkled skin came dangerously close to the blade. Her hands moved furiously, and after a few minutes, she cut through the stuck cloth.

Len and I had struggled for ages, and neither of us could get the zipper to budge. We'd even used a knife we'd seen in the canteen. This was truly a mountain woman who knew how to survive. Then she pulled out a sewing needle and thread and sewed up the torn jacket. What an amazing lady!

I was so thankful that I repeated "Thank you" three or four

times in very bad Bulgarian—probably the equivalent of "I thank, I thank." But she just laughed and seemed happy enough that she had helped us. She asked us what we wanted to eat for dinner and babbled off a list of food she could cook up. The first word Len recognised was "omelette," and so that's what we had for dinner. Omelettes with sliced tomato.

We ate ravenously, then played an uninspiring game of "I spy" before deciding to go cosy up in our bunk beds.

Up in our frigid room, we set about starting the fire. It should have taken only a few minutes to get a stove fire started, but our inexperienced hands took about 20 minutes to get the damn flames going. We eventually felt the welcome blaze, then buried ourselves in several layers of dry clothes, sleeping bags, and blankets.

The room was dark, and the flames cast eerie, orange, flickering light against the wall at the foot of our beds, feeding into a dark and sinister ambience. Outside, the wind picked up even more and seemed to slam against the hut with a vengeance. It rattled the windowpanes and sounded as angry as thunder. My thoughts returned to the dragon we'd imagined, restless below the icy lake.

I slept very little and woke up every few minutes it seemed. Fearful of the banging from the wind and a little uncomfortable with the isolation of our hut, the kind but kind of creepy old Bulgarian Gollum lady downstairs, and the uneasy memory of the abandoned axe in the nearby hut just down the slope from us. It was almost 11, and we planned to wake about 6 a.m. to continue up and over the mountain peaks, toward the monastery. I rolled over in the top bunk and tried to get some rest.

The Storm

WE DID WAKE UP at 6 a.m., but then we each fell back asleep until a little past 9. I don't think either of us had slept well with the wind screaming outside the windows and shaking down our hut. I know that "howling wind" is an overused metaphor, but there, above, in those lofty mountain peaks, huddled amongst the frozen lakes, we could hear it unquestionably.

Loud, relentless, and cold. The wind *howled*.

Len and I still had a couple of sandwiches remaining for our day. We borrowed a plastic bottle from Gollum, and Len filled it up from the fresh water flow of melted snow outside our hut.

We each ate a piece of bread and an apple for breakfast then began the next segment of our hike. Len asked Gollum about the trail over the peak, and to our surprise, she just laughed. Then she blew her lips out and made a series of gestures with her wrinkled hands, shook her head, and said something that sounded like "snitch, snitch."

Snitch?

More charades ensued. A few minutes later, we determined that "snitch" meant snow, and from her somewhat frantic gestures and lip-blowing, we gathered that the snow was *bad* snow. We understood that it was unsafe to continue along our planned route that day. We were a little disappointed, but if this woman could survive winters in isolated huts on Bulgarian mountain peaks all on her own, and *she* said it was unsafe, then it probably was.

We devised a new plan to walk three hours down a different trail toward another hut where we could stop in for "chay." Afterwards, we would walk further down to another village where there *might* be a bus, but if there were no bus, we could walk from that village for 13.5 kilometres to a final village where there would *definitely* be a bus.

Easy. Downhill. We had our tomato and ham sandwiches still and now a bottle of clean, ice-cold water.

I was limping a little that morning as we started off. The hiking from the previous day had given me a giant blister that had burst and was then bleeding on my right heel. Just putting on my boots was excruciating, but, as Len assured me, once I started walking, I wouldn't suffer from it after 20 minutes. He was right, but it was a painful 20 minutes.

Day two proved to be more of a treacherous hike than we had anticipated. The wind blew with full force gales, and this time, instead of heading out under a crisp, blue winter morning, we walked with lowered heads into the cold, grey wind.

I had to stop and brace myself when an uppercut punch of wind threatened my balance while trying to walk. The wind blew with unexpected might and seemed to be trying to knock us off our feet. The downhill trail we had chosen was very steep, and it had been snowing for a couple of hours already, completely transforming the scene we had traipsed happily through the day before. The snow continued to fall rapidly and heavily at our backs, and our progress was slow-going. Each step we took was manipulated over either frozen, icy rocks or through slushy, muddy snow, the wind a constant force.

The yellowed, rocky landscape we had admired from the mountain peak the day before had become completely white overnight, covering the entire mountain slope. Fresh snow hid protruding jagged rocks and deepened holes or ruts.

The greying clouds pressed low above our heads, and the snow whipped around our frozen faces, making it difficult to see too far ahead. We continued clambering down, checking every once in a while for a marker pole rising from the snow to be sure we had stuck to some kind of trail. We were hundreds of metres above the tree line still, but I couldn't enjoy any kind of view; full concentration was needed to determine where to solidly place each step.

Within about half an hour, we were completely soaked through. The snow fell as hard as pellets and froze to the back of my hair and neck. My backpack had several inches of thick snow draping over it like a frozen cape. Even though my waterproof coat kept my torso dry, my jeans were saturated. Snow found its way inside my gloves so that my fingers went numb. Wet snow trickled inside my boots, and so my feet were sloshing with each step, my left foot in cold water, my blistered right foot in cold water and blood.

And then, our trip became a little scarier.

Len had been walking ahead, slipping and sliding forward in his tennis shoes through the ice and frozen mud; I had been watching the ground and carefully overseeing my steps when I heard Len ask, "Was that lightning?"

I looked up, "I didn't see anything."

As if on cue, a rumble of cracking thunder roared at our backs. The wind blew even harder, and the snow fell suddenly faster and thicker. Our concentration turned to panic. Then another lightning bolt—this one I saw—flashed through the sky and struck the ground about 6 metres away from us. The thunder rolled and grumbled like a furious beast.

We were at least a 45-minute climb above the treeline still, which meant we were the tallest thing on the mountain. For the first time, I actually felt fear that I might be in real danger, that serious injury was just one treacherous slip ahead.

We had already been moving downhill for over an hour and were far from a place with any other people. We were without phone service and couldn't possibly turn back and reclimb the snowy slope to the frozen lakes. I couldn't remember if the advice, when caught in a lightning storm, instructed running towards a tree for safety or keeping away from them. Len and I decided that we needed to stay low, keeping against rises in the landscape and try to make a straight bolt towards the tree line where we could find shelter from the storm in the forest. It seemed the safest and quickest way to escape from the fury of the lightning snowstorm we'd unwittingly hiked into. This we did, but our escape route into the trees took us off the trail.

After a few minutes of heart-racing running and slipping without having a clear path to follow, we stopped to get our bearings under a canopy of dark forest. We were still high above the thicker trees, but it seemed a little calmer there, and we needed to see where our trail had gone and how we could find our way back to it.

I say it was calmer, but it was that quiet kind of calm that does little to ease your nerves. Nothing had changed; the weather was still bad, and just as I was thinking it was too quiet and calm, as if nature had just been inhaling a breath, another bolt of lightning flashed just metres away and lit up the low-bearing sky.

We ran.

Down, down, over mud, slipping through snow, towards the dense forest, the snow and wind pushing and blowing and freezing, my feet sloshing, fingers aching, breath gasping.

With a pervading feeling of sheer terror, we crossed from the open slopes into the thicker trees. Even Len, my adventurous, thrill-seeking friend, told me he had felt scared back there. How do you hide from lightning? How do you see it coming? We'd had no place to go and only the choice to either lie down still and freeze or to run and hope we would not be struck.

Searching around a bit, we discovered a trail through the forest that seemed a surer bet, but the falling snow had covered up the painted rocks that kept hikers clearly on one trail. Because of the fast-falling snow and the wind, it was sometimes difficult to see where we were going or to even make out which clearing in the forest was the trail meant for us. At times, we had to search through the tangle of tree trunks and curtains of snowflakes for life-saving signposts. Some signs had nothing written on them, or when they did, they of course were in Bulgarian, and it took a few minutes for Len to attempt to decipher.

Panic has several stages for me, I learned. The first stage of panic revealed itself in the form of flight. My body had refused to fight or freeze but had instead acted rapidly and without thought to remove itself from danger by fleeing.

The second stage came in the form of giddiness. About half an hour after having reached the relative safety of the forest and continuing our hiking descent, I began to laugh. I'd been about 15 paces or so behind Len, thinking over our situation. I don't think I've mentioned bears yet.

I'd read somewhere that the Bulgarian Rila Mountain range has the largest population of bears in Europe—and wolves for that matter. I had briefly worried about them the day before, but in the excitement of the hike and the beauty of the woods, I had forgotten about them and dismissed their threat by telling myself that bears had already gone into hibernation. And surely, the wolves were fattened up enough from summer still to not yet be a bother. It had been easier to brush this aside in the beginning.

So, as I was trailing behind Len, carefully placing my steps as my thoughts wandered, a fit of the giggles struck me. There we were, two foreigners in the Bulgarian wilderness, hiking through a snowstorm that even Bulgarian mountain people wouldn't venture out into. I had no phone. Len's phone worked only sometimes. We had not packed a first aid kit. We had one bottle of melted snow. We had no flashlight. No tools. Len was wearing trainers. I was bleeding and frozen, and both of us were soaked. We had just run from and dodged lightning bolts, and there, rising in the back of my mind, came the nagging worry about the wild animals in this seemingly untouched tangle of the mountain.

If something were to have happened to Len, if he were to have slipped in his trainers and broken his foot, we would have been *hours* from other people with whom I could not communicate. I couldn't have read the Bulgarian maps or trail markers to find my way. And if we did find ourselves in serious trouble and in need of help, all Len could do would be to say, "Can I...?"

At that moment, our situation seemed so silly and struck me as incredibly funny, and I burst out laughing at the ridiculous impossibility of our situation until I almost peed. The laughter felt terribly good after enduring so much fear, and Len joined in too, realizing the stupid hilarity of it all.

We continued hiking down, following the trail as best we could for about three hours through dense woods until we came into a clearing and saw ahead a large building with low light in one of the windows.

Relief flooded me. I was soaked from head to toe and had been for most of the journey. The snow hadn't let up once over the prior few hours. Len and I were more than ready to enjoy a cup of hot chay inside the hut, so we sped up our pace a bit and romped over a snowy clearing towards the hut.

We had to cross a fast-flowing stream using a make-shift rail-free bridge of frozen logs with every other cross plank missing. I was a little worried about slipping or losing my balance and falling off the poorly constructed bridge and into the stream. Then I realised that if I did fall, the stream probably wouldn't be deep enough or strong enough to carry me away. Injury or pain from the fall didn't occur to me for some reason. A fall into an icy river would only leave me cold and wet when I was already both of those things, so over the bridge I went. Slowly.

This hut was much larger than the one we had left earlier. It squatted a little above the clearing. We had so much snow stuck to our clothes; we must have looked like snowmen making our way towards the building. But when we arrived at the front, we found the main door locked.

We walked around back to check the other doors, but they also were locked. There were no cars. No footprints. No signs of other people. I banged on the window that had the light on, peered through the glass, and called out. Through the window, I could only see one abandoned teacup forgotten on a dusty table. Nobody home. No chay.

The feeling of heavy letdown replaced any momentary joy and dissolved our hope. There was an open shed underneath the porch, and, disappointed, we decided to take shelter and eat the last of our sandwiches. I was so cold.

The shed was full of ski equipment and yard tools: rusty saws with snow stuck to their teeth, old tires, and miscellaneous tools you would expect to find in a shed. I tried not to think about how this was the perfect setting for a horror film: Two exhausted hikers find their way through snow-filled woods seeking relief from a harrowing lightning storm but find only an abandoned hut littered with stained and rusting saws and axes...

I sat on a stool, under the shelter of the shed roof, looking out at the white trees and falling snow. Len shuffled through his bag. I slowly ate my sandwich, focusing on lifting and lowering my frozen, wet toes.

Right foot, lift, down. Left foot, lift, down. Keep the blood moving. Try to get them warm. Ignore the ache in the fingers. Drink the melted snow.

Len chose this moment to chirpily say, "It's really cool that you're here and doing this! Not many of my friends would be here in these conditions, especially none of my girl friends." Encouraged, I smiled at him and bit into the last of my sandwich.

We sat and ate for 15 minutes or so but didn't want to stay still for too long for fear of freezing. We weren't sure how far we still had to travel, and we needed to keep moving, so we did. This is when the third stage of panic set in for me.

I followed Lenny for about 10 minutes. As per usual, he led the way, and I was trailing behind. The temperature had warmed slightly, turning the falling snow into heavy rain. I was soaked through and aching and was colder than I could ever remember having been.

Our conversation had momentarily stopped, my silence due to focusing on each treacherous step, as probably had his. The trail narrowed at this point and followed along a steep side of the mountain, rising sharply to our left and dropping starkly to our right. Stacks of boulders elbowed out from the side of the mountain, and trees stood so close together the forest became far too dense to see through. Even though it was daytime, the trail was very dark.

My emotions began to downward spiral. Thoughts drifted to just how painfully cold my body felt. I tried to stave off the blow of disappointment from having discovered that the first hut had been abandoned, and the image of the rusty saw in the shed only added chills to my fears. My thoughts began to terrorise me. They started retelling stories of bears attacking humans and unearthing images in my mind of clawed-up tents and scattered limbs.

As I walked, I reminded myself that bears are noisy creatures, and I would hear them before any attack. Bears are frightened of humans from years of being hunted by them. Bears are probably not hungry this time of year because summer eating is over, and they are probably sound asleep by now anyway. Bears hunt the weak and slow...and I am far enough behind Lenny that I looked like the weak and slow of the herd.

So the cold, the wet, the tiring hours of climbing on little sleep, exhaustion from the day before, dehydration, the lack of relief from the closed hut, the pain in my feet and hands, my overactive imagination, and the lack of comforting conversation as we walked in silence—and probably a post-traumatic reaction to our flight from the lightning storm—all of this hit at once.

I tried repeating to myself that I was brave, to not be scared, that I was a strong girl and not to be silly and afraid of the cold, the dark, the snow, the woods, the isolation, and the bears, but I could feel the panic rising with each uncertain step. My cold lips trembled, and hot tears began to spill. And then..."Lenny!" He turned. "Lenny, I'm psyching myself out back here!"

He stopped, and I let spill everything that I was holding in. I truly was frightened at that point—and I *am* strong and brave, and very rarely reel from the danger I often find myself in, but rather love the thrill of every minute.

Not this time.

This time I was scared. It was the first time I can remember actually being frightened while on a camping trip, hiking and exploring nature. I was seriously worried I was fated to be one of those hikers you hear about on the news. The ones that go missing and their remains are discovered when the springtime sun thaws the ground.

Len began to talk to me at that point, engaging me in conversation as we continued walking. He started to talk to me about any topic to lift my spirits. He told me bears would probably run from me if we saw them. His tone was calm and friendly, and the kind-natured story-telling he began soothed my nerves. He let me walk in front as we traversed the steeper part of the trail.

After about 15 minutes or so, the woods opened up a bit, and everything seemed a little lighter. The trail smoothed out and wasn't as steep, and all the walking had warmed up my fingers and toes. The light conversation had helped immensely. I became calm again— and eager to find the next hut where we could finally (hopefully) find ourselves a hot cup of chay.

I'm not sure how much time passed, but we finally arrived at a hut that we thought *might* be open. This hut seemed more kept-up than the one we'd left earlier with the abandoned saws and closed doors. This new hut had two cars in the drive, and as we got closer, a man wearing a black coat walked onto the porch holding a mug between both of his hands.

He was the first human being we'd seen since we'd left Gollum on the stormy mountain peak hours ago. It was still raining and cold, and I raised a frozen arm. He raised an arm back, and a giant woolly black German Shepherd bounced gleefully around him. This was it! The warmth and rest our bodies so desperately needed and our anxious minds had sought. We sighed with relief and we were happy.

The man welcomed us right inside, his only guests. He sat us down and made us some hot chay. Then, seeing the soaked condition of our clothes, piled more firewood into a stove and, within minutes, had a warm fire roaring. Our clothes began to steam. I held the mug of hot chay, finally, in my pink and clammy fingers. My hair was completely wet. Everything ached. We still had 13.5 kilometres to walk until we arrived at the next village with a bus that would take us home.

After a few minutes of thawing, we heard shouting from outside, then a huge, muscle-y man boomed into the hut where Len and I sat soaked and steaming and shivering, holding our cups by the fire.

And then, there he was. Kostas. The broad-shouldered Bulgarian was a big man. Tall, with hard, round muscles. He seemed nonchalant about the cold, and wore no coat like the rest of us had donned. He was the cook and a friend of the hut owner. The two Bulgarians chomped loud and fast to each other—maybe about us, maybe not. Then Len somehow communicated to them where we were headed, and Kostas said a string of words we didn't understand, followed by exuberant gesturing, and then said "car."

Car?

Yes, he had a car and was offering to drive us down the mountain. After all the unknowns we had been through this day, do we take a ride from a large, muscly stranger in the snowy Bulgarian mountains? Yes, we do.

Kostas quickly became one of my favourite characters from my travels. Booming and boisterous. By the time Len and I had stood up and reached for our coats, he had already loaded both our bags into the trunk of his car and was waiting. The rain had stopped.

We jumped in. I took the front seat, with Len buckled in the back. The car was a brown, creaking junker with a cracked and glued dashboard and an engine that died at least four times en route. Kostas popped in his favourite CD for us, Bulgarian rock and roll, which I think consisted of electric guitars and accordions. Kostas talked loudly and enthusiastically and gestured excitedly around him, pointing out the scenery and explaining to us how beautiful the mountains were, shiny and colourful from the recent weather.

I think.

I don't actually know for sure that those were the things he was saying. Turning to the backseat, I asked Len what the word for bears was. "Um, мечка" he said.

So I turned to Kostas and asked, "мечка?"

"Мечка?" he replied. "Oh! Мечка!" he shouted with understanding. Then nodded animatedly and repeated the word with much gusto as if to say, "Bears? Oh yes! Bears are here! Bears are everywhere! Lots and lots of bears! All through the woods! In the trees, on the paths, along the trails! Bears here and there and everywhere! Bears, bears, bears!"

I decided then that I was much better off in this rattling car with this huge Bulgarian stranger than I was on the mountain trail, freezing and stalked by hungry bears.

Kostas drove us the entire 13 km to his house, located in the destination village we'd hoped to reach hours ago at the start of our day back in Gollum's canteen. As I climbed out of the car and as Kostas removed our bags, I heard a crash and yelp behind me. I turned to see Lenny entangled in a stretched out seatbelt lying on all fours on the ground just outside of the car. He'd tripped trying to escape the back seat, fell against the car door, and landed on the gravel. Of all the dangerous and treacherous climbing we'd done the past two days, Lenny fell over then, igniting roars of laughter from both Kostas and me.

Kostas was extremely hospitable and led us into his house, where he literally jumped all around his small den, sat us by a metal heater, and encouraged us to take off our shoes by pointing excitedly and practically doing it for us.

He had two teenage children who were home, and he kept shouting at them to come and translate for him ("Poncho! PONCHO!!"), and there was a furry little kitten curled up near me, hiding from the commotion. In the background, we heard water running.

I whispered to Len and asked him what he thought was going on, and Len said, "I think he's running a bath for us."

Well, here we were, in some remote mountain village, in a Bulgarian chef's house, who was forcing his teenage children to communicate in English with us for him. We declined the invitation to bathe and sleep, but his kids were very helpful in drying us with a towel and a heater, and then showing us the way to a bus station.

In the never-ending exchange of confusing but energetic conversations that overran our entire time spent with Kostas, we learned a lot about him. It turns out that Kostas is a local celebrity. He was in the 1993 Guinness World Book of Records for winning a 100km race barefoot somewhere overseas. We were impressed. But I have yet to find him in that book.

After a few more minutes of awkward but endearing conversation, we headed out to catch our bus home. Kostas and his kids were friendly and helpful, and after the day we'd had, they were a much-welcomed comfort.

In all my travels, encounters with the kindness of strangers have far outnumbered the encounters with crooks or thieves. Here was one more warming example of humans looking out for other humans who found themselves in a bind.

We boarded the bus, and after a couple of hours of a drive,

we found ourselves back in the city and in Lenny's cosy flat. We ordered pizza, and then I crashed for over 12 hours of much-needed sleep.

The Last Days

I AWOKE TO MY last full day in Sofia, a little sore but rested. Len had work to catch up on, so I planned to wander through the city and indulge in a little souvenir shopping.

As I always do, I managed to get lost in the streets, but also managed to find my way back, as I usually do.

There were several markets I found with stalls piled high with winter vegetables and packaged meats. One stall sold only honey; honey in small jars and honey in gallon jars. I had never seen it sold in such quantities. I wanted so much to buy a giant gallon to return to London with, but there's no way I would be able to fit it in my suitcase or risk a spill so impossible to clean. So I took a picture instead (my camera had decided to work again in the warmer climate) and then bought a small jar.

In a stall selling various Bulgarian pottery, a rectangular ceramic piece caught my eye. The entire piece was painted a shiny bright yellow, all the way to each edge, and had a deep blue sun painted in the middle—the opposite of what we see when we look up on clear days. I purchased this souvenir for myself. A bright blue sun in a shimmering yellow sky.

I had booked myself a massage at Lenny's gym for the end of the day. It was a swanky gym, and the massage felt great on my sore muscles.

That night, Len and I planned to hit up a tacky and traditional restaurant called "The Jolly Village." It was a favourite among the locals and decked out with giant pumpkins and other gourds piled into corners, with baskets of root vegetables and dried flowers hung from the ceiling.

It was the type of place that keyed up the tacky tourist attraction vibe but in a way that seemed to add to its charm. We sat at a table and ordered red wine. The dishes were tantalising. Every plate of food we ordered came served on thin round bread like a giant pita, but solid, chewy, and tasty. We ordered three plates to share and allowed the bread base to soak up the flavours of each dish. Feta cheese, roasted tomatoes, eggplant, we ordered grilled baby octopus, and lamb meatballs—it was a feast!

And then, the pinnacle of the evening! Well into our entrees, the entertainment began. Traditional Bulgarian music started to play. Fiddles, drums, guitars, and men and women in bright coloured greens and yellows and reds of traditional dress spilt out into the busy dining room and started dancing up and down between the tables.

It was fantastic! We then noticed that the music was playing over speakers, and the instruments the dancers had in their hands weren't actually the source of the music. They were only pretending to play. The entertainers weren't all that coordinated, as sometimes the drum would sound between beats—but never mind, it was still loud and lively, and entertaining to be sure!

After the dancing musicians, out came the belly dancers! They were captivating in their bright blue and red costumes that shimmered with dangly jewellery. They also were accompanied by an entourage of men and women dancing and "playing" their instruments.

The belly dancers went from table to table, picking up tips as they gyrated in their bright and flashy costumes. The lively dancers grabbed unsuspecting diners by the hand, including mine and Len's, and a chain of diners and dancers step-step-kicked throughout the entire restaurant to the tunes of traditional Bulgarian folklore songs, hand-in-hand in one long, looping, joyfully clumsy and hilarious line. Eventually, the whole restaurant joined in. It was brilliant.

Our entire food bill and bottles of wine and entertainment at this upscale restaurant cost us each £8. Nothing at all. We paid our dues and, wound up from dancing and wine, walked down the road to seek out a bar that we'd heard had booked a gypsy band. As we approached, we soon realised that the bar was a little quiet. A burly security man guarded the front door.

"Is there a gypsy band playing tonight?" Len asked in English.

"No gypsy band," came the monotone, deep-voiced reply.

"*No* gypsy band?" I asked again.

"No gypsy band." He said. Again. Humourlessly.

"Is there a gypsy band at another bar, maybe?" we asked.

"No gypsy band." A straight-mouthed frown.

Ok. No gypsy band, but we decided to stay for a drink anyway.

Turned out there was live music, but in the form of a Bulgarian Elvis look alike.

As we sat down with our drinks inside this dark, cavernous bar, a gorgeous, dark-haired man walked in, and everyone else in the bar began to cheer. His cheeky grin greeted the crowd. A gold hoop pierced each of his ears, and he carried an electric guitar in his hand. He strolled to the back of the bar, and his voice broke into song. He sang renditions of the Beatles, the Rolling Stones, Bob Dylan. Every song he sang for the first 40 minutes was in English, and he sang them with flirtatious confidence and talent. The bar crowd loved him. I loved him. I wanted to marry him. We had a brilliant final night in Bulgaria.

Of course, caught up in the fun of our last night, we drank too much and ended up sauntering home at a late hour, as we had typically done while living in Brighton. I was determined to avoid a hangover and lined up nearly every glass Lenny owned on his counter and filled them each with water. It amounted to 10 or 11 full glasses of water, which, I figured, would flush out the alcohol so that I'd feel fine the next day.

My attempt to deflect a hangover failed, and I still woke up the next morning with pounding almost-regret. I fumbled around with my things and packed, found my way to the post office to send off a few postcards, then back. I returned in time for Len to take me to the airport to catch my onward flight to Stockholm for another one of my back-to-back travel adventures. Tired, hung-over, achy, but incredibly grateful and happy with every turn our reunion had taken.

Living my life out as an expat living in the UK, I immersed myself in new experiences, travelled often, learned about myself, came to understand more about the world, and met people from vastly different backgrounds and cultures than mine. It was all so enriching.

But it also plunked me into a lifestyle where my family was such a distance from me that my efforts to deepen friendships were more purposeful. Friendships became a source of family. Roommates and friends felt more like siblings; each individual mattered more. This is especially true of those friends who were also expats themselves.

It seemed that even if our objective for such a lifestyle may have differed, the fact that we lived in a land foreign to us created a unique bond. Holidays were spent together, as were routine weeknight dinners. We connected on a level that just wasn't possible with friends at home.

While my blood family was not to witness first-hand or be a direct part of my life during these seven years, my friends and roommates were involved in those life-shaping and impressionable years each day. My friends inspired me, encouraged me, explored with me. We travelled together, revelled together, we laughed and cried together. Whether we were studying, off adventure-ing or just cooking a "family" meal together, these moments were treasured.

And so, I hugged my dear friend Len goodbye, still buzzing from our snowy adventure and reeling from our hilarious escapades. Smiling as I boarded the plane, I was already looking forward to the next time I'd see his kind grin—wherever that may be—and exchange each of our stories over hot tea or too much red wine.

The Elephant's Journey

WHAT IS IT THEY say? That elephants never forget? That they recognise their own, their friends, and their enemies even after decades of absence?

Travellers carry this same truth. We don't forget. When travelling, we tell stories to strangers of the home we've left; when home, we tell stories of strangers we've met when travelling.

The wanderers that leave home, and travel far and wide to the ends of the earth and over strange seas, eventually find themselves on the road that leads back home. We remember where we came from, and one day we circle back.

Sometimes laden with riches, or sometimes broken and weary—sometimes both.

But when the final destination has been ticked on the map, the journey towards home begins. The traveller goes, intent on reuniting with loved ones, or perhaps finally brave enough to confront past fears.

Perhaps feeling they have grown into who they are ready to be with a seasoning only other travellers will recognise.

Elephants, as far as we know, don't circle the globe in their lifetime, experiencing other elephant cultures, collecting stories of hardships and triumphs. But still, they travel. They migrate and move about, stomping through the heat of sandy deserts and tropical jungles. Their modern journeys, long and dusty, are played out roaming up and down on one continental stage. They don't travel quite so far as us humans.

Or do they?

Just south of Nashville resides a pack of elephants. They roam the green Tennessee hillside, befriend the yipping ranch dog, and graze on lush grasses. The herd of retired performers and leather-skinned labourers are well cared for now as they spend the rest of their days in the good graces of southern hospitality.

Not a likely thing, to come across elephants living free and happy in the continental United States, but there they are. And there they will stay until they die peacefully of old age, and into the elephant graveyard their bones will settle.

I wonder, is it strange to be buried in the earth so far away from your own kin, and in dust so different from the ground where your feet first tread? Maybe.

But that's not what's happening with these Tennessee elephants. They're not so far from their native home as it would appear if we expand our perspective of time and distance.

In 2010 in a suburb of Nashville, a family had contracted diggers to build a swimming pool in their backyard. As the bulldozers and tractors tore at the earth, the broken remains of a Trilophodon were discovered.

These prehistoric animals had once stood ten feet tall and resembled a modern elephant. This species was believed to have been widespread in the Americas over 12 million years ago, travelling up and down a very different continent than their descendants eventually would.

So it is here in the deep south, in the 21st Century, these modern elephants roam. Native to Africa and Asia but ending their days in a sanctuary in eastern Tennessee, not too far from where their ancestors began their journey millions of years before.

Perhaps these southern elephants had found their way home after all. Does it matter that they didn't walk to Tennessee on their own four feet? No more than it matters that most of us travellers choose to fly, rather than walk, to the destinations we seek.

As a traveller, I don't know where my bones will eventually rest, or where my dust will float, but I'd like to think that wherever that may be, it will be a place familiar. That those I rest amongst will be kindred flesh and bone turned kindred spirit.

It might not be the same land where I began this life, but I imagine it will be a place where I know in my heart that I've come full circle. When I've traipsed and climbed and danced and laughed and loved and cried and fully immersed myself in this beautiful life in every way and every place that I possibly could. The journey ended, the backpack set down, the travel tales told. I will be home in a place I know I'm meant to be. As do these elephants, I will rest amongst my familiars.

Travel isn't always pretty. It isn't always comfortable. Sometimes it hurts, it even breaks your heart. But that's ok. The journey changes you; it should change you. It leaves marks on your memory, on your consciousness, on your heart, and on your body. You take something with you. Hopefully, you leave something good behind.

ANTHONY BOURDAIN

PART FIVE

The Pilgrimage

Camino de Santiago, Spain
2008

WHEN I HAD FIRST set out on the Pilgrimage, my travel bag weighed about 12 kilos. I felt this weight not only on my back and shoulders throughout the 27 days and more than 300 km that I would eventually journey by foot, but also in my heart. It was not the sort of heart-heaviness where our emotions sink to the bottom anchoring in place in some form or another, no. This heavy-heartedness pulled and heaved through every chamber, every vessel, where each beat stacked on beat felt no less than a brutish pound in my chest, filling a newly vacant void.

For 27 days, I had walked the Camino de Santiago with this heaviness. I had walked through tangled vineyards and dirty city streets and over dusty, sunlit, lavender-strewn fields and along quaint, cobbled roads. I had walked up forested mountain trails, hiked steep, rocky hills, and had passed soft, wind-blown pastures and broken-down, rusted barns. I had walked against the cold wind, under a merciless sun, and through forgiving rain. One cold, rainy morning, I had walked along wet concrete departing from a dismal train station, insistent but reluctant to attend the funeral of a dear, sweet friend. And then again, I had returned to dusty, winding, foot-worn roads to walk the remainder of the Camino.

By the time my journey ended in Santiago de Compostela, almost a month after my start, my feet had blistered and bled many times over. From the outside, it might seem that was about all that was different about me. My emotional and physical load weighed more or less the same—my heart was still heavy. These things had not changed.

But crossing through the city gates of Santiago, I sensed my strength as something honed—something seasoned. I did not buckle at the weight of my bag or fold over from the heaviness of my heart as I once had.

Now I carried my load with the dusty grace and forged strength I had earned and learned along The Way.

JULY 31ST

Saint Jean Pied-de-Port

WE SAT AT A wooden picnic table in a small, shaded courtyard outside our hostel in Saint Jean Pied-de-Port. It was the first evening of our long, much-anticipated Pilgrimage on the Camino de Santiago, and other healthy, rested, and as-of-yet uninjured travellers were mingling about. We were all preparing for the crossing by foot over the emerald green Pyrenees mountains early the next morning.

A French nurse sat just a few seats down from me on the picnic bench, holding a cup of herbal tea in her hands. She was a pilgrim, too, relaxing for the afternoon with the rest of us. I remember her slight, slender frame and short, soft brown hair, acknowledging me with kind blue eyes. Unlike the pilgrims staying in Saint Jean Pied-de-Port, she had travelled east on the Camino, away from Santiago, hiking in the opposite direction of the standard route. She had walked for about four days, hiking alone, even though she had two small boys waiting for her in another part of France. She was one of many intriguing pilgrims I would come to meet along the trail. I'm not sure what struck me more—that she was travelling in the direction that she preferred, walking against the current of other pilgrims on the Camino, or the fact that she was a mother who set off without her children.

Back then, I had only known children to be the members of the family who set off to explore and travel on their own. It was the children who did the leaving behind. She demonstrated a reversal of expectations I had become familiar with. Gentle, kind, unimposing. But she was clearly leaving the duties of her motherly role, even if for just a few days. She shaped time into her own and walked the direction of her choosing.

These thoughts did not surface in my mind back then; so busy was I with my own internal musings, the distracting scenery, and new encounters. But of the dozens of pilgrims I met, this brief meeting made an impression that I was not to forget.

Setting my mug down on the wooden table, I asked her why she did not keep her boys with her as she walked. She replied in careful, slow-spoken English, "Because I am not a...chicken mother" and smiled at me over her cup.

At first, I didn't understand her meaning.

"Mother hen," Haley explained from across the table and smiled at me as well.

24.2 KM

St. Jean Pied-de-Port to Roncesvalles

THIS FIRST DAY OF the Pilgrimage, I climbed eight hours straight up the steeper French side of the Pyrenees. The heavy weight of my bag was a new sensation that I was certain I would never fully get used to. Though they had been worn in plenty during previous hiking trips and mountain treks, my hiking boots were now subjected to a steadier pace and longer distances and were consistently rubbing on my skin.

Haley, a friend who had taught at the same school as I, had been a regular hiking partner in the UK. She was keen to experience the Camino and dirty her own hiking boots along foreign trails. As she and I started off, we were initiated into the spirit of the Camino with a light morning drizzle that, soon enough, dripped more heavily into a mild rain as we walked. It was cold. By the time I'd reached the first albergue, (Spanish for hostel, or shelter), I would discover no less than five shiny pink blisters on my feet and one chafed inner thigh. I hadn't given myself any bruises or been afflicted by bug bites—yet.

Despite the rain and the first signs of physical hardship, we had taken great delight in the landscape along the walk. Through the rainy mist, we had spotted herds of dark horses in the green pastures, flocks of woolly sheep and spotted cows, and giant, fat liquorice slugs splayed out along the muddied rock path.

As we trekked along the damp hillside, my thoughts billowed about in my mind. The landscape was dreamy, with soft greens and low cottony clouds, but at the same time, ever so real. As lightly and as surely as the rain, a feeling descended upon me—the kind of moment when, while moving right along with life's current, making decisions, and playing them out over time with order and a process, we suddenly feel the sensational movement of all that we are. This feeling brings us a moment of presence when time slows, and we are allowed to take a good look around and observe where all of those decisions have finally taken us. Walking through the rain those first hours on the Camino, my thoughts reflected on the past seven years of choices and chance meetings.

"How did this kind of life shift into existence? Each friend, each adventure, all the learning, all the love. How did I get myself *here*?"

For more than eight hours that first day, I walked 27 km uphill to reach an elevation of 1,410 metres—the highest point I would reach along the entire Camino Frances. The fog was too dense for our 5 a.m. start to have been rewarded with a spectacular sunrise, and we had spent most of that first day wet—our clothes, our bags on our back, our faces and hands dripping.

Near the peak, I crossed into Spain by foot, the French side bordered with barbed wire.

On the trail that day, we had befriended Eugene, one of many pilgrims we would encounter along the way. He was tall and strong, with overgrown, dark curly hair tumbling around his unshaven face like a black mane. We ambled along beside him for a while, offering him conversation, and he offered us his package of nuts. He planned to walk 1,000 km, which was three times the length of the Camino Frances. He was Russian but had been living in Germany studying communication systems. His story was that he had been a soldier for six years, but now, free from study and work and war, he was intent on a more personal mission. He carried his pack, a sleeping bag, a tent, and kerosene, which all must have been very heavy. Unlike me, his strength for these things was toughened already, and he was prepared for what the Camino would bring him. He, like us, had a reason to walk.

The entire walk from St. Jean Pied-de-Port to Roncesvalles was muddied and shrouded in mist. It was a mist that felt magical, mysterious, and cloaked the trees. The mist also robbed us of our panoramic valley views. But from the nature that we could see surrounding us, the foliage creeping at our feet was a bright green, and the damp fog, though blanketing us with cold, softened the scenery we could take in.

We passed a few more pilgrims, and a few pilgrims passed us. Perhaps six hours or so in, while walking along a dirt path that hugged and curved into the hillside, I thought I heard the sound of a harmonica faintly breathing a melody in the distance. Perching on a rock, I listened and peered down the path behind me into the mist.

Through the fog, led by a tune, emerged a Spanish or maybe Italian, dark-eyed man. He wore light brown clothes and revealed a three-day stubble underneath a fedora. His thick black curls were tied back in a neat ponytail at his neck. His arms were swarthy, and his legs looked strong in their muddy boots. Easily, he was the most gorgeous thing I'd laid eyes on in days. As he approached, the notes of his harmonica gently floated through the fog more robustly. The scenes from a storybook came to life at that moment.

I can't remember if he stopped playing when he saw me, offering a nod and a smile as we locked eyes. Or perhaps we only locked eyes, him nodding as he continued playing and carried on his way past me and on around the mountain. Either truth, he left me behind, mesmerised by the moment, the pieces of his song in my ears and in my heart, until the fog thickened back up where he had been, and he and his harmonica were gone.

We slept in a monastery that night. Actually, it was the large barn inside the monastery. The old barn, no longer housing straw or livestock, had been repurposed and filled with 60 bunk beds, lined up side by side by side, each only about two feet apart from the next. It had the capacity to sleep 120 pilgrims. 120 strangers. 120 reasons to walk.

Dinner was included with the stay and served promptly at 7 p.m. We dined on pasta and wine, fish, and homemade bread. Lights out promptly at 10 p.m. was the welcome rule, and from 10 p.m. onwards we were secured in our barn until 6 a.m. the next morning.

The barn was a stone building dimly lit inside with low chandeliers that hung from the vaulted ceiling. The thick walls, medieval with their high, slotted windows, had been designed for days gone by when shooting arrows from them might have kept us all feeling cosy and safe.

Occasional flashes from cameras struck the monastery walls like lightning, and an orchestra of snores soon filled the darkened room. I wasn't sure if it felt more like we were at camp or in an orphanage. There were so many different nationalities fumbling with their bags and beds. Every age group was present—all of us weary from our day's trek. An American girl was in the top bunk next to me. Alex, an Italian actor we had met at dinner, was sleeping opposite, and Eugene bunked nearby. I had discovered one bug bite.

In the morning, we would awaken to soft choir music played through large speakers I hadn't noticed before, followed by the loud rustling of my waking fellow pilgrims and a cacophony of clumsy flashlights and loud zippers.

That first day had worn me out. We had been warned it would be the hardest day physically, but now, looking back, I am not so sure. The walking had been challenging at times this first day, but I still felt good, despite the blisters and backache I could feel beginning to grip. Sleep came easily.

My thoughts traversed from the scenes of the day, ahead to the plans for tomorrow, and back to the events of the past summer. I thought about Lenny all the time. *How could his heart just stop?*

~

BEFORE I MOVE INTO the next day, there is another character to introduce. He was not a pilgrim, and I have neither a name nor an age for him. I can't be sure where he is from, but I presume he was a local, living in a Spanish Pyrenees village. I can't even remember exactly what he looked like. I know he was older, kind, and spoke to me in Spanish. But whether his hair was dark or grey, or if he wore glasses on his face, I cannot recall.

He did speak a little English, and, like most people I encountered along the way, he was curious as to where I was from and where I was going.

Sitting for a few minutes over a glass of red wine in the café in Roncesvalles, waiting for dinner to be served, I'm not sure how much I showed him of myself in our brief but friendly encounter. Did I show him the teaching career that I had just closed a chapter to? Room 9.13 and each student I had left behind in the classroom? Did I show him Over Street family dinners with my colourful cast of roommates over the past seven years? Did I show him red wine lit pub nights with friends and musicians on the streets of London? Exchanging stories of lovers with Tanja? Dancing in ballrooms of Castles? Did I show him Lenny?

I must have shown him a glimpse of that life I had chosen to say goodbye to. I must have given him a glimpse of my mother, my sister, my brother, my family on the other side of my trek, who I would see again soon.

In just a few moments of his broken English and my embarrassing Spanish, I must have given him a glimpse of where I had been and where I was going because he looked at me with soft eyes, paused, then said to me, "Tu corazón está en dos piezas."

Your heart is in two pieces.

26.5 KM

Roncesvalles to Larrasoaña

THIS IS WHERE THE pain sets in. Twenty-seven kilometres more beneath my belt, and I'd earned two very bloody, very rashy, bumpy feet. I was also a little sunburnt by the time we arrived at the next albergue in Larrasoaña.

That morning, as we left Roncesvalles, we were gifted a gorgeous sunrise with a golden sheen lighting up creamy coloured cows grazing in the nearby fields. The villages we walked through were sandstone and still sleeping beneath the blanket of the morning light.

As I walked, my stride became synchronised with others walking along the Camino, and so we naturally fell into conversations with other pilgrims that lasted hours, sometimes days. It was rare to actually sit down at an albergue and meet someone whilst *not* walking because exhaustion from the day's trek meant food and sleep were all anyone really wanted upon arrival.

Mostly, I met whoever's pace fell in line with mine. "Buen Camino" was the friendly greeting along the road. Pilgrims would smile, nod, and say these words to each other as we headed out in the mornings, as we passed along the route, and as we dropped our bags at the end of the day. All nations, all religions. *Buen Camino*—have a good journey.

On this day, I met Mary, a Japanese-Canadian who was soon to marry her French boyfriend. First, before any vows were exchanged, she was walking solo to San Sebastian, where she would land a solid few days of surfing before heading to Paris to plan her wedding. The ceremony would have three translators, French, Japanese, and English, and would take place in Switzerland.

We also met Ryan, from Florida, who had been living in Barcelona as an English teacher and was fluent in Spanish. He, too, was soon to be married, but to a girl who was half Brazilian and half British. He would frequently pause his walking along the Camino to spend time in meditation, and I enjoyed several lovely conversations with him—mostly about Buddhism, life, love, and what it all is supposed to mean.

When we arrived hot and sweaty in Larrasoaña, the line of pilgrims around the albergue was discouragingly long. Because no one can ever be quite sure which albergue we would arrive at, depending on how far we could walk each day, it didn't make sense to make reservations, nor were reservations accepted. First come, first served was the rule.

The doors of the main albergue in Larrasoaña did not open to receive pilgrims until 2 p.m., and when they did, I could see there would be far more pilgrims than the venue would be able to house. Haley and I were among a small group that arrived too late to stay, that needed to find our own beds somewhere else in the village.

We were lucky to have met Spanish-speaking Ryan, who trekked throughout the village, all of us failed Spanish students following behind him until we found a house that agreed to put our newly formed clan up in their spare bedroom. By then, we'd grown to 10 bed-less people. We celebrated Ryan's successful find as was fitting— with a dip in the nearby river, cold drinks, and a watermelon seed-spitting contest on the lawn. There was no dinner included at this local home-turned-albergue, so I made myself a dinner of lettuce, tomato, cheese, red pepper, and grapes. But I didn't mind, as this place had perks the other albergue couldn't offer. This pension was much more private than the albergue would have been and offered a sunny back garden where we could do a little yoga and practice kung fu.

Every single day walking the Camino was a full one spent discovering the unexpected topography of the trails, facing new difficulties with either food or board or blisters, and encountering fascinating new people, all pilgrims on the trail. For a day, I found a kind of camaraderie with Mary and with Ryan. Like me, they were both North Americans who had been living in Europe and were now moving back to the continent. Like me, they were closing one chapter and opening another, using the Camino to voyage them from an ending towards the next beginning.

The Pilgrimage was not just another travel experience or adventure through a new country. For me, the Pilgrimage was to help me with my transition. The weeks on the trail, I had hoped, would give me the time I needed to think about the newness of all that awaited me: new jobs, new locations to begin living in, and the potential for new relationships.

My intention had been that this walk might help to create space to dwell on these things and consider what I wanted next for my life. I had ideas, but I was also unsure and still mourning the fact that my life living in the UK had come to an end—even though it was a choice I had been ready to make. The Pilgrimage, I'd decided, would allow for the dust to settle. It would allow me the time to remember with fondness and gratitude everyone I loved who was still in England. Time to let go of things that it pained me to remember.

It seems like sometimes life spins you so fast and the momentum of your choices jostles you so rapidly that you have to be sure you have a firm grip and that the momentum is moving you forward. Even from its very beginning, the Pilgrimage provided me with a welcome relief to check in on the life I was gripping and be sure it was a life I wanted.

Every passing day, every passing kilometre, I sought to sink deeper and deeper into assurance. And comfort. After all, my choice to leave the UK had not been easy, and even though I was sure bringing my UK life to a close was the right thing for me, I was still a little anxious as to whether I would land on my feet in the US. I wondered what the next part of my life would deliver and if I were positioning myself in the best way.

The all-day walking did just as I had hoped and enabled uninterrupted thoughts to roam. And even though the terrain often left me short of breath, taking time to breathe on the Camino was the best thing I could have done to help me ease from one kind of life into the next life unknown.

It felt good to meet so many captivating strangers along the road each day, sharing our stories. As we exchanged bios, I realised each pilgrim was a mirror. As we told each other about ourselves— who we were, what we did for a living, where we were from, and what we anticipated would come next, I realised we were really giving voice to how we viewed our own self. Most of us were not travelling with our families or friends and, like the French nurse back in St. Jean Pied-de-Port, had left our roles behind. On the Camino, we were only ourselves—however we chose to present that to others during the select kilometres that our journeys overlapped.

As I walked the Camino, I was in between homes, in between jobs. I had no address, no title. I was weightless—except for my too-heavy pack on my back. I felt both free and unsteady.

By only the second full day of walking and thinking and talking to strangers, I realised what I had done and where my choices had led me. After the commotion of goodbyes, the packing of bags, and the planning of trips had settled, I began to realise what it meant to leave the UK and start moving towards life back in California—the different rooms I had backed out of and closed the doors to. Even though I trusted my decision and was ready for the next thing beyond my life in the UK, it still felt like I had jumped blind off a cliff into darkness. Thinking about this darkness ignited a slight panic that could swell if I let it.

As I walked, as I met other pilgrims, as we shared stories and compared blisters, I realised something comforting: As I was falling in the darkness, I recognised from their stories that the others had jumped blindly too. We all had. None of these strangers walking in line with me, carrying our bags and our burdens, our dreams and our memories—none of us could truly know what was waiting for us next. We each were there on the Camino because, at some point, we had decided it was time to leave, to close doors. At some point, we had decided the next thing—whatever we envisioned that next thing to be—was waiting for us at the end of the trail.

And then, as I kept walking, and kept sharing and kept listening to others, I realised that I wasn't falling at all. I was floating. Floating from one chapter of my life into the next. I exhaled a bit more throughout that day's walk, and I remembered that it was okay to float for a while.

We land when we're ready. We land where we should.

14.5 KM

Larrasoaña to Pamplona

WALKING TO PAMPLONA WAS one of the greatest physical challenges of the entire Pilgrimage. It was only about 15 km, and not too bad uphill. However, I awoke in the top bunk of our room in Larrasoaña with my ankles stuck to the sheets with the puss and blood that had been seeping from wounds while I slept. I had to peel the cloth off my open wounds before leaving the bed. My heels were raw and bloody, and the constant friction of roughened leather on wounded skin was agonising. My sweaty blisters screamed inside my boots. This third day on the Camino was a hot one, and my ever-growing blisters were squeezing out of my toes and burning into my heels.

Moodiness crept over me, and I'd started to sink a little further into my sadness from moving and the saying of goodbyes. My emotions had caught up to me on my travels, once again. I'd been grieving for Lenny. Walking is therapeutic, yes, but part of therapy is that so many of our thoughts—not just the positive and affirmative thoughts—are given more time to dig their claws right in. Along with grief, I also felt loss, fear, and anger, and every twisted version of these emotions was flaming in my mind with each sorrowful memory. My feet felt the burn with each strenuous step.

During one stretch of the trail that day, I'd had a good chat with Ryan about Buddhism, human suffering, and the reasons bad things happen to good people. His outlook was positive and told me there were always reasons we can't see, that we must trust in the good. Our conversations gave me something to think about, and if I'm honest with myself, something to learn from: "Focus on the good", "trust that everything happens for a reason", "believe that everything will be okay in the end"—shit like that.

I was just so sad about Lenny.

Because I was so moody and in pain, I felt like I was being a bit of a nuisance to my travelling companion. To get our minds off our feet, we set off to lightly explore Pamplona a bit more, the city of the running bulls—and possibly find some cold beer.

Pamplona turned out to be a city that offered quality distraction from the stinging pain in my feet and the heavy pain in my heart. Penis drawings on city walls were an overwhelming theme found throughout Spain. Alex the Italian, who earned a living as a waiter but was an ever-hopeful and eccentric actor, accompanied Haley and me and kept us amused with his never-ending and hilarious commentary on such an art theme. He could spout Shakespeare lines on cue, he vowed to marry me in California, and very seriously told me I was older than my companion because I had very wise eyes. Perhaps he sensed I was an old soul.

A small group of us pilgrims-turned-friends found a bar just off one of the main plazas in Pamplona where we ordered Kalimotxo, a new drink for me. Kalimotxo was a Spanish tradition of blending Coca-Cola with red wine. As awful as it may sound, it tasted surprisingly good and refreshing and most definitely released me from my heavy thoughts and my painful injuries.

I ended day three locked into the Jesus y Maria Albergue by 10 p.m. I wrote in my journal for a bit on a bench in the courtyard and took in the peaceful surroundings. That day was the last one I would spend with Alex the Italian, Mary, Ryan, and a few others. Haley and I would continue only a little ways the next day, and would no longer be in sync with these same travellers.

The albergue was very busy in Pamplona and heaving with energy. Again, like in the monastery barn in Roncesvalles, the bunk beds were lined up a little too closely. More beds, more pilgrims, more euros. It was here that I noticed how much trouble some pilgrims were having with the trail already. A tired-looking fellow slouched nearby announced he was giving up. I passed by the bunk of a small Italian girl whose feet were both bandaged up so completely that her bandages could have been mistaken for socks. She sat by herself on the bottom bunk, tears streaming down her face, unable to continue the walk.

The albergue was massive, with five or six floors and an expansive communal kitchen. However, the beds were unhygienically close together, and there was very little privacy. I acclimatised quickly to this lack of privacy and close-sleeping with strangers. I had a sleeper-bag, but it was too hot in Pamplona to even use that, so I slept on top of a mattress that held a different person each night. The pain, the heat, and the exhaustion all helped to lower my personal standards without resistance.

The next morning, I woke up on my side on the top bunk, my bare knees touching the bare knees of a sleeping stranger, a man probably in his 40's, curled into his own dreams in the bunk next to me. I was so tired, I didn't even care, and rolled over.

Day three had left me feeling pretty miserable on and off. Haley and I decided day four would be a much needed down day. My feet looked as if they'd been chewed on by small, sharp-toothed sharks. Everything ached. Cizur Menor was the next village down and only 5 km away, and that was all I thought my feet would tolerate.

We sipped a leisurely coffee at 8:30 a.m. while we waited for the shops to open. I badly needed more comfortable shoes. I decided to search for sandals sporting a gripping sole for traction. By 10 a.m. I could buy new bandages and my blistering boots would mercifully be off my feet. Because our days had usually begun at 5 or 6 a.m., we felt a little guilty about not being on the trail yet. Mary had left early, and by the time I finished my café con leche, she had been going for three hours. By the time I finally finished coffee and shopping and started on the Camino, she'd be about done with her trek for the day.

Our group, bonded after only a few days, had now splintered and broken apart. I was sorry to see Mary go. I hoped to catch up with Alex the Italian and Ryan, but who knew? I hadn't seen Eugene since Roncesvalles. We were offered a lift from a nice German couple in a shiny car, who were happy to drive us the short distance to Cizur Menor. Tempting, but I wanted to walk the Camino, and chose to tough it out.

4.3 KM
Pamplona to Cizur Menor

CIZUR MENOR WAS ONLY a 5 km walk from the buzzing city of Pamplona but cultivated a small village feel. This refuge along the Camino hosted only one cosy restaurant, one post office, and, at most, about twenty pilgrims. It was just Haley and me who had set out from Pamplona. Everyone else we had journeyed with for the last couple of days had either headed home defeated or surged onward. We had limped a meagre 5k and were very happy to end it at the first place of rest we came to.

The albergue here nursed us to health—literally. A vibrant, short, plump Spanish woman quite happily welcomed us. Her check-in desk was simply a weathered wooden table with pencils and papers loosely scattered across the top. She jubilantly arranged for Haley and me to recoup in a room where she had already checked in "English boys." She was exuberant about her match-making. "Three English boys," she exclaimed, seemingly proud of herself to have mashed the English speakers together in the same shared room in her albergue.

The Albergue Roncal, while easily missed along the Camino, was the perfect tranquil resting place that we so sorely needed. It enclosed a lovely flowering garden and a serene and swampy turtle pond. The bright green grass, the lovely trees, the mossy pond, and the endless supply of free bandages are what made this place so exceptionally memorable. It provided us with everything we didn't fully realise we had needed. The fussy but endearing host cleaned and freshly wrapped my feet. She had a fully stocked first aid kit at the ready, and other resting pilgrims were very happy to promote her kind attention to us once they had a look at our injuries.

After our feet had been freshly gauzed, we practised a little restorative yoga in the garden, immersed ourselves in a bit of reading, and relaxed on the soft green grass under a warm and orange sun. It was lovely to spend the entire afternoon this way. Dinner that night was enjoyed in a local restaurant—the only one. We shared a table and some wine with an Irish couple and three solo travellers; they were the English boys that our enthusiastic host was so insistent we meet. Everyone at our table had only just met while on the trail.

In truth, only one of the "English boys" was actually English. Of the other two, one was from Sydney, Australia and the other from Pretoria, South Africa. They were a bit older than the last crowd of travelling companions we'd had but possessed the same traveller's spirit. And while not claiming English heritage, everyone at our table was an English speaker, and their company proved hearty and friendly as we exchanged stories of how the Camino was treating each of us (and our feet). After dinner and revelry, our group found its way from the table to our beds in our shared room, and I took up my pen and journal. The others were ready to crash for the night, but I couldn't sleep.

The night outside was peaceful, but I needed just a bit more light than the stars to track my thoughts. My £6 flashlight had failed me, so quietly leaving the dorm room, I crept outside to the patio. I found a clean place on the floor and leaned my back against the wall. The evening proved to be as peaceful as the day. Stars and crickets and sleeping turtles were my only company as I sat out on the open patio. Church bells clanged a lullaby in the distance, reminding me the 11th hour had arrived and was fast fleeting. The vending machine hummed along to it all, and I scribbled away in my journal, cross-legged on the floor, under the dim light.

I remembered a scene, still bobbing on the edge of my memory, of an incredible message I had passed by sometime in the last two days, a message sent from one pilgrim to another:

Emerging from the shaded wood at the base of the Pyrenees, I came across it, legs wobbly from the rugged descent. I looked ahead as the epic emerald forests soothed softly into lush hillsides that sloped below. The path guided me slightly right as the tall conifers and shrubbery shone a lovely green in the late summer heat. To the left along the path, in the distance, stood a stone wall, maybe 8 or 10 feet high. More thick trees crowded in behind and rose above it, a tangle of foliage so dense there was no guessing what the wall was hiding or protecting behind it.

I don't quite remember where my mind had been wandering as my feet wandered down this particular stretch of the Camino trail that afternoon. But I do remember the message scrawled hugely on the wall before me. In giant letters, spray-painted in thick, bright, peachy neon, were the words "EUNA, YOU IMPRESSED ME SO MUCH. KEEP ON GOING."

There were a few other black graffitied words on this seemingly forsaken wall out there in the woods, but those faint scribbles were muted by this bright message.

On the Camino, we cross paths with so many. Sometimes faces and stories would be forgettable, sure. But more often than not, one pilgrim's steps would fall in line with another's whose story was so penetrating, so inspiring that this story and the storyteller could not easily be forgotten.

I was so deeply moved by this spray-painted message, out here in the Spanish wilderness. After walking past the wall for several minutes, the significance of the words sank in. I felt compelled to turn around and walk back to the wall to snap a quick photo.

The neon graffiti struck my heart warmly, and I felt connected somehow. Some other pilgrim had been so inspired, so deeply moved by another's story, and possibly concerned that this person, this Euna, might falter somewhere on her journey. That perhaps one morning she would feel the heaviness in her legs or her heart, and she would set her bags down and call the Camino off.

Whoever had scrawled this message had clearly left Euna behind somewhere along the way. They must have realised they wanted to send her a message so impactful and encouraging that it would reflect the impact her story had made on them. A message more impactful than a text or an email from some unkempt internet café in the next albergue.

The graffiti artists had paused their journey for just a few minutes to warmly vandalise the backside of some Spanish farmer's wall for a worthy and heartwarming cause: encouragement to keep going. Praise. Validation. Support. Friendship. There was so much in their words. They didn't want her to give up.

And also, I wondered, when was this message left? It had been painted on the wall, so it could have been written the day before I arrived, or the week before, or even painted years and years ago.

Did Euna pass by and see it? Did she make it this far? Did it give her the emotional boost she needed to keep going? Did she smile and pick up the pace when she read it or even shed a tear at the kind yet criminal message left just for her?

I wonder these things. I wonder if she finished the Camino entirely and if she remembers this message left for her as much as I remember it. As much as I'm sure many other pilgrims might have felt connected to it that came before me or passed by after me. There's no way to know.

I wonder if, all these years later, the message is still there, painted on that wall in the brightest letters for all to see. For every weary pilgrim that passes by to look up from their journey and read the words, "You impressed me so much. Keep on going."

~

IN CIZUR MENOR, I experienced my first changing of the guard on the trail. At least for me, I couldn't help but notice the energy change and a shift in momentum.

My enthusiasm traversed to feeling grumpy due to tiredness, pain, and sinking thoughts. Our familiar, friendly pilgrims had continued on, and we now had new companions around the dinner table; I would have to remove one pair of shoes and purchase a second if I were to continue without causing more pain to my brutalised feet. And also, we'd paused our walk and taken a day to rest. While day one had seen us climb the steepest leg of the Camino, uphill, for 27 km, this day, day four, we'd enjoyed a much-needed pause in the Pilgrimage.

Journaling away far too late into the evening, I took in these unexpected shifts, feeling that "out with the old, in with the new" would have to be the theme of our short trek on this day. Yawning, finally, I pulled myself off the floor of the patio and crept back into our quiet dorm to seek sleep.

26.8 KM

Cizur Menor to Cirauqui

MY SLEEP WAS A restless one that night. Writing out my thoughts to the sound of church bells while the turtles dozed in their pond outside did little to put my mind at ease.

As we rose from our beds at 5:30 a.m., we discovered that the South African and the Aussie from dinner the evening before were already well on their way. We'd see them for coffee on the trail soon enough.

Of the weeks I spent on the trail, I remember that morning especially.

It was still dark and starry crisp when Haley and I set off from the healing gardens of the Albergue Roncal to continue on the Camino. Haley's knees were aching, and she wanted to take it easy and slow her stride, leaning a little more into her steel walking poles. My bandaged feet, in the comfort of my just-purchased, well-fitted flip-flops with gripped soles, were feeling renewed. I was confident with the new fit and eager to make progress, so after a couple of kilometres meandering forward in the sleepy dark, I arranged to wait for Haley at the first open coffee house we came across. I picked up my pace, venturing out on the trail and walked a couple of hours ahead on my own.

The sunrise was gorgeous that morning, with tangerine light pooling easily over the Spanish hills. The gravelled dirt path was bordered by quiet fields that hosted acres and acres of sunflowers. All were bathed in golden light over dusty ground. I put one bandaged, flip-flopped foot in front of the other and let my thoughts flow as I soaked up the sun, the sunflowers, and flowed with the morning as it awoke and opened around me—and around Haley, not far behind. I believe it was here where Haley laid a flower for Lenny.

Along the Camino, even from the very beginning of the trail, which had been, at that point, five days and forever ago, pilgrims had laid down rocks. They had laid small piles of stones, pyramid style, unmissable as we walked past. Sometimes, the pilgrims who built and left these piles of stones along the side of the trail left words behind too. They wrote on papers and tucked them under the heaviest of stones.

Some say these piles of rocks served as art, tokens for the Camino, or humble memorials. But as I understood the meaning of these piles of stones left along the Camino roads, these stones were burdens. They were the worries of pilgrims and the sadness they'd carried. The stones were the reasons they walked. The piles of stones were their anxieties, insecurities, or shame. They were frustration and grief. The stones were loss and tragic heartbreak. And all along the dirt-paved Camino, I would pass these burdens and heartaches that pilgrims had left behind on the road. I would pass by the goodbyes. I would pass by the release. I would pass by the letting go of things. I would pass by what others decided to leave behind in heavy piles.

As I walked and the sunlight softened and lit up the sky, I thought about the rocks that I carried in my pack. I thought about how we all have burdens we carry, burdens that ache, slow us down, and tire us out. The burdens we burn to set down. But, when we allow ourselves to even acknowledge there are rocks to leave behind, it's not so easy to know when. Or where.

We'd brought some rocks for this very purpose from Brighton Beach. Before we left, Haley and I had walked along the pebbly beach of Brighton and picked up special-seeming stones and pocketed them. I don't believe I assigned a purpose or burden to my stones just then. I only carried them, trusting that when their purpose was made clear, I would understand the ritual and intent behind the stones and create a pile of my own to leave on the trail when the time came.

On this quiet morning, I still carried mine. But somewhere along the trail, underneath the golden sunflowers and sunrise, Haley left a few stones for Lenny. Later, when she confided what her solo walk had compelled her to do for my friend, I found that gesture hard to take. Only knowing of Lenny outside of friendship, acceptance came much quicker for her. But I just wasn't ready to leave anything or say anything for him just yet.

Lenny had died days before our departure. He and I had planned to indulge in our own separate travel adventures before reuniting in North America to begin the next exhilarating stage of our lives. Him pursuing a new career that his study of quantum physics had prepared him for, I in pursuit of something I hadn't yet defined. He would hike and explore the Atlas Mountains; I would walk the Camino—our last adventures this side of the globe. Our plan had been to meet in Toronto, celebrate our 30th birthdays in tandem in early September, then off we'd go, charging through whatever door life was holding open for us next.

On that sunflower morning, I still hadn't understood exactly what had befallen him and caused his untimely death. It had been weeks since we had news. For all I knew, his body was still in Morocco.

When you travel, time shifts and shapes around you. Four days living a professional life in the UK seemed mechanical and paced in familiar, comfortably timed ways. The days pass with a quick regularity. Here, four days into the Camino had seemed like weeks, but after all of the thinking, reflecting, walking, limping, and sharing with strangers, I was nowhere near ready to leave any of my rocks behind. I kept them all, weighted snuggly in my pack on my back. Up until that point, throwing rocks into the sea was the closest I had come to attaching memory to a stone and then releasing that stone.

The night before, sitting on my own by the vending machine, part of my late night journaling resulted in flipping back a few pages and rediscovering a few lines I had written just a week or so before. I don't have a memory of ever doing this, but it seems that sometime after learning what had happened to Lenny and yet before I had begun walking the Camino, I had taken myself to the sea. Grieving and no doubt angry, I had hurled those soft, rounded Brighton rocks as fiercely as I could into the choppy, cold sea. This—the symbolic stuff—I understand can sometimes help cement an acceptance of something we struggle to fully acknowledge. The throwing of rocks into the sea served as a physical act of refusing a truth I couldn't bear, a truth that seemed too unreal to accept. Symbolically placing my rocks down would have been a far more peaceful response, rather than hurling them away, or stubbornly carrying them with me, day after day. But acceptance or acknowledgement was as far from me then as was Santiago.

What am I doing? I remember thinking as I walked on my own, looking at the stone piles I passed and feeling the weight of the stones in my pack as it dug into my back. *Leaving piles of stones on dirt I won't ever revisit? Throwing rocks into a sea I won't swim in again—for Lenny? Is my friend really dead?*

No. Forget about the rocks.

I walked on my own all that morning, turning every rocky bend and summiting the sloping Spanish hills. At the top of the highest hill on that expanse of trail posed a surprising piece of art. Metal artworks, to be clear. The piece was crafted from flat iron and shaped into the life-size silhouettes of trekking pilgrims. Each pilgrim flat, dark, iron, and shadowed no matter where the sun hit, appeared ageless, nation-less, and without identity apart from what they were doing. They were walking the Camino. One led a donkey. They were all travelling along, west, toward Santiago. Toward Compostela.

In the morning light, I noticed a couple of pairs of actual leather hiking boots contrasting with the flat metal of the forever pilgrims' feet. There, the boots rested, worn and forgotten on the dirt. Why? Of all I had seen so far on my trek, this was the strangest. I was no longer wearing mine, but I had strapped them to the side of my bag until my feet could heal. Why would anyone abandon their boots? I looked around for the owners, should they have taken some temporary relief for their feet and enjoyed the panoramic view of the hilltop. But no. I was alone out there. So I just carried on.

Of the nearly 800 km I planned to walk of the Camino from St. Jean Pied-de-Port in France to the Compostela, I was only about 100 or so kilometres into my trek. It wouldn't be until around 700 km of the trail, or about 63.5 km short of Santiago, that I would find myself without question as to why anyone would abandon their boots on the Camino.

A few hours later, past the metal statues honouring pilgrims, and just as shops were beginning to open their doors, the path led me to the first coffee shop with a welcome sign. I marched right in. Sitting at the bar, enjoying a couple of flat whites, were Casey and Johan, the Aussie and South African "English boys" from the evening before. They were both surprised to see me. I guess they'd written us off after seeing the condition of our semi-mutilated feet, but here I was, and Haley was not far behind me. More coffees and muffins were ordered, and I sat down.

That day of walking from Albergue Roncal in Cizur Menor to Cirauqui was a scorching one, and the latter half of the walk proved to be an excruciatingly tough climb.

Just a few kilometres before our destination, Haley and I found ourselves arriving in a lovely village by the name of Puente de la Reina. We bumped into the Irish couple who'd also been at dinner the night before. Looking down at my exposed, flip-flopped feet and bandages, they questioned my toe ring. Of all the suffering indulged by my feet, how had the toe ring not given me a blister? I don't know, and truth be told, I hadn't even thought about it.

Wandering into the welcome vibe of the village, we recognised a friend from a previous day, poor Alex the Italian. Last I had seen him, he had been bursting with exuberant emotion, spouting hilarious Shakespearian one-liners, boasting both a comical gleam in his eye and a liveliness of spirit in his step. But now? Now, he was leaning against a low rising wall of the city, a frown on his face, and completely spent of any energy or enthusiasm. Or comedy. His right knee was caving in on him, and I remember him acknowledging to me that he would be heading back to his responsibilities as a waiter very soon. His knee injury would stop him from walking too much further. Poor Alex the Italian. I waved a tired hello and opened a friendly, minimal chat with him, but that was the last I ever saw of Alex the Italian.

There was no sign of Eugene, the Russian soldier, or any other familiar faces I had connected with since we'd begun just a few days back. We pressed on through another field of sunflowers, this one boasting pumpkin-sized blossoms and bright yellow petals that towered and flagged way over my head. We tripped over an old, stony Roman road, crossed a lovely, scenic bridge, and clambered up a steep, dusty road, sweating and thirsty and dirty and tired.

After a 26.5-kilometre day, one that had begun in a cool dark leaving behind snoozing turtles to walk in the company of sunrise-drenched sunflowers, we came to arrive at our next albergue at the top of a dusty hill peppered with Olive trees in a village called Cirauqui.

Cirauqui

CIRAUQUI EASILY BECAME THE most memorable of albergues. Cloaked in the scent of sweet, fig-infused rain lightly blanketing the sun-kissed dust of the centuries-old village roads, the stonewashed churches and taverns, the slow-paced streets—all of this cosied into the folds of the gentle Spanish hillside. Cirauqui was quiet, an embracing tuck of earth that warmly welcomed weary pilgrims from their walk and into the home-like feel of peace and, even during a late afternoon storm, offered us a deep, reassuring calm.

After claiming my bed and clean sheets for the evening and cooling off with a shower, I left the albergue and wandered on my own through the quaint hilltop village. The lazy afternoon was perfect; it was hot but tempered with a slight breeze rising. I felt I could be easily lulled into a deep afternoon doze by distant thunder.

Meandering through a stone maze of narrow roads buffered with sandstone homes and shops, I could hear church bells clanging a melodic and haunting tune. The dusty country roads were vacant, with every shop seemingly closed in the lateness of the afternoon.

The village was dotted with charming tree-lined squares where locals could relax. The elderly would have a coffee with a neighbour or enjoy the tranquillity of the day while local children played their games into the early evening. The village square just outside the albergue was dominated by an old church whose bells rang every 15 minutes all through the day. And, irritatingly, all through the night as I would come to discover hours later from my bunk.

After sitting for some time in the square and sinking into the peace of the place, I decided to continue my wander uphill on a dirt road until I found myself at the trail's end. The road became less of a road and more of a patch of earth that blended drying grass and stamped dirt until it decidedly ended, revealing a vast, panoramic view of the greens and browns and copper of the rolling Spanish hills below and away. A stone table had been erected under an inviting, leafy fig tree where it sat for who knows how many years. I couldn't resist.

The light wind was warm, and no one was about. Encroaching over the horizon and distant hilltops threatened the dark rumblings of a slowly approaching storm. Stretching out on the stone table, I allowed my gaze to soften over the valley below me and listened to the sounds of birds, trees, and thunder. I relaxed into a nap in the comforting wind. I'm not sure how long I slept the hours away there, but so good was the feeling of solitude and beauty, any number of hours spent there could never be too much.

At one point, I sleepily noticed a very old, wrinkled man in weathered overalls. He walked slowly and approached, carrying a bucket of wilted greens to scatter on the ground perhaps for some kind of animal. Step by aged step, he returned down the path, smiling kindly at me as he left. A cat leapt among the shrubs, exploring on her own. The black thunderheads began to flash and rumble as they picked up speed and charged and rolled towards the village.

Not too long after the slow-moving old man had departed came the arrival of three Spanish men: Ramon, Emillo, and his deaf brother whose name I can't remember but who boasted the sweetest smile of the three. I sat up from my stone-table bed and greeted them with a sleepy, friendly smile. We had what was to become a typical conversation during my time in Spain—that of my child-level Spanish and their broken English. I learned how to say lightning (relampago), thunder (trueno), storm (tormenta), fig (higo), fig bread (pan de higo).

The old man returned just then, but this time instead of some feed for free-range farm animals, he returned with some walnuts in a plastic bag and a hammer for the cracking. Walnuts, local Spanish farmers, a shady fig tree, and an approaching storm; it was a storybook setting for our friendly chatter, overlooking acres of countryside, deep valleys with the fresh rain scenting the air. For a few moments there, a peace descended soothingly over me—I was no longer in my thoughts and carrying fears or sorrow, no longer in pain or tired from the trek. I was travelling, connecting with friendly strangers in the most scenic of spaces, and I felt infinitely at peace.

And then, it hit. The storm was rapidly upon us. Even though we could sense it encroaching, the farmers nor I seemed to have fretted the impending weather until the moment the sky cracked open. Down came the rain, its accompanying lightning forking and thunder roaring. The wind and the water were so deliciously strong and so very fragrant as they pelted us from our calm and onto our feet in seconds.

As much as I'd treasured my afternoon moments, I couldn't remain reclined on my stone table under the fig tree in the claws of the storm. Smiling an adios to the farmers, I began my descent back into the village. The dusty, sloped roads had become slick, muddying streams. My quick movements to take cover couldn't be that quick at all, and the refreshing shower quickly soaked me through. For shelter, I popped into a small tavern—the first welcoming, open doorway on the main road that I came across. On the inside, I found a few locals, and of course, my companions from the Camino: Casey, Johan, and a pilgrim named Carl, all enjoying a beer and watching a bullfight on TV. I ordered a red wine and sat down to join them.

The day was not over just yet, though. After the bullfight, the four of us returned to the Albergue for the pilgrim dinner included with our stay—pasta pitted with meatballs in a red tomato sauce, more wine, and fresh homemade rolls served up with butter in the cellar of our albergue. In the spirit of the evening, I enjoyed a little too much wine. Casey entertained us with tales from Australia, and the stories that tumbled over our plates filled the evening with more hilarity. We told jokes that earned me a few shushes by the "mama-owner," and Haley and Johan and I polished off the bottle of locally grown wine.

At some point, the dinner conversation tainted with bawdy jokes gradually became more serious talks about religion. We were four nationalities (UK, USA, Australia, South Africa), four continents even, and all possessed a different view.

Haley didn't believe in a God but that every person is blessed with a soul. Johan was very Christian and believed that Jesus lives and all else the Bible told him to. Casey believed in none of it. I was a blend of all of the above.

It wasn't my first conversation about religion where each person at the table suggested a different belief than another sitting on the other side. I suppose that religion was also a very normal and prominent conversation for pilgrims on the Pilgrimage to turn to time and time again. But the lightness and calm I had indulged in all afternoon had been a welcome distraction, followed by a jubilant dinner. This turn of our chat into religion, life, death, and life after death gave way to the aching in my heart.

The sadness I had harboured the entirety of my Pilgrimage crept back heavily, made buoyant by the wine, and the dinner time talk of the afterlife wound me round to Lenny. Still uncertain of what had gone wrong for him and struggling to accept or understand, I ended the night in tears.

22 KM
Cirauqui to Villamayor de Monjardín

THE NEXT MORNING TAPPED me awake from a sleep that had been interrupted throughout the night with clanging church bells. The sunlight greeted me with a slight hangover.

It was not the cheeriest of moods with which we packed up, but our foursome—Haley, Johan, Casey, and myself—banded together and began the day's trek towards the next albergue.

We walked along an old Roman road as the day grew brighter and the heat grew stronger. Flies landed on every part of us as we walked. My blistered and toughening feet were holding up okay in my three-day-old flip flops, and as long as I changed the bandages once or twice a day, they wouldn't rub too much into my raw skin.

By now, walking the Camino had become quite routine despite that every day was filled with unexpected sights and encounters with pilgrims who shared their histories, stories, and dreams for where their Pilgrimage would lead them. That part was always intriguing, but it, too, was a regular part of our days. The scenery changed with every kilometre—new albergues welcoming us with warmth and refuge had become a happy expectation after a hard day's walk. We would awake sometime between 5:30 and 6:30 a.m., pack up our bags, bandage our feet, walk about 5 km or so, stop at a café. We'd continue walking the remainder of the morning and into the afternoon toward the next destination. Arrive, launder clothes—usually in a sink outdoors—chill, nap, yoga, or read. We'd fill our bellies at family-style dinners, refresh with cold drinks, head to bed and be asleep by 10 p.m. in shared rooms with strangers-turned-friends. Usually.

It was along this stretch from Cirauqui to Villamayor de Monjardín where we met another Italian pilgrim travelling with his girlfriend. They were a somewhat sombre pair and seemed more tired and weary than other travellers we'd encountered. They were travelling with a tent for camping alongside the road in one of the farmers' fields we often passed, in case they did not arrive in time to secure a bed at any of the albergues.

His reasons for travelling are why I remember him, even though we didn't necessarily travel together for too long, and his name escapes me. Although we each carried our own maps of the Camino (my story takes place long before GPS or iPhones were around), the Italian was travelling with a self-made guide.

He had drawn his map himself, treated with every artistic detail, and complete with gradients, iconic details surrounding local villages and sites, and basic needs for hygienic survival, such as bathrooms, beds, and water fountains. On the cover of his map, he had pasted a photo of his friend's father, recently deceased. The deceased father was the reason this Italian had ventured out. He was walking the Camino for him.

Everyone we met along the way had their own private reasons for walking the Camino. I think he was the first person I came across who shared that they, like me, were walking away a loss—walking through grief, walking because someone once close was now gone and the Pilgrimage had become a walk in memoriam; it had become an homage rather than a journey.

And so we journeyed. We walked, we pilgrims, and we sunk into our thoughts as we took in the sights.

The sights this day included walking the Camino amongst more sheep than I've ever had the pleasure of passing through a pasture with. The field alongside the Camino was populated with hundreds of them. They were being herded across long, sloping grass plain and onto our path, directly in front of us. To the left of our path, where the sheep had come from, lay an outstretched field. To the right of our path, the hedges grew high, somewhat hiding access to the grass likely greener on the other side. The herds of sheep gathered and grouped toward the hedge, and then jumped, noisy and baah-ing four or five sheep at a time, through the high brush wherever they saw a small break and finally carried noisily onward toward greener pastures.

While this was not something one sees every day, even for the Camino, it wasn't just the swarms of stomping and baah-ing sheep we found ourselves amongst that entertained us as they crossed our road. In the distance, beyond the conversational baahs of the flock as they moved in unison in front of us, bellowed a high-pitched and rapid baah-ing that was far, far from the other side of the field behind us where the sheep had first emerged from. It seemed some poor, young sheep must not have been paying close attention to the movements of his herd and had frantically realised he had been left behind.

We watched with amusement as the poor little thing, all on its own, ran from across the farthest end of the field until he reached the fence. His panicked cries called out to his herd as he raced back and forth along the fenced-in pen until he finally figured his way through an opening the others had gone through before. Then, with all his woolly might, he pounded his hooves all alone through the stretch of pasture, heading straight for us and baah-ing all the way, running intently to catch up with the rest of his flock. By the time he reached the path where we were standing and watching, the rest of the flock had all bounded through the high brush. The little lost lamb crossed the road, distraught to find himself very alone so near strange humans. He was clearly confused as to where the opening could be found in the brush.

As we continued to walk along the path towards him, he only panicked further until after what must have seemed like a very long time for him, he found an opening in the brush and quickly, clumsily, hurtled himself into the pastures on the other side, toward the safety of his flock.

I thought then of the solitude the Camino offered us, alongside the closeness with strangers, but also, how desperate we all can be when we realise just how far away we are, how lost we can feel, and in a panic, hurtle ourselves towards home.

~

APART FROM THE SIGHTS we'd take in, or the stories each pilgrim would share, sometimes conversations with others were filled with stories about the Camino itself, and the stories told of other pilgrims from days gone by.

Sometime during this day's walk, I found myself engaged in conversation with Johan. This South African man was tall, his eyes deep and dark, his hair short but thick. He carried a quiet, intelligent, and yet warm demeanour about him. At the end of his Pilgrimage, he'd told us, he was headed to a friend's wedding, and so amongst the 17 kg of weight on his back, with day-to-day needs, clothes, and survival gear, was also packed a tuxedo.

Before he had departed on the Pilgrimage, Johan had brushed up his knowledge of the Camino folklore and read the stories, legends, and history that enveloped "The Way." He knew a bit about St. James and his role in the wars with the Moors. St. James was a religious and national icon, and Johan knew the reasons why a scallop shell was used as a symbol of the Camino that all the pilgrims in centuries past would have carried. He educated me on what "Compostela" really meant. In truth, I should have studied this a bit more myself. However, my past travels for my own purpose had always been, and would yet prove to be, to *just go—see what happens*. I have a deep love for the language, culture, and local histories of every place I travel to, but no book or article or podcast could ever feel as authentic or real as an unplanned conversation with those I meet on the road. As it turns out, I never fail to fall into the company of those whose historical and cultural knowledge of the places I go enhance my entire experience.

And so, I nodded to Johan to carry on.

The destination we were all walking towards was known in full as the Santiago de Compostela, or "St. James of the Field of Stars." The legend of the Compostela goes that the pilgrims who walked towards Santiago in search of healing, blessings, and good fortune were so great in number that, as they walked the Camino, the dust from their feet flew up high into the night sky and became embedded in the atmosphere as stars twinkling their light back down to the Earth. These specific stars made up the Milky Way, which was another map the pilgrims of long ago knew to follow, and which showed them the way to go. They would look up at the sky and follow the stars.

It was a lovely, romantic, and timeless image. I don't know that any dust from my bloodied feet would have made it that far into the heavens, but it was an uplifting thing to believe that we were all a part of something so human, so celestial, and so ageless.

Our destination that day was Villamayor de Monjardín. It was along this route that we passed the famed fountains of wine: the Fuente del Vino. The Fuente del Vino was, in truth, a monastery run by monks, and homemade, monk-made wine from local vineyards, free for the thirsty, would flow out of a fountain in the courtyard outside of the main entrance. It was not an eternal flow, however, and only early bird pilgrims who arrived first were welcome to fill up their wine cups or bottles until that days' offering had run dry.

Along the entire Camino, free-flowing water fountains had been set up wherein pilgrims could refill their water bottles. Fresh, pure, Spanish mountain water. Spanish wine would have been just as welcome. However, even with a 6:30 a.m. rise and what I thought was a pretty good hustle, we still arrived at the fountains far too late, and there was no wine left for us parched pilgrims. We carried on.

A little further along the way—and this might have occurred the day before; in fact, I think it did—we had rounded a corner, obedi-ently following the painted yellow arrows on tree trunks or light posts indicating which turn in the path to follow along the entire route of the Camino. We passed a fellow pilgrim sitting on the ground to the side of the road. He had long legs and a dishevelled, hairy beard. I remember his aviators were perched on his nose, and headphones sat atop long, tousled hair. But what we *all* remembered from this easy-going pilgrim was the sandwich he was eating, held firmly between both of his hands.

For the past six days, we'd pretty much only dined on pasta, ham and bread rolls, and crisp apples as our daily lunch and energy source. Those were the items of food readily available to buy at markets and shops along the way. But this guy was enjoying a sandwich—and a pretty good-sized sandwich at that. It was wrapped in shiny, silver foil, with the freshest red tomato and greenest leafy lettuce ruffling out the sides of soft, white French bread. He waved a friendly hello as we passed him and continued on.

Whatever conversation we had been carrying halted. Instead, we talked about that sandwich for at least the next kilometre. *Where did he get such a sandwich? How did he get it to look so homemade? Did he make it himself?* We didn't see him for some time, but his long legs and energy from his sandwich must have enabled him to pick up speed and catch up to us. It was at one of the many frequent water spots, well past the Fuente del Vino, where we recognised his beard, aviators, and friendly smile.

His name was Cam, and he was from Melbourne. Another Australian. He had been making a living working with teenagers at a youth centre in Ireland, but was a writer by trade. Fresh from Dublin, en route to San Francisco, he was game to travel with us along the Camino for a bit. He was lively, clever, and also kind, and the conversation easily picked up a friendly tempo. I don't think I ever found out where he got his sandwich.

Now a company of five, we carried on to Villamayor de Monjardín.

Villamayor de Monjardín rests atop a very steep hill, but rewards pilgrims with another panoramic view of the plains below. It seems this stretch of the Camino led us from one hilltop albergue, down the valley for the walk, and up another hilltop to the next albergue. We booked out our beds inside the small, family-sized albergue and made ourselves at home. Doctoring my foot that day included cleaning, medicating, and slicing off a respectable chunk of dead skin with my pocket knife. I engaged in this grisly self-operation while having the first of many conversations with Cam. Cam was not phased or horrified as we casually got to know each other, and I sliced away at my beaten feet. My flip-flops were holding out okay.

The afternoon lent itself to good afternoon writing. Often, after a long day of walking in the heat, hydrating where we could and taking journeys in our minds while listening to the stories of other pilgrims or taking in the passing scenery of sheep, shops, or fountains run dry, our resting spot would become a scene for the surreal. To be fair, many moments along the Camino felt surreal, but this particular one found me relaxing on a wooden rocking chair, half dozing under the open patio of the albergue in the Spanish heat, overlooking the hazy browns of the hillside. Below me, in a somewhat scant village dotted with homes and markets, was another old church, this one with bells that rang mutedly.

In a window behind me, I could hear people I had not yet met nor seen—a group of pilgrims perhaps. While the words were difficult to discern, the tunes were well-known to me. They were singing old hymns—songs I was familiar with from attending church in my youth. I couldn't see who they were, but it sounded like a girl playing a guitar and singing, and a guy who was singing along but seemed a little uncertain about the lyrics. The song was sung half in English, half in Spanish, and their joyful melody was the only noise around.

The albergue in Villamayor de Monjardín turned out to be a Dutch-run hostel populated with Protestants. It was the not-so-perfect setting for the bawdy jokes and indulgence of wine that seemed to be the emerging theme of this leg of the Camino. With two Aussies, a South African, and Haley and I enjoying every minute of their banter, our band of pilgrims quickly shifted into a band of merry-making revellers. We sang our own noisy hymns that night, words out of sync and out of tune, but just as joyful as the Protestants.

30 KM
Villamayor de Monjardín to Viana

IT WAS ONLY DAY seven, but we'd travelled about 150 km walking the Camino since we'd left St. Jean Pied-de-Port.

The five of us (myself, Haley, Cam, Casey and Johan), had begun this seventh day with an especially early rise at 5:15 a.m. to walk a long, hot 31 km all the way down the hill from Villamayor de Monjardín, through a valley, and up another hill to the town of Viana. This would turn out to be another thriving rural city but with a bustle that reminded me of Pamplona, where we'd slept several days back.

We started when the stars were still dusting the sky, with not a single trace of the dawn. I'm not sure how we managed to follow the dirt trail before us in the dark. Walking single file, quiet and sleepy, we followed the bobbing flashlights of others just in front. The only noise rose from our boots on gravel and the clang of water bottles swinging from metal backpack straps. The descent on the path was not smooth, and I kept my focus on avoiding twisting my ankles or stumbling and mangling myself on the encroaching thorny bushes. My feet were throbbing, and even though my flip flops kept their form and grip, I aimed to keep my feet in as healthy a condition as possible. I still had a long way to go.

While dark and precarious, it was still an excellent morning walk, and we managed a whopping, fast-paced 12 km in only two hours as the night eased into dawn. By the time we reached the next village along the road, I was starving and very ready for my first café con leche.

But this was not to be. We had arrived too early, and not a single place was open. Only the stunning sun, rising between the towers of a quiet church steeple, received us with any warmth. As we passed on the road below, the only other forms of life I noticed were two large dogs perched stolidly atop their doghouses in the yard alongside the road. They seemed like furry sentinels, watching us silently as we trekked by.

Haley needed to stop for a few minutes to drain and re-bandage her pained feet, but after that, we continued along our way as the day began to heat up with the steadily rising sun.

As had become typical, each of us pilgrims would fall in stride with others who walked at a similar pace. Sometimes we walked with one companion or would branch off with another, walking just ahead of the others, or sometimes just behind. Sometimes we walked alone.

On this stretch of the trail, past sunrise but before breakfast, I found myself walking with Casey. I remember this part of the Camino being especially dry and rocky with very few trees and only flat, empty, yellowing land stretching out before us. Casey had the most competitive nature of the five of us, and during one of our chats, he asked me how long I could continue walking forward while keeping my eyes tightly shut. I took up the challenge.

I can't remember how many paces he walked, but I remember walking and walking and walking, feeling the gravelly path under my blistered feet, step by step. I did not even see the darkness of my closed eyes because, behind my eyelids, I still imagined the road I had just shut my eyes to stretching straight ahead. I simply carried on, following the road that I could now see only in my mind—step by step. In fact, I only reopened my eyes, not because I doubted my actions forward or grew nervous, but because Casey had started speaking to me again, having quit several paces back to open his eyes and be sure of his direction. He was certainly surprised I had walked so far ahead without being able to see the path.

This I found to be ridiculous. I had closed my eyes knowing the path ahead was straight and narrow. There were no trees, boulders, ditches, or other pilgrims coming toward me to be wary of, and I guessed I would have an easy 10 minutes of walking straight ahead with my eyes closed, as long as I didn't start slanting my stride sideways and off the trail. And even then, had I lost sense of direction and leaned to the right or left, I would just have wandered slightly off the path.

I should have kept walking. I should have waited to open my eyes when I felt fear or had fallen, just to see how much longer I could trust myself. I should have kept going until I needed help rather than stop my own progress to look back on the progress of others who questioned how I could possibly do it. I wonder how far I would have gone.

A little bit later, the five of us came across another pair of travellers. They were two English lads, brothers from the UK named Liam and Neil. Their addition meant we finally were travelling with actual "English boys" in our company. One had a sore-looking and tenderised black eye, and the other had a torn and scabbing neck where he had been brutally scratched in a recent attack. Turns out the two had got drunk on too much rum and had one hell of a fistfight the day before, which had been their first day of the Camino. They had started their walk mid-trail and were not the typical roughneck English blokes I had come across more than once in rowdy pubs when I lived in the UK. They were sophisticated graduates of University College London, both very clever and neither short on entertaining us with that witty and ironical banter that British humour never fails to deliver. They were in their mid-twenties and had never had a fistfight before in their lives.

These two spiced up our band with a welcome brew of British comedy. The crew Haley and I had collected was impressive. With its combination of rugged handsomeness and dirty jokes balanced with intelligent conversation, we'd done alright for ourselves on this leg. These two brothers added to our posse. It was like sitting front and centre to our own personal stand-up show as we continued along on our Pilgrimage, engaging in more sharing of stories and backgrounds, hopes and dreams, and hilarious misadventures.

We eventually arrived in Viana, set atop another very steep hill under the oppressing heat of the Spanish summer.

The main street that led into the city was lined with weary but jovial pilgrims perched along walls, sitting on curbsides and enjoying cold beers while getting off their tired feet. There were familiar faces amongst the pedestrianised street, albeit dirtier and far wearier than when I had first met them.

Eugene, the tall Russian soldier I hadn't seen since the first day en route to Roncesvalles was sitting along a wall, his tent and sleeping bag toppled over near his feet. He had met an eastern European girl, and they were now travelling together, day by day, making their way. I gave him a big hug when I saw him. The few American girls I had met from the first day were also there, and one of them called out to me from her third-story window of the albergue, waving and smiling under a blond ponytail. The albergue here housed hundreds.

Again, we were hot, sweaty, tired, relieved, and limping as we checked into the albergue and moved into our daily routine of leaving each other to tend to our own time, shower our filthy bodies, and bandage our aching feet.

A perk to arriving in a bigger city? Internet cafes were available and open. Refreshed, I left the albergue and walked down the main road toward the nearest cafe to check my email.

Five weeks had passed since Luis, a friend and neighbour, had arrived on my doorstep that night in Brighton with the news about Lenny. For all this time, we had been waiting, waiting, waiting. Lenny's friends, his partner, his parents—we had been waiting. We still didn't know how he had died in those mountains in Morocco, or when we would finally be able to mourn him, or hold a funeral, or bury him in peace. Now, in Viana, well into the high deserts of Spain, so far from any main roads or trains or planes and with only poor cell phone reception, I received word in my inbox from Lenny's father. Lenny had finally been returned to England. His funeral would be in four days.

The news I had been waiting for had arrived, but still, it carried a punch that took my breath. Lenny was finally home. And I was so far away.

Reacting with rapid panic, I immediately emailed each of my friends to send my regrets. I was in Spain. I was in the middle of the Camino, stopping for the night on a high hill down a dirt road. I would not be able to make it.

Wandering out from the café, dazed and forlorn and on my own with my journal, I sought a place where I could be alone. Perhaps I needed to cry, or let my thoughts drift to Lenny, or think about the funeral plans being made across the sea in England. I was upset, there's no doubt, but I just was unable to talk to Haley or anyone about it. I must have been a real burden to travel with, and in hindsight, thinking of all the baggage I carried, I should have walked the Pilgrimage alone in the end. But who can ever guess that such a thing would ever happen? Lenny was only 29, healthy, smart, athletic, and kind.

I found a quiet patch of green grass under the shade of a leafy tree behind an old church where I could lay down in peace and write. Pilgrims and locals were milling about, so there was a pleasant buzz, but not an invasive frenzy. I remember closing my eyes. I'm not sure how long I stayed there. Time had a way of playing tricks on us during those long days, and minute moments could easily stretch into hours.

Even though I had sat down in the shade with the intention to write in my journal, to process, to record, to reflect—to do all the things pilgrims do between walking and sleeping—I wrote very little that afternoon. I remember my reason why. I came across Johan.

We had all split to tend to ourselves after the tiring day that had begun at 5 in the morning. I had left the shade tree and decided to walk across the plaza and found Johan sitting on his own along a wall. For some reason, he looked absolutely gorgeous to me just then. Dark, thick, and wavy hair newly washed, his broad, tanned, muscular build peeking out beneath his clean, unbuttoned shirt. Johan smiled up at me and suggested we grab a beer. *Sure.* We found an outside table along the main strip and ordered a couple of cold pints. It wasn't long before Haley, Cam, Casey, Neil, and Liam, in staggered order, came traipsing along the front walk and found us. The beer we grabbed was soon followed by another cold beer and, true to form with this Camino crew, another beer after that.

The email from a couple of hours ago and all it meant hovered in my mind, but I shoved it to the back. I didn't want to think about it or let it in; I shoved it to the bottom, closed the door, and left it in the dark. Instead of journaling, or calling home, or sitting with sadness, I rejected it. I decided to use the night for distraction. I drank with my new friends and then drank more, chasing the joy at the bottom of each glass. I laughed at stupid jokes, told hilarious stories, and behaved as if nothing so tragic and unfair and horrific had ever happened. I laughed as if I had every reason to feel untarnished happiness in those moments and that no one so important to me was missing from the world that night.

As the conversation flowed, so did more beer, and so did more wine. So did more jokes, more stories, more laughs. On and on and on, we drank and laughed and drank and laughed. Later, I could never recall any of the jokes or exactly how much wine we indulged in. With our numbers of bawdy pilgrims growing, we knocked over plenty of pints and apologised for more than one broken wine glass.

This probably was not very pilgrim-like behaviour. Photos from this night trigger a few hilarious memories, but mostly we drank an exorbitant amount—enough to punish us all the next morning, as we attempted to resume our roles as pilgrims along the Camino.

At one point during the height of our revelry, my mother called. Because Viana has been built at a higher elevation, sometimes the cell signal was stronger than on other parts of the trail, and calls would come through to my phone. I left my rowdy friends at a table full of wine and fish and bread to go outside and found a place I could hide in the shadows of the medieval town. I wanted to be away from any strangers passing by, where I could talk to her in the quiet.

I leaned against the darkened side of a shop, and when I heard my mother's voice on the line, I just couldn't hold back any longer. I had no words for her, only cries. I cried every aching cry that had been quickly mopped up or shoved aside the last few days on the trail. Cries that were spinning and brewing and growing in strength until I finally undammed them from my heart. Now, given space and time, triggered by a crushing email and fueled by Spanish wine, I cried out for my dear, lost friend. Down into the phone, over the continents and across the ocean, I cried out every hot tear to my mother, listening on the other end. I told her about the news I had received that day, the funeral I wouldn't be able to attend, and every little thing I loved about Lenny and how sad and unfair and cruel it all was that he was really gone. Maddened with the loss and needing so much the comfort of my mom's arms, I sobbed and sobbed in the shadows. The sound of her voice was a comfort as my own voice raged and mourned, distorted with the broken cries of the drunken and grieved.

After, when the tears had subsided and the calm had blanketed my mind, I returned my body to the table with my still-partying fellow pilgrims. My face would have been reddened, but theirs was as well, as they had not slowed down from the wine or the banter one bit in the time I had left to take my mom's call. I shifted myself back into the welcome distraction, greeted again the present joy, the reckless abandon, the cheering our drinks, the laughing, and reassured my mind it was best to be present in the moment. I knocked back another glass of red.

The details that followed the rest of this night are admittedly foggy. I remember being embarrassingly late for our albergue's 10 o'clock curfew, and having to track down security to unlock the main entrance. I remember making out furiously with Johan in the dark outside the church walls after he had accompanied me back from whatever bar we had finished off the night in. I only just remember clumsily climbing the metal rungs to my bed, precariously balanced at the top of a three-tier bunk, and trying not to wake fellow bunkers or step on their sleeping faces as I finally took my exhausted, drunken, and wildly grieving self to bed.

That was the last night that our group of seven would travel together. I'm glad it was one of the most frivolous nights on the trail, blowing our savings on fish we don't remember savouring and wine we don't remember tasting.

Except for the two British brothers, the rest of us had treated the Pilgrimage with a sense of respect and sacredness since we had first met. We were to pay for our sins. The next morning, a very worn out Haley set her mind to take a bus north to Bilbao and take a break from walking for a few days. With an aching head now added to her aching knees, she needed a rest. I did, too, in all honesty, but I couldn't bear to leave the trail just yet. Lenny had helped me map out my trek on the Camino, with the intention of celebrating with me when I finished the walk. With his funeral only three days from now, the Camino seemed more important to continue doing than anything else.

So, with a sore head I deserved, new bandages on my blistered feet, and a fresh hickey on my neck, I headed west out of the city into the pink dawn with Casey, Johan, and Cam.

20.6 KM
Viana to Logroño to Navarrete

-11.9 KM
Navarrete to Logroño

127 KM
Logroño to Bilbao

ON A BENCH JUST outside Logroño station, waiting for the next bus north, I sat alone trying to script into my dirt-stained journal the events of that day as best I could. I had some time before departing to Bilbao to find Haley and leave the Camino for a while.

I should probably say here that there are many things about the Pilgrimage I wish I would have done differently.

I wish I had done it solo, without a walking partner, and left finding any companions to serendipitous encounters on the trail. The Pilgrimage became one of self-reflection, private growth, and personal mourning that a companion seeking lighthearted adventure just couldn't—or shouldn't have to—connect with. We all walk for different reasons.

I wish I had prepared my feet better and invested in higher quality bandaids.

I wish I wouldn't have taken the bus from Logroño just yet. But everything happens for a reason.

I had walked over 20 km that day, down from the hilltop of Viana and into the valley of Navarrete. Anyone paying close attention to the dotted stops along the Camino map would notice that Navarrete is about 13 km *past* Logroño. Haley had left by bus that morning from Viana, and I had carried on with Cam, Johan, and Casey, while the English boys slept off their hangover. As we departed, the stars had still been glittering the sky, with a creamy pink dusting in the dark distance. The earthy smell filled my nose while my head throbbed with the worst hangover I had experienced yet while on the Camino. But I felt compelled to go on more urgently than ever before and to stay on the path. I knew it had everything to do with my sadness over Lenny. So, head aching, feet wrapped and oozing, back aching, and heart crushed, I trailed along behind the boys into another glorious crystal dawn of a morning.

We were a ragged and frayed crew, but onward we went for about 9 km until we arrived in Logrono for pastries and coffee and to replenish our stash of band-aids.

About a kilometre before the coffee stop, Cam and I had fallen behind the other two. I remember crossing a bridge over the clearest water—a small lake, or perhaps a pond—and as I passed over the rounded, upturned middle of the wooden bridge, the sun seemed to suddenly burst over a hilltop opposite the clear, still body of water. So brightly and joyously, it doubled itself on the horizon. Mirrored in the stillness of the water just below, we were gifted a double, spectacular sunrise. I almost didn't notice my foot blisters pop. Almost.

And pop they did. There was a quick sting, and then an oozy wet spread underneath my foot. And then more sting. The grippy flip flop shoes and protective mummifying of my feet with bandages that had served since Pamplona had expired. Blisters had been doubling at what seemed like an alarmingly inhuman rate. Cam provided a bit of encouragement, but by the time I arrived for coffee, I was limping. A muffin and a latte later, refuelled and rebandaged, the four of us again set off. Cam made it, oh, I don't know, not too far. A kilometre more, maybe? I think we were still in Logroño. He was a trooper, ploughing on despite his equally massive hangover, but he suffered a busted knee that proved to be his downfall. His knee pain had become too agonising for him to walk. He called it quits after another hour and decided to seek out the Logroño albergue for the night.

And then there were three.

Johan, Casey, and I continued to walk. Past pristine green lakes, down more dirt roads, past vineyards scented with Rioja. We came across a friendly, elderly man wearing a grey, floppy cloth hat who had set up his own hospitality stand for pilgrims. He was giving away apples picked fresh from his tree. Simple, yes. But we'd grown accustomed to a diet of fish, pasta, bread, and wine, and so fresh fruit was so very welcome—especially from a kind and sun-wrinkled smile. His face was weathered and bearded, flowing long and grey past his chin. He personally handed red apples to each of us pilgrims as we passed, us smiling and grateful, he smiling back with kind eyes. Later, while chatting to other pilgrims, I was told that he sets up his apple cart every single day, wishing a "Buen Camino" to travel-weary pilgrims. God bless him.

Walking onward, we followed the yellow arrows of the Camino, painted on the ground or a tree or a pole, indicating the turn we should take next. Through fields, up hills, down hills, past chain-link fences with broken bits of stick criss-crossed into them to resemble a cross.

One section of this fence posted hundreds of crisscrossed sticks that shaped into hundreds of crosses that were crudely fashioned and endearingly simple. Piles of small stones and rocks demarcated the trail every now and then where pilgrims had laid their burdens. Pilgrims with walking staffs and the Camino scallop shells tied to their heavy packs leaving behind blessings, burdens, and reminders of why we were all walking.

In the early afternoon, Johan, Casey and I arrived in Navarrete. The albergue had not yet opened, so travellers had lined up outside, leaning on their dirty bags to wait for their showers and food. I was oozing and limping and bleeding through my bandages again, so I set off for the green "plus" sign that by now I realised represented both a Spanish pharmacy and ultimate relief and healing for me. This time, when I peeled back the dirty bandages, what I saw was nothing less than *ick*.

The tiny spaces between each of my already squat toes were filled with sacks of stinging puss, swollen, burning, and in some cases, broken and split. The sides of my heels had long ago rubbed raw and were now blistered with a second layer of blisters pushing through the top of the original blisters. It was as if my toes had broken out in a rash of blisters—blisters that were bursting.

With my bandages, ointment, and pocket knife, I set out determinedly to nurture my feet and continue walking. Casey and Johan saw the pitiful state of my feet and sat down to help me out.

For the first time on the Camino, the cutting and cleaning and wrapping were doing very little for my feet. After cleaning as much as I could, I still looked at my feet with despair. All I wanted to do, more than ever now, was just keep going. Keep walking. Continue on the Camino. But my feet were deteriorating by the hour. Johan looked at my feet with a sympathetic expression and told me I needed to rest them. They just weren't going to get any better. Casey just looked down at me, hands on his hips, and seeming a bit sorry for me, finally said, "Take care, Christy."

And that was the last I saw of them. I think they carried on to Ventosa for the night, another 4 km away. I had no choice but to trek backwards to Logroño, where the closest bus station was. A helpful concierge in a nearby hotel called me a taxi that would cost me €20, and I waited pitifully on the steps by myself. Exhausted, hungover, sad, alone, my feet leprous and diseased. In the cab, I looked out the window at the passing scenery I had just walked through that morning. I saw a stork flying low.

I wanted to cry. I had walked farther than I had originally planned to on this day, but somehow I still wanted to be on the trail. After so many days on the journey, it felt so wrong not to be moving forward and walking towards Santiago.

Each morning that I set out carried the air of something meditative and rejuvenating— a purpose rising each day with the need to continue walking across foreign land, following the yellow arrows forward, kilometre after kilometre. But now, my blisters had become so numb that I could no longer feel some of them. They were much worse than the shark bites I had tried to heal in Pamplona. Most of the new blisters hadn't yet popped, but I knew I would be in such pain when they did, and I didn't want to feel that again. I realised that it was time to take a rest in Bilbao and join Haley. Still, I felt like I had failed.

Over the next four or five hours, this failure would gather, double, and lay heavy on my mind and shoulders. All I had been through on the Camino ebbed and flowed in my mind. The past week I had travelled felt like months. From sitting on the hotel steps in Navarrete to sitting in the torn leather backseat of the cab, to waiting on the metal bus station bench, to sitting in the hot bus headed north, I let the events of the prior few days sink in.

As per usual when I travel, I had found myself alone in a foreign place with people I felt like I had known for years. They were funny and handsome and kind and intriguing, but it was as if I'd known them for ages, and the Camino was our home. It's so easy to miss someone you've only known for three days when the three days feel like time has turned in on itself and stretched out so far. Or when, in that time, you've shared so much of yourself and experienced such

a unique depth of friendship—even momentarily—and found camaraderie in strangers.

Since St. Jean Pied-de-Port, I had walked 180 km. I thought of
the hot, sweaty walks, the fellowship, the never-ending joke-telling
sessions, the epic views, the iron church bells, Liam and Neil's cease-
less banter. I thought about the brief romance with the burly-chested
and chisel-jawed South African, his deep blue eyes, and of Cam's
defeated knee. I thought about the scenic walks down endless roads
and alongside crystal clear lakes, dusty villages, and creaky bunk
beds in shared rooms. I wondered if I would ever see any of these
pilgrims again. I wondered where their lives would take them.

I don't remember how long I waited on that bench, and I don't
remember how long the bus journey was or what time I finally arrived
in Bilbao. I just know that I was devastated from needing to stop.
My heart ached from it.

Looking out the bus window as I travelled up the Northern
coast of Spain, the opposite direction of where my map or the yellow
arrows directed me to go, I remember seeing thick clusters of green
over the hillsides. I remember feeling sunken. The farther north
the bus took me, the worse I felt. I don't remember ever feeling this
dejected and crestfallen. Everything inside me insisted I should still
be on the trail, taking step after blistered step towards Santiago. In
my mind, if I couldn't be in England during these next few days for
Lenny, if I couldn't attend his funeral and honour my friend in that
way, then I would at least be on the Camino for him, walking the
same trail he had once walked, walking the same trail he had helped
me to route. I should be destined for Santiago, then Lyon, then
Toronto, where he was meant to have been. Instead, I was on a bus
going the wrong way because my feet had failed me.

When I arrived at the northern Spanish coastal city of Bilbao,
a more refreshed Haley greeted me at the station. She had found us a
Pension with a room at the top of five flights of stairs. There was no
elevator. It was a cruel, ironic joke to be played on our feet and aching
legs, but it would have to do.

Settling in, we then set to work ensuring our blisters were
cleaned, punctured, drained and iodised. Leaving the room, we hobbled
about the city, limping through squares and plazas, covering very little ground over the long hours of the afternoon. We decided to rent
bikes for the next day and cycle around. There was a food market we

could visit, or we could chill in the city for a few days before visiting all of the best beaches along the city coastline. I didn't know much about Bilbao, but the reset for my feet and distraction for my mind would be welcomed.

Then, come Thursday, in three days, our plan was to take a bus southwest, back to the Camino, with just over 100 km to Santiago, and finish the Pilgrimage. The plan was also to bandage the shit out of my feet and try to wear my hiking boots again from Sarria. These boots had been tied with the laces to the back of my bag, dangling for the last several days. I wanted to wear them once more.

In Bilbao, resting on the cheap mattress in our dingy hostel, I made another list of my achievements from August 1 to August 8:

190-ISH KM COVERED FROM ST. JEAN PIED-DE-PORT TO NAVARRETE

120 KM OF THAT IN FLIP-FLOPS AND MUMMIFIED FEET

1 CHAFED THIGH

2 RASHY, ECZEMA ARMPITS

8 BLISTERS ON 5 TOES

2 BLOODIED, BLISTERED HOLES IN HEELS

3 DAYS OF MENSTRUAL CRAMPS

2 DAYS OF HANGOVER

10 JAMÓN Y QUESO BAGUETTES

16 CAFÉ CON LECHES

1 KNIFE CUT

1 BROKEN NAIL

1 STUPID CUT FROM MY STUPID BROKEN FLASHLIGHT

2 BUG BITES, ONE ON EACH ELBOW

2 LEGS OF STEEL

14 PHARMACY STOPS. MAYBE MORE.

The Beach Fox

A FEW WEEKS EARLIER, before departing for the Camino, I went walking close to the dark sea-salt water, lapping onto the pebbly Brighton Beach. It was a chilly July evening. Often I took these walks alone, as a way I could find solace, gather my thoughts and centre whatever emotions had been roused of late.

The sun had long gone down, and every dreg of summer light had leaked from the sky. All but enough to turn the beachside benches into silhouettes and shadows.

I had meandered maybe a mile along the shoreline, headed west, when I spotted the fox.

It was dark, and I was surely in a shipwrecked state, but the fox was unmistakable. Too slinky to be a dog, with a head too boxy for him to be a cat. It was a fox. It moved quickly, bolting away from the shore, across my path, and off into the shadows beyond.

Brighton is a city in the south of England, boasting part beach, and part hilly green, and fairly close to the countryside. I had seen a fox once before in daylight to know they creep into town every so often, but still. A wild fox in town was a bizarre sight. A fox who had chosen to forage so close to the beach was unlikely.

But there he was, a sly fox, scooting away from the frigid shore. He was quick, but I hold a fleeting glimpse of him in my memory. Once in shadows, I imagined he would scamper across the rising pavement, behind shadowed alleys, and eventually return back towards the safer haven of the hillsides.

An hour before, I had a knock on my door. A tall friend stood on my porch, his Spanish face drawn long and sad behind his black-bearded cheeks. With stumbling words, he gave me the unthinkable news that lovely Lenny had died.

He'd lost his life hiking and camping atop the Atlas Mountains in Morocco. It was sudden, tragic, and the details were infuriatingly few.

Shaken, I had left the house and began walking alone along my familiar beach. It was all I could think of to do. To head towards the water. To start walking.

I remember a cold, sharp wind. Amidst the storm of tears and confusion, shock and grief, and sadness and anger whirling through my mind, I looked up and just ahead of me, I saw a small fox bound across the cold beach.

The shock of coming across this woodland creature on the seashore held my attention just for a snap.

And then he was gone, and I descended back down into the flood, thinking about my friend and how untrue it had to be.

That's all I wrote about in my journal that night. Two lines. My friend's too soon, and unexpected death, and the unexpected beach fox.

An entire year later, my mind returned to that night again. I had lived in Brighton for 7 years and had seen a fox only once before, and nowhere near a beach. What was the little guy doing there?

A few minutes of rummaging online lead me to a site explaining animal folklore and ancient Oriental myths. The discovery left me with warm chills.

There is a significance in sighting animals in unusual places, and fox sightings in particular. These creatures symbolise spirits of the dead and gone, and their appearance is an affectionate gesture towards the living.

A fox sighting is a soul in the afterlife, reaching out to other familiar souls still walking this life.

The fox appeared on my beach on the day I found out I had lost my dear friend. He darted out of the dark for a moment, and then too quickly, he was gone.

Bilbao

RETURNING FROM A SHOWER to my room the next morning, I was horrified to discover a large spider smashed into the white sheets where I had just been sleeping. Its appearance now could have been due to any of the following possibilities:

1. I had crawled into bed with a dead spider and had been too exhausted to take notice.
2. It had been hiding in the sheets, alive but then crushed by my sleeping body rolling over onto it sometime in the night. (It looked withered, and one of its legs was broken off next to it.)
3. The spider had spilt from my bag, dead already amongst my stuff, and its corpse just happened to shuffle out from my pack and into the bed sheets as I was digging around.

Dear Lord.

I have left out much of these insect incidents throughout the retelling of my journey, but bugs, spiders, worms, wasps, and all sorts of creepy crawlies were a daily part of our experience. The dead spider that I had likely slept with was the worst.

The exploration of Bilbao turned out to be a pretty lame attempt on our part. Literally. It took me 40 minutes to hobble on my wounded, swollen feet down the five flights of metal stairs to the entry of the Pension.

What I craved was cool, creamy Greek yoghurt and fresh, juicy fruit outside in the warm sun. However, after circling the area a few times, feeling pathetic and lost, I could find no such treat. I settled for something inside the same coffee joint Haley and I had found the night before. Morning cigarettes from other patrons made for a smoky flavoured breakfast, but at least the coffee was good. The croissant was good, too, even if it wasn't good for me.

My feet were hideous to look at. They were black, roughened, and aching. My mood was agreeable, I suppose, but I still felt cloaked in failure as I sat eating croissants in a cigarette-stained coffee house, watching a bustling city pass by outside, the Camino hours away.

I did manage to wander a little way to people watch and take in a few sites of the city. The sun felt warm on my shoulders, and so I sat down on a bench with the other cripples also resting and enjoying the sun. The other cripples, in this case, were no longer travellers on a Pilgrimage, but rather old, wrinkled, Spanish men, leaning on their canes, the youngest of whom was probably 80.

Later, I managed to stumble down to the riverside, taking in the sights over the water, the Nervión River flowing busily on its way to the Bay of Biscay. I hobbled quietly along. As I did, another aged Spanish man approached me from the opposite side. As he passed, he looked me in the eyes and in clear, slow English through a thick, Basque accent, kindly spoke to me. "My god. You. Are. Beautiful." His unexpected compliment lifted my spirits some, but I don't think he noticed my feet.

~

I DON'T PRETEND TO understand fate or how the Universe or higher powers band together to help us pilgrims on Earth when we are in strife. I don't understand how guidance works when we are lost or how miracles manifest. But I have learned that there is no such thing as a coincidence.

Leaving the Camino when I did, and as I did, had felt devastating to my spirits. I kept thinking of the faces that I would likely never see again. I wondered how they were doing and what events had occurred on their travels without me. On a whim, I limped to an Internet café and decided to send Cam a friendly hello. How was his knee? Did he rest, or had the English boys caught up with him and coerced him into more obscene shenanigans? He must have been at an Internet cafe at that exact time as well because, moments after I emailed him, still sitting at the computer, I received a reply. In his email, he entertained me with a story about how he'd caught up with Liam and Neil again in

Logroño, and again, drank too much wine. Between the booze and the bruises, he was going to have to call it quits on the Camino for good. He told me he was headed to Bilbao to catch a flight to Dublin to nurse his wounds.

I caught my breath. *There was an airport in Bilbao? There were easy flights to the UK?* I had been steeped in so much sorrow, pain, and failure that I hadn't even looked up. My mind had been clouded with my emotions rather than in a state of clear thinking. But with Cam's email on the screen in front of me, I didn't have to think for too long. I had believed that if I couldn't be in Canterbury to attend my friend's funeral, I would at least be able to honour him and continue the Pilgrimage in Spain. But I no longer was on the Pilgrimage. I had, without realising, been bussed to a city boasting an international airport. My timely hello to my bearded, sandwich-eating pilgrim friend had revealed to me another option. Within 10 minutes, I had booked a flight to London that left first thing the very next morning—a Sunday.

Are there angels looking after us? Does the Universe or a God or some form of higher power conspire in our favour? If I hadn't emailed Cam at all, or even just at that moment, I would never have known that I was 20 minutes from an airport with cheap flights direct to the UK. If I hadn't seen this lanky, bearded Melbournite devouring his tasty sandwich on such a hot day, I might not have befriended him in the same way. I might have spent the next six days lingering in this city, trying to heal, but feeling all the swampy sadness of loss, failure, exhaustion, and grief. I might not have thought to look up, discover I could fly from Bilbao and land in London in just over an hour, and arrive a day before Lenny's funeral.

I emailed a few friends in Brighton and Horsham to let them know I was going to be in London after all, but my choice had been made so quickly that I would arrive before emails were checked. Fortunately, the next morning as I sat in the terminal, my feet still bandaged, my bag still dirty, I was able to reach one of my dearest friends who I had taught school, enjoyed adventures, and read tarot cards late into many a night. Yes, she was home this weekend, and yes, she could pick me up. Yes, I could stay with her, and yes, she could loan me a dress to wear. We would also have a lovely, much-needed talk, watch a movie on her couch, and eat some dinner that wasn't pasta or fish. We would also buy better socks and new bandages for my feet.

I boarded the plane.

1,192 KM
Bilbao to Canterbury

THEY SAY THE CAMINO de Santiago can be split into three different trails: The Trail of Joy, the Trail of Sorrow, and the Trail of Glory.

The first leg of the trip is where not-yet-weary pilgrims set out, their spirits high, muscles strong, their feet clean and unwounded. Excitement is in the air as every step brings newness into the setting in the conversations with other pilgrims, in the freedom and fresh air. There is a camaraderie and vibrancy that each person experiences during the first part of their Pilgrimage. This is the Trail of Joy.

The second trail is the Trail of Sorrow. This is where the to-pography changes. The mountains and climbs up hilltop after hilltop take their toll on travellers. Blisters form upon blisters, and knees and backs ache. Muscles grow tired, sleep is not as sound, and pilgrims grow bored of the same carbohydrate-packed dinners. We miss home, comforts, and the companionship of those we know well. Here, the land flattens out for days, with no change in the scenery, and a less stimulating view. The heat is comfortless, our moods become crankier, maybe hot-headed. This portion of the trail is the hardest because not only are our bodies burdened but our minds are also exhausted. For many, the emotions swing from joy and jubilant energy to fatigue, loneliness, and hopelessness. On this stretch of the Camino, Santiago de Compostela is still so far away.

Early the next morning, I left the warm, comfortable home of my lovely friend and navigated the rail connections, boarding a train that would take me all the way to Canterbury. I had been off the actual trail of the Camino in Spain for maybe a few days now. But as for me and my journey, I was very much walking the Trail of Sorrow.

Even though it was the early days of August, summer in England still promised rain, and the rain poured down on my train the entire journey. I looked out the window, watched the quaint villages pass by, the signs for British franchises that line the High Streets, and watched as the manicured green hills folded away from the rails.

I sat alone in my booth, with my bag and my boots on the seat beside me, and cried. I wept for nearly the entire two-hour journey as the tracks led me to an unexpected and unwanted reunion with friends I had said farewell to just over a week ago. My time in Spain felt like months, and even though it had been so quick to journey back, the Camino felt another world away.

The sadness clung. It streaked down my cheeks, washed into my borrowed black dress, and flowed over my hands as they wrung soggy tissues, my face as wet as the rain outside. There was no stopping my tears or hiding them from other passengers. I surrendered to them and let them roll and fall as I grieved for my friend while the world whirred by outside.

In Canterbury, the church was filled with almost everyone who had been both Len's and my friend. Everyone except for our good friend Miles, who was on his honeymoon in Rome, and Luis, who I think had travelled to Madrid. Lucy had flown in from Mexico. I still carried my pack, my hiking boots dangling by their laces from the back.

We were all just standing around in small circles of awkward mumbling. We were in our twenties and thirties, dressed for what should have been a summer wedding instead of a funeral. The cold wind blew through the grey, rainy churchyard. Sadness weighed heavily in the air. Our faces were gloomy and without smiles as we conferred in low-spirited and uncomfortable conversations. We were all so young. And then, the hearse was suddenly there, pulling slowly into the parking lot. The hearse and the coffin and Len's parents and brother, his partner Ana and her family. The people who our grief-stricken eyes would settle on, sympathetic and sorrowful.

I have never attended a funeral that felt as surreal as this. It felt as if I was in a terrible dream. I chose a seat in a church pew behind Ana and next to Pete, four rows from the front. We watched as the pallbearers carried him in and set the coffin down under a cross. Len's friend Ben played the violin, and his best friend Bill delivered the most beautiful eulogy. He barely got through it. Later, I would ask him to send me a copy. It was heartbreaking to listen to and read again, but I didn't want to lose a single word written in honour of my friend.

The things that were said about Lenny in a church filled with both familiar and strange faces nodding at Bill's touching words—these were all a tribute to show just how genuine a guy Len had been with everyone he met. Young, kind, funny, compassionate, brilliant. He was the kind of person the world needed more of. Bill had been with Lenny in Morocco when he died. I think he had tried to save him.

The rest of the service moved forward, crushing us with each shared memory: How he secretly enjoyed playing the French horn, called in sick to work from Brazil, stole a trophy from Cambridge on a dare when drunk (he gave it back). His brother spoke; his broken father spoke. Candles were lit, and "Old Man Time" played in a haunting but comforting sound through the church as we cried. The worst moment came near the end when we were all asked to rise as the curtains closed in the front of the church, Lenny's coffin disappearing behind them.

And he was gone.

Afterwards, I spent a couple of hours at his parents' house. The calm and strength demonstrated by his parents was moving, as they dutifully attended to their guests with grace, filling their house with Lenny's friends. I spoke to his parents some, and we each swapped stories of Lenny, as mourners tend to do. I talked with his mom for a while, exchanging stories of Bulgaria, where I had last seen my friend. I remember placing my hand on her arm and telling her that her son was so loved. He was so, so loved.

~

I FLEW BACK TO Spain the next day, taking an early train from Canterbury to London, and then flew back to Bilbao. The tears continued to flow, but amongst the grief now flowed gratitude. I had been forced off my feet and stopped from walking, surprised by an informative email, and delivered so swiftly back amongst beloved friends to honour Lenny and to say our goodbyes. For this, I was grateful.

My Trail of Sorrow took me north, across the sea, overland, and back again.

I was ready to keep going.

The Trail of Glory

UPON LANDING IN BILBAO, I bussed west to meet up with Haley in Gijón, a town sitting under the hazy, overcast sky on the northern coast of Spain. Despite the London-like weather, the beach was still bright and inviting. Cafes and bars dotted along the promenade and bustled with travellers, holidaymakers, surfers, and lifeguards.

While Gijón wasn't very warm, I spent most of the day wandering along the harbour, the scenic lighthouse views reminding me of other Mediterranean travels. I purchased a blue leather wallet imprinted with the sun. It reminded me of the blue sun ceramic I had bought the previous October on my visit to Bulgaria.

In the morning, we would take another bus and rejoin the Camino Frances at Sarria. From there, it would only be another 127-kilometre walk to Santiago de Compostela. There was a section of the trail we would have missed between Navarrete and Sarria, but Haley wasn't so fussed, and I had definitely endured enough emotional sorrow to account for the skipped-out physical distance.

Perhaps I could finish the Camino in just six more days on the trail. Having been off the trail for almost as long, I was anxious to pick the pace back up. While in Gijón, I received a text from Johan, who was somewhere behind me now on the Camino. We'd routed around him and Casey when we took time to heal. What an uplifting thought to learn that some of my fellow pilgrims were thinking of me too.

The bus ride to Sarria took six and a half hours. Once we arrived, we had to trek up and down through the town to find an albergue that wasn't *completo*. We finally found a room that was *disponible,* and settled in.

In the evening, Haley and I spent our time strolling around the quaint, sunset-lit village, cobblestone roads, wooden doors, and leafy shade trees. Along part of a wall leading just off into a field, I spotted a swastika painted directly next to the Camino's golden yellow arrows we were meant to be following. Horrified and shocked, I checked this with Haley. Likely, the modern connotation of Nazism and the holocaust had nothing to do with what a swastika truly represents. Before the 1940's altered the emotions that this symbol would spark, in Hindu, the swastika symbolises prosperity and good luck—both gestures much appreciated by pilgrims on the Camino. The Camino Frances had been in use for centuries, long before the swastika had been rebranded.

In the small village of Sarria, we couldn't help but pick up on a different feel amongst the other pilgrims. They were not as weary. Sarria felt like a quaint tourist destination—one that was motored to. As we had done too, I suppose. A couple travelling by motorcycle, all leather and silver buckles, flashed bright grins at us as they passed. The 5 o'clock church bells rang out, and the day began to turn down. I was ready to go.

We watched the sunset while cigarette smoke drifted up outside the albergue doors. Workmen on horses clip-clopped down the narrow, cobbled roads. In my head ran Johan's mantra that he had picked up from some other pilgrim along the way and taught me during one of our walks.

> *We know the way*
> *We go the way*
> *The way we go*
> *The way we know*

I'm remembering this wrong. I believe there was a second verse, but I was unable to commit it to memory. Johan took the words with him.

> *We know the way*
> *We go the way*

The way we go is uphill.

28.1 KM
Sarria to Gonzar

THIRTY-THREE KILOMETRES.

Well, according to Michael the Austrian. Thirty-one kilometres according to Dan from London, and about 30 km according to me, when I gauged the distance we'd trekked that day.

I looked down at my dirty, swollen feet, blisters re-emerging with a vengeance. *Fuck it. Thirty-three kilometres it is.*

It had been a tiring day. Re-entering the Camino came as somewhat of a shock to the body after taking a few days off to not walk very much at all. But, even though the familiar pain had returned, walking the Camino again felt good for my soul.

I had purchased Compede, a skin-like bandage meant to hold together every tender piece of flesh that burned or ached from rubbing against my hiking boots. My heels and toes were completely padded over with the stuff. They still were tender and swollen, but this time there was no blood oozing from open wounds between my toes and no new blisters.

I only had 80 km more to go before I reached Santiago.

The afternoon heat had begun to dwindle when we settled into our bunks in the farmhouse-turned-albergue. More and more each day, as we arrived at our destination for the evening, we discovered that our places of rest were small barns set up with beds and amenities set up to shelter pilgrims rather than the massive monasteries we'd stayed in before. Our albergues became cosier, homier, and more familiar. As we fell back into rhythm, I became less diligent with our daily routine. On this day, arriving in Gonzar, I don't think I even showered. Instead of tending to myself, I ditched my pack upon arrival and decided to see what and who else was around, sleeping in this family farm-like albergue for the evening.

We wandered into a courtyard across the dirt and passed cage-free chickens pecking for corn to encounter a few other pilgrims who'd arrived before us. They were a collection of men, faces overgrown, clothes as dirty as mine, sitting around a round, wooden table, drinking cheap, cold beer in frosty glasses. Exhausted from covering such a massive stretch of the Camino, I just couldn't be bothered to clean up and delay sitting down with a cold cerveza and some friendly conversation.

There was a weathered Austrian man with shaggy hair, a floppy hat, and a walking stick leaning against the table. His demeanour was quiet, but his eyes were kind and deep. His smile greeted me as I pulled up a wooden chair. A large, bearded, chubby German was sitting next to him, boisterous and lively, and his ruddy complexion lit up as I ordered a cold one and introduced myself. They didn't mind the intrusion.

During our exchange of hello's, I practised my greetings in German. "Wie geht es dir?" As much as I would have enjoyed a friendly banter in German, "good day," "good night," and a few food items were all I could pick up, so we continued our introductions in English.

The German, whose name I sadly can't recall, was jovial, fleshy and round; his personality was so...cheerful! I thought for sure he was ol' St. Nick, spending the summer months in more physically active pursuits. I wasn't far off. After an amusing guessing game that he cajoled us into playing, we tried for quite some time to figure out his profession. He wore a bright orange, sleeved shirt, buttoned down underneath suspenders, and he happily knocked back pint after pint of cold beer as we threw down incorrect guess after incorrect guess on the table. After enough of our losses, the German finally gave in and professed to be a preacher of a church in Germany. His flock was, according to his story, proud of him and his endeavours to walk the Camino. He followed this game with beer jokes, belly laughs, and stories of his travels, his life, and his friends far off.

Our other afternoon companion was Michael, the Austrian, and he quietly shared with us that he had begun his Pilgrimage by foot, all the way from Austria, so much further than St. Jean Pied-de-Port. There are routes to Santiago stemming throughout Europe, and he had been walking his Pilgrimage for nearly four months. He was very near to finishing now, this lone pilgrim. I remember looking closely at his deep-set eyes, which didn't meet mine for very long, glancing down at his half-drunk beer, held between both of his roughened hands. His journey, his reason for walking was unknown to me. But without him speaking, I could tell he was on this journey to relieve himself of burdens heavier than I had yet to understand. He had a Lenny—or a few Lennys—he was walking for, too. I could feel he had left his share of piles of stones on the trail.

~

EARLIER THAT MORNING, HALEY and I had left our albergue in Sarria strikingly early. As per usual, I suppose. Once again, we stepped out onto the trail, packs on backs, hands-on sticks or backpack straps, and feet fully bandaged. Out, again, we ventured into the early morning time of night.

The air we breathed was chilly and a smoky dark. I had long ago given up on my flashlight. The road we embarked upon had been frightening, as the first part of the trail directed us down a shadowed dirt lane and alongside cemetery walls.

The cemetery was not the modern, flat stoned, manicured cemeteries we leave potted flowers in, bedecked with flags or windmills. Rather, these were old, century-aged headstones that had crumbled and moulded over hundred-year-old coffins, deep in timeless earth. These cemeteries are bordered by broken bricks, viny and graffitied, enclosed with rusted iron gates creaking on their hinges and laced with dusty vines. The headstones inside were overtaken with weeds, uneven mud, and statued angels. Sarria's cemetery was no different, and in the pitch-black morning, with its broken, hinged gates crookedly open just wide enough and lurching as it was against an even darker forest, I did all but shit myself.

I would have run past it all if I could, but the morning was still too dark to even see the ground in front of me. The best I could do was a hurried walk, keeping my eyes faced forward, imagining blinders to block my peripheral vision from any ghouls or spirits still lurking from their midnight haunts. In the black, cool Spanish breeze, I stumbled down the broken road, past the spooky cemetery towards the dark, arching trees. I blocked my vision and then my mind from the horrors that seemed to claw at my imagination and focused on stepping one booted foot in front of the other as quickly as I could through the dark, trusting it was only a matter of time until I felt at ease again.

Even though most of our mornings began before dawn, in previous days on the Camino, there seemed to be some sort of chirpy welcome as the sun broke over the horizon, sleepily announcing its arrival over the hills. That was not the case on this particular morning. As the sun rose over the dark forest that we now walked through, the cemetery at our heels, the shades of sunlight beckoned uneasily, and I struggled to shake the feeling that something had watched us pass. Once we were a good ways beyond the cemetery, and through the branching, tangled trees (which were not as dense as they had first seemed, once the sunlight climbed upon them), the dirt track turned uphill, the trees became less sparse, and the space in front of us opened up. We'd been accustomed to fields of sheep, endless rows of sunflowers, or even vineyards, stretching out for miles on either side of our path. This time, lining the road were cornfields.

Cornfields, it turns out, are just as terrifying to me as cemeteries. I never would have settled on this thought had the Camino trail not led me along an extended patch of high, ripening cornfields so early in the morning, having just survived the horrors of a night-time cemetery.

Corn stalks—they loom. And they proved to be denser than any haunted forest we'd yet had to survive our way through. Their shadows are militantly tall, whispering towards you, teasingly, sinisterly, mercilessly as you brusquely walk past their faceless rows, silently faking brave thoughts to yourself until it's over. There was so much in my surroundings to fear.

However, I do have one lovely photo from this terrifying morning walk that brightened up the whole morning's experience. As the sky began to lighten and we left the cornfields and the cemetery behind us, the fields transformed into pastures. Along one such pasture, a small, pretty pony was standing right up against the fence near a bend in the road. She was a curious little thing, dark colouring with a white, patchy nose, and she whinnied as I walked near. I just couldn't help myself. In my pocket, I carried an apple meant to be my midday snack. Instead, I pulled out my apple, reached up, and fed the pretty girl from my palm. It was a sweet moment, interacting like this with a spirit animal, and it dispersed any lingering fear or shadowed memories that remained from the morning. It was, however, also the only snack that I had packed for the entire day, and I would eventually come to regret having given the well-fed horse my only piece of fruit. The rest of the day, we travelled just Haley and I, walking through dairy farmland that smelled at times overpoweringly sour.

This next part of the Camino was cast with lovely and interesting characters, whose presence spiked our days with pleasant chats. But, for reasons I can't quite stitch together, these figures did not weave themselves into my narrative, nor were they as strongly bonded to my memory as was true for the first eight days of the Camino. Perhaps the Trail of Joy carried a friendly enthusiasm, and the Trail of Sorrow bound us in a "misery loves company" anthem. But the Trail of Glory (which we had embarked upon unbeknownst to us), while still friendly, seemed more of an insular and private journey. I had yet to sink into any glorious feels.

Many pilgrims we met along this section of The Way were doing the "short" stretch toward Santiago, only walking for a few days, treating the trail as if it were some recreational excursion. The people we had met who had begun their walk from St. Jean Pied-de-Port, walking on through Pamplona, and on still through Viana had planned for a much longer Pilgrimage, their outlooks becoming more solemn with each passing day. Somehow, that made a difference in how travellers perceived the Camino and how pilgrims perceived each other. Some of us journeyed. Some of us were on holiday.

Arriving in Gonzar, we'd find both types of pilgrims. Haley and I had ended our day's walk from Sarria, and I sauntered straight for the wooden table to meet new beer-drinking, story-sharing friends.

The Stone Marker

THE NEXT MORNING WE LEFT our slumbers and mechanically moved into our familiar drill. Awake, pack, bandage, go. Except this morning, rather than set out in the crispness of peeking dawn, we left in the dark *and* in the pouring rain.

Our pace was frustratingly slow. Where on a typical morning we could move 6 km in about an hour, the rain trickled into our travels, and it took us three hours to go only about 10 km. After about 40 minutes of walking through mud, we came across a four-pronged fork in the path. The cheap flashlights we had been using continued to fail us with their dimming or absent light. The rain blinded our faces, and the water had washed all kinds of debris, rocks, and sticks onto the path. We were chilled by the wind and searched a good, long while for the yellow Camino arrow painted on a rock, on a tree—anything that would show us the correct way to go.

Our spirits were low and our moods irritable that morning as we fumbled around cold and wet and lost and blind. Eventually, other pilgrims caught up with us—pilgrims with much stronger flashlights—and we were able to backtrack until we found the muddied yellow arrow we had missed.

We carried on but stopped at the first open café we found so that we could dry off and order a hot drink. This seemed like a good idea at the moment—a chance to find warmth and calm and rekindle our dampened spirits. It was so nice to come in out of the rain for some hot coffee and a friendly chat. But then, 20 minutes later, we had to put our jackets back on, still wet and cold, lift our sodden bags onto our aching shoulders, slip out from the cosy, warm café, and head back out into the relentless storm.

Hours of walking the Camino later, we had left behind the

storm, or the storm had left us. Finally, we had dried out and warmed up. But I now faced a different, if not totally new problem: My hiking boots were not working out so well. I had hoped my boots would take on a more seasoned shape around my hardened and torn feet once I was back on the trail. But two days after we left Sarria, my boots were crippling me.

I stopped at one point and pulled out my pocket knife—the same knife I'd been using to slice cheese and fruit and to cut away dead skin. I now used it to slice through the leather along the back seam of my boot heel. The £100 hiking boots with the "heel-lock system" had served me through the marshy woods of the New Forest in England, over the frozen peaks of the Rila Mountains in Bulgaria, and up the smoking rocks of the erupting Mt. Etna, plus many other weekend treks through the wild. Now, less than 100 km from my destination, the snazzy heel support was no longer effective. With my little knife, I began to saw through the tough leather of my expensive hiking boots in an attempt to create more space between my heel and the inside of my boot.

The relief my feet felt once I'd sawed down the middle and released the seam was instant. There was far less rubbing of skin along roughened leather. With happier feet, I carried on. A little more room in my shoe went a long way.

But not that much longer, I was dismayed to discover. My feet filled the extra space in my shoe with more swelling. They ached as much as ever. A few kilometres before we reached Cassanova, we passed through another town. A town with shops and cafes and supplies. One such shop caught my attention. Within view of the front windows were several pairs of shoes for sale. Ten minutes and €15 later, I was the proud owner of the ugliest pair of sandals imaginable. They were an unappealing fashion choice, and horrible to look at. I felt like a stupid little kid in them: they were grey plastic sandals with two Velcro straps across the top. These ugly, cheap, Jesus sandals worn over my filthy socks would just have to do. They would carry this pilgrim the rest of the way to Santiago. No skin touched leather. No blisters were exposed or rubbing. They were hideous. But they were also perfect. I tied my beloved, betraying boots to the back of my pack, and carried on following the yellow arrows and Camino shells drawn on trees, light poles, rocks, and street curbs. Blisters no longer bleeding, feet no longer swelling.

For some time, I had been walking by myself. Haley and I were at different stages mentally and different paces physically. It was better for our camaraderie if we woke, walked, and felt completely content as we drifted and the distance between us on the Camino grew. There was always a coffee shop ahead to catch up in, or the next albergue. We each walked at our own pace.

The boots dangled from my bag for a few kilometres after I left Cassanova, swinging back and forth behind me, once again adding a heavyweight to my pack. It was about 64 km outside of Santiago that I decided to leave the boots for good and say goodbye. A memory came flashing back to me—that scene of tall metal artworks adorning the top of the hill outside Cizur Menor, the pilgrim silhouettes. Just next to them had been several pairs of abandoned boots, lonely and empty. Now, my feet ravaged and my boots used to their max, I could completely understand why this had been. The small piles of rocks and stones that had marked the Camino for the entire way, the handmade stick crosses we'd seen jammed into fences, the stories and the faces from every age and every country—we all carried burdens along the Camino. We all carried something we needed to set down. I had been able to walk about 250 km of the Camino, and it was time to drop my boots and my burden for good.

The dirt path I now trekked along was canopied with a lovely shade from trees and vines. The morning was neither overly hot, nor too damp, nor peopled with companionable pilgrims. In fact, the bend in the road I came across was sheltered with leafy overhang and welcome quiet. I stopped for a moment and set my bag down. Carefully, I worked at the laces that I had tightly tied around one of the straps of my pack. I wouldn't leave piles of rocks or sticks on my Pilgrimage. My boots were what I would leave for Lenny. He and I had survived Bulgarian snowstorms in those things. Screw the rocks. I set the travel worn pair of boots by the 63.5 km stone marker, honouring the pilgrim who'd gone.

Even though I was on a Pilgrimage, prayer had never been part of my journey—not much, anyway. But I took a moment and said one there. I had removed the laces from the boots and stuffed them into my backpack pockets to keep. Strapping my pack back on, a little lighter now, I carried on down the trail and left the boots behind.

21.1 KM

Gonzar to Ponte Campaña

NEXT, WE WERE INVADED by Italians. There seemed to be more and more of them as we journeyed closer to Santiago. Boisterous Italians, loud and jovial, and who I would have happily fallen in stride with and joined in the banter if I could have kept up with their language.

We trekked just over 21 km from Gonazar to reach Ponte Campaña. This rustic albergue proved to be another private home turned pilgrim abode. Friendly, but tired pilgrims dotted throughout the grassy back garden. Somewhere, new-age music was playing, the melody drifting through the air and filtering through the leafy trees and onto our tired heads. Inside, as we waited to pay for the night, I took a look around our resting place. The cosy room was filled with weathered wooden tables and well-read books; an assortment of woven baskets was set around the place. Pieces of corroded farm machinery had been repurposed and were fastened high on the stone walls. This place felt centuries old.

Another pilgrim with us was a Spanish girl who was travelling with her mother. She sat at one of the tables, nursing her feet. Her heels were far worse than mine ever were. Hers were blistered and had also become infected, scabby, and bruised in a serious way. I decided to stop complaining about mine.

We'd been fortunate. Most of the albergues had been so welcoming. Warm showers had always been available (even if I chose not to use them). Sometimes the albergues were lively, sometimes they were calm and offered a chilled-out vibe.

Somewhere along the way, I had befriended another German named Patrick, who was travelling with his younger 17-year-old twin brothers. I had guessed Patrick to be about 27. He hadn't fared so well as far as his albergue experiences had gone. He complained about one of the cheaper albergues he'd stayed in, and how he had slept outside one night on the porch because there were no more beds available for him. Haley and I had switched from staying in the larger, cheaper albergues to staying in the private albergues. They were a little more costly, but the comfort was well worth the extra euros.

The albergue in Ponte Campaña we had chosen for this night created more of a "family night" feel, which at this stage along the Camino, we were both grateful for. There were eight of us that sat around the table for dinner. Dinners with strangers usually consisted of poorly spoken English, Spanish, Italian, sometimes French, and German. I don't remember what was on the menu, but I do remember dessert. The Spanish girl's mother had decided enough was enough for her poor bruised and blistered daughter and decided to liven up the mood and order *queimada*.

Queimada is the traditional fire drink of Galicia. It is made by filling a huge ceramic bowl with strong, clear liquor. Next, the bowl is filled with coffee beans. Then the rinds of an orange and a lemon are sliced into the mix, followed by copious amounts of sugar poured in without measure. Finally, the entire bowl, placed in the centre of the table, is set on fire and burned until the flames spiral high and wildly blue before being consumed in a special ceremony. This...this was just spectacular! The handful of pilgrims, the Spanish mother and daughter, Haley and I, the hosts, we all sat around the dining table and watched the magic potion as it was created in the centre of the dining table right before our eyes.

The concoction burned a purple, fiery flame for several minutes, rising high above the bowl and heating our upturned faces. The flames shot with gusto up into the air while we ooh-ed and awed at the show in the centre of the dining table. The drink kept burning purple for about 10 minutes or so until finally cup-fulls were scooped for each of us to enjoy and get a little drunk. The smell and steam coming out of my cup completely burned my eyes, but the hot sweetness of it was worth any sting. The *queimada* burned all the way down to my belly.

After the *queimada*, anyone at the table who struggled with their English or Spanish or German or any other language we were learning—our skills instantly improved, and it turned into a lively evening of *queimada*-infused conversation in many spiced and sweetened tongues.

24.8 KM

Ponte Campaña to Ribadiso

THIS DAY, I ARRIVED at the Albergue Ribadiso de Baixo after another 20 km or more of the Camino. Even though the usual wine with dinner had been replaced with the much stronger *queimada,* we still began quite early. We walked through the still-dark morning through the eerie, fairy tale woods of the Spanish north. There was no rain this time, so it wasn't too challenging to keep track of the yellow arrows pointing the way. It was a much longer hike to the first open café. Being a Sunday morning, every potential resting spot was closed.

I spent the afternoon at Ribadiso doing my usual lounging. This place offered a larger albergue, with a comforting, shaded creek running alongside it. I did yoga in the wispy cow fields, stretching every muscle that had come to ache more and more with each passing day.

While wandering along the property, I discovered a grassy slope by the creek under an apple tree where I could inspect my blisters and catch up on my writing. My poor toes were completely misshapen and still needed regular first aid and Compede.

It was at this juncture that I made friends with another German. This German was young, wore a straw farmer's hat, and went by the name of Markus. He had a sweet disposition but was also quite shy—even without speaking much English. He had begun the Camino from St. Jean Pied-de-Port two days before Haley and I, but he had been walking the entire way, without any resting or bus trips to Bilbao. His fast pace was incredible, surpassing the speed of any other pilgrim I had met. He had even walked 54 km in one day. What should have taken the average pilgrim about 35 days to cover, he had done in about 20.

On this quaint and pleasant stretch of Camino, we were accompanied by a sweet Camino dog. The dog had befriended the pilgrims along this part of the route and seemed to be just as intent on reaching Santiago as the rest of us pilgrims were. First, he had followed Patrick, the German with younger twin brothers all the way from Sarria. The Camino dog looked like a slim St. Bernard with ears flopping cheerily on either side of his face. I had seen him at Portomarín two days prior, and he'd now attached himself to an Italian for the last 20 km. It looked like he'd planned to stay with all of us for the night, swapping masters and following the trail— sweet old thing. I wondered how long he'd been on this Pilgrimage.

This serene scene chatting with a shy German under an apple tree and making friends with dogs was as calm as the afternoon would get. A mischievous band of fellow pilgrims, Spanish, new to the trail, and only along for a few days' hike arrived, boisterous, loud, and full of far more energy than any of us seasoned pilgrims could display. Those who joined the trail with only a 2-or 3-day walk to reach Santiago were a different breed. They were adventurers, sure, but also vacationers and holiday-makers. They were on the Camino for a good time, not a long time. Their minds had not been enchanted or distracted by the Camino in quite the same way. They also had not had their feet beaten down and subdued by the path. These pilgrims had not travelled along the Trail of Sorrow. This group was to co-create the noisiest night I had experienced the entire journey—as a sleeping pilgrim, at least.

The Spanish travellers, impassioned by local fruity Rioja, cluelessly stomped up and down wooden stairs at all hours of the night, accompanied by jovial shouting in Galician dialects, and the dropping of metal things that sounded to me like a thousand forks falling into a metal basin late into the night.

Combine the Spanish cacophony with the Camino dog's gallivanting gleefully through the albergue dorm rooms, the Italians shooing the dog away, someone's phone ringing from the dark corners of my dorm, ceiling lights near my pillow that confusingly stayed on all night, cameras flashing, and outside laughter wafting in all made for any attempt to rest futile. Another Italian in the bunk next to me was suffering from a nasty coughing fit throughout the night—so much so that at one point I thought he was actually throwing up on himself.

Confusingly, somewhere in the deep recesses of the room, some fortunate pilgrim was loudly and enviably snoring away. They sounded like they were drowning, but at the same time, I wish I could have sunk as deeply into my dreams as they seemed to be. They were not perturbed by the noise of the night—not one bit.

Meanwhile, in the land of the wide-awake, I was drowning in the discordant melodies of the wild frivolity carrying on throughout the popular albergue.

36.6 KM
Ribadiso to Pedrouzo

THIS LAST LEG OF the trip was different.

There were more conversations with pilgrims I met on the trail, specifically from Spain and Germany, but even these cross-cultural connections were growing tiresome for me.

During the seven years I'd lived overseas, I most often would naturally gravitate towards the opportunity to communicate in what ways I could with others from a different walk of life, a different culture, and a different way of thinking. But now, nearly at the end of my journey, the effort for even the mildest of chats was exhausting. My friendly greetings were limited to Camino conversation topics—where I was from, how far I'd walked, my painful blisters, etc., etc., etc.

On this Monday, I walked alone for most of the day. Without Haley, without strangers for companions, without music or podcasts in my ear. I just walked, accompanied only by my thoughts. I wasn't unravelling any complicated life questions, submerged in grief, or struggling with important career decisions in my mind as my feet carried me forward. My thoughts were set free to drift, to dally in recent memories, and reconnect with meaningful moments. I allowed my mind to miss people, to miss places other than where I was. I walked along the Camino, through rugged, rural paths, but, in my mind, I was miles away. Miles away, that is, until my senses took over, and I'd shift back to the present. My thoughts would then quietly respond to the scenes revealing themselves before me: the sloping green hills and the rugged trails of the endless Spanish countryside.

For lunch, rather than apples I'd packed or roadside watermelon, I managed to get my own table at a café in Arca O'Pino—the very last albergue on the Camino—as well as some wine in my glass and calamari on my plate. I had bought some nice cheese to enjoy along with my solo indulgence.

The Camino dog was still travelling with us, cheerful and tail-wagging. He'd made a night of it the evening before, crashing through the door and romping up and down the aisles of bunk beds. I remembered my own recent experience in Viana, crashing and romping and hooting it up with Cam, the Aussie writer with the busted knee and the bruised up but articulate English brothers, Casey and Johan, who'd witnessed my worst moments. I watched the Camino dog with warm affection and recognition of his selfish joy, bounding as he did amongst the bunks of sleepy pilgrims. I swear his furry face was laughing, even as he was shooed at by the owner of the albergue, who only wanted quiet for his guests.

However, this upcoming night, with the last 18 km of the Camino just one sleep away, would be my final night. I had risen in the morning knowing I had one full day of travelling ahead. It was the last full day that would roll out with the same daily routines I had grown accustomed to. The last of my starts before sunrise, coffees bought on the trail, thoughts or chats or adventures in unfamiliar places before I arrived at the next albergue to wash my clothes, bandage my feet, dine on pasta, and rest my head amongst strangers.

The last day of encouraging fresh blisters to plump between my toes. My poor feet seemed disfigured, so severe were the bulging pillows of flesh along my suffering skin.

The morning cracked open the sky. Being the last of my Pilgrimage days, I was distracted as I packed and left my only shirt hanging on a hook in the shared bathroom. That morning, I set out on my own and walked the long, hot, sunshiney day to the final albergue.

I know I passed through beautiful forests. I know I walked through quaint villages. I know I exchanged friendly hellos with other pilgrims, with locals, with whomever my eyes made contact with as I passed. But I can't remember exactly what I saw. I was so ensconced with my inside world as I spun around within the rivers of my mind and the caverns of my heart. The outside world didn't concrete in my memory as my inside world did.

So much was ending.

At home, at work, within whatever routine we find ourselves dedicated to, the efforts and energy we exert shape the project, the job, the relationship—the life we aim to create. But weeks of walking had shifted my efforts from carving an outside life to reconnecting with myself, and getting to understand how the internal mechanics of my thoughts worked—important things I wanted to understand and to lock onto like my purpose, desires, all my joys, all my sorrows. Walking the Camino gave me space, time, and a healthy balance of solitude and connection to realign myself with who I was and the maps I create in my mind and attempt to follow.

Somehow, and sometimes, who we are gets lost in what we're doing. Ebb and flow, drift and dream.

I cannot tell you details of each of those thoughts, but they most definitely ebbed back to England, my life in the Castle in London, teaching my high school students, my life in my house on Over Street, live music in Brighton, the embrace of my lovers, the faces of each of my lovely friends, my adventurous travels abroad to Amsterdam, Vienna, Paris, Edinburgh, Dublin, Brussels, Rome, Venice, Pula, Athens, Crete, Bulgaria, and of course, returned to the crushing loss of Lenny. My thoughts surely flowed as well to my family, to the California sunshine I'd fly back to, to my brother, my sister, my mother waiting for me at the end of the journey; to our family desert trips and new career choices and jobs I needed to find; and, too, to cars I needed to buy and all the things my new adult life in America would soon demand of me.

So much was beginning.

After several hours of walking on my own, Haley caught up with me, and we arrived at our final albergue too soon. It hadn't opened yet, and so we joined the queue of pilgrims sitting on or leaning against their backpacks in a line along the stone wall entry. We took our heavy bags off our shoulders and perched them up along the ground so we could sit and lean against them instead of bearing their weight. Around us, about 40 or 50 pilgrims waited in the sun for the albergue doors to open and let us in.

While we waited, I had a chat with Patrick the German again. Patrick was a skinny guy with stringy blond hair he kept back in a low-tied ponytail. His younger twin brothers were still walking some ways behind him.

Patrick's arms, legs, and torso displayed some wild tattoos. While we sat waiting, he explained the spiritual meaning of each of them and told me stories of their significance. Patrick was full of stories. He was a walking canvas of inky symbolism and purpose.

He continued revealing parts of his personal narrative and shared with me his experience of Shamanic dancing in Germany during a temazcal ritual. He'd erected a large tent, wide and expansive, but sheltered and cosy. In the centre, a pulsing fire blazed over round, hot stones, and naked dancers writhed around the heat, sweating out all of the badness inside of them. That's how he explained it to me. They were sweating out the badness.

The afternoon wore on, and we were finally allowed to enter the last albergue we'd encounter before reaching our final destination of Santiago de Compostela. After being assigned to my bunk, I wandered a bit through the small town and into the nearby wheat fields that border the roads. I was torn between the desire to explore my final village and resting place on the Camino, and the desire to sit still and rest my aching legs and feet. It was a feeling I had struggled with every afternoon on my journey when I reached an albergue: Rest or explore?

Sometime later, in the dwindling light of the afternoon, Patrick the German discovered he was one twin brother down. One had shown up, the other hadn't, and hours had passed by. In just a short expanse of time, I had watched my new friend Patrick shift from a calm traveller to an animated storyteller and then into a worried and distressed older brother. The only phone between the three brothers had been in Patrick's possession, as had been most of the food, and all of their money.

What worried Patrick especially was that the twin who had shown up at the albergue had been the slower twin. He'd been dragging his feet the entire journey, and so, Patrick deduced, if twin number one had been injured or stopped along the way, then slower twin number two would have caught up, and they would have carried on together, or at the very least, understood where along the trail each other would be.

This wasn't the case, and slower twin number two had not come across his quicker twin brother. Patrick worried that his brother could have missed the turnoff to this albergue, and carried on walking to Santiago on his own.

With no phone, no way to ask ahead or ask around, nor a way to rest peacefully, a decision had to be made. So a very fretful Patrick asked me if I would kindly look after his present twin brother while he continued on his own down the Camino towards Santiago in hopes of finding his lost brother. I didn't mind. On the trail, even after only a few hours of meeting and exchanging stories with others, we quickly could discern who the good humans were, and strangers were quick to place trust in each other when we needed to—with phones, with our only belongings, and with kin.

The younger twin was quiet and seemed to be even younger than his 17 years, but he'd be okay staying in the albergue by himself. I had learned only about five words in German, but Patrick assured his brother that if he needed anything or became upset, or worried, or scared to just let me know, and I would help him. Patrick and I traded phone numbers, and off he went. No rest for the Shamanic dancer with his tattooed stories on every bit of revealed skin. I imagined after walking what would be a 42-kilometre day that by the time he finally reached Santiago, he would have sweated out every drop of badness left in him.

In the meantime, I had aligned myself with some very friendly travellers. Haley wasn't feeling social, so I left younger twin number two to his bunk, and befriended the other travellers by myself. Markus was among them. The shy German with the straw hat had found a couple of Austrian girls with friendly faces, two spirited Spanish girls, and one tall guy in his mid-twenties, who was Spanish by blood but had grown up in Germany and spoke fluent English. In fact, he was fluent in all three languages—Spanish, German, and English. He was also tall, dark, and lively. His animated character thrived in this perfect triangle of cultures. He utilised all three languages necessary and decided to host a dinner party catering to our specific cultural dynamics. He took the lead amongst this new circle of pilgrims, who had migrated from the dorms to the kitchen area, and he commandeered the evening.

This last night, he declared, *this last night before we all end our individual journeys, our treks, our Pilgrimages, and conclude our reasons for walking, this last night before we arrive in Santiago, this last night,* he decreed, *should be celebrated with paella and with Spanish wine!*

Of course, it should.

In German, he instructed the Austrian girls and Markus which fruits and vegetables we would need for the famous Spanish dish and sent them off to shop. In English, he told me he needed to buy and prepare the rice. My task was to find and purchase the rice. In Spanish, he told the Spanish girls that he needed to find a local butcher and purchase a chicken—and then? And then he could prepare for us the paella! He emphatically and kindly shouted these plans to each of us, flitting between languages and changing the tongue, but never losing the charisma, the energy, the excitement, or joy he found in this opportunity! We each listened to him and did our best to keep up, laughing and agreeing to his suggestions. Flowing as one boisterous bunch, we set off into the village roads, in search of each ingredient.

In a modern city, most of these purchases could be made from one shop in a familiar location, and all dialogue needed for an exchange of money and goods would be communicated in one language. For this bunch of travellers, because we needed to inquire about shops, needed directions to these shops, knew nothing about the ingredients that go into a paella, nor were we fully familiar with how to prepare this particular dish, we accomplished the shopping for dinner in the least efficient way possible. Roaming streets, laughing while having incomprehensible conversations in three languages in at least as many dialects, getting lost, finding our way again, and eventually finding each of the shops we needed.

But, we also had nothing else to do.

With blistered feet and aching legs, us pilgrims-turned-dining-companions, limping aimlessly around unfamiliar Spanish villages was something every pilgrim had grown accustomed to. Each of us fell into conversation with someone else, either meeting for the first time, or speaking in our native tongue with fellow travel companions. But, speaking, we were. Loud, multi-lingual, jovial, friendly, curious, and hungry. We were excited about the dinner that everyone was eager and preparing to be a part of.

Vegetables and rice were bought first, then the Spanish-German guy who spoke English (Luis? I regret I did not write down his name.) He led us zigzagging through the streets, telling stories in Spanish, laughing away, shouting in German, pointing and gesturing, and asking me things in English every now and again about my life. Where was I going? What had I been doing for seven years in a country so cold as England when my family lived in Southern California? The usual set of inquisitions.

The Spanish-German leader of our posse found his way into a local butcher shop, and our posse followed him. Inside, the shop was small and plain, but it was there that our chicken lay, whole, frozen, and waiting.

Rapid Spanish was exchanged between our self-proclaimed head chef and the lady, the butcher behind the counter. I only caught a quick glimpse, but as she opened the door behind her to reach into the large freezer for our paella chicken, I could see the other animal carcasses hanging by their feet from the ceiling in the freezer. I cannot be sure now which specific animals I saw. From memory, I picture pigs and cows, but in reality, I had only a quick glimpse. Sometimes, acute memory fails, and then our minds embellish with whatever horror our imagination allows.

The butcher returned with a whole frozen chicken corpse. A whole chicken. Feet, neck, head. Strung out and stiffened. It had been de-feathered, but that was about it. She slapped the hardened thing down onto the counter in front of us, and quicker than I was able to reach into my bag and grab my camera, the lady butcher went to work. Cleaver in hand, she expertly hacked away at the neck, the legs, the chest. She hacked off all of the parts we would eat from this bird. I was struck by how quick and forceful she was as she mutilated this poor farm animal into something we would heat, season, and add to our Spanish rice. I was certainly horrified to view the raw reality of the beginnings of our meat dishes, but also, I was so curious to see such a thing. It was gruesomely spellbinding.

Now stocked with Spanish red wine, local vegetables, bags of rice, and chopped-up chicken parts, our quirky group returned to the albergue and invaded the kitchen to prepare our last supper.

Cooking has never been one of my favourite things, but I will happily grate cheese, set tables for large numbers, mix ingredients upon command, chop vegetables I wouldn't buy, and chat away with whoever is actually in charge of the cooking, happily refilling any empty wine glasses. We were all in high spirits, and after a good hour or two in the kitchen, listening to our chef instruct us in German, English, and Spanish, we finally finished preparing a meal for every one of us to sit down to and enjoy.

Our army of chefs and kitchen help migrated to the nearby dining room, where we invaded the space once again, armed with plates, forks and serving utensils. We arranged ourselves, jovial and chatty, along one long dining table, and with wine glasses lifted high, smiles bright on our faces, and full plates of food before each of us, we cheered a "Buen Camino" to everyone and dug in. It was one of the most enjoyable dinners I had indulged in along the Camino, and I couldn't have concocted a more perfect last meal to experience on the trail.

About 10 p.m. that night, long after the dregs of wine had been poured and drunk, and we pilgrims had been worn out, we found our way to our bunks. I was lying with my thoughts on my pillow, the albergue had locked its doors and turned out the light. I thought about Patrick, who had set off in search of his missing brother. I sent him a text. It had been hours since he'd left. He quickly sent me back a message saying that he had reached Santiago but had found nothing. He'd been walking for so long, the entire day, and now so late into the night. Twin number two had gone to bed, so I didn't worry him, but I couldn't sleep, worried myself. I laid in my bunk, trying to doze, but my thoughts continued to spin out on the beautiful hilarity of my last dinner, the miles I had walked, the pilgrims I had met, and the plans waiting to unfold for me in the upcoming days.

One restless hour later, I received a second text from Patrick. He had found his brother.

The lost twin had travelled all the way to the cathedral itself. He had been found sitting on the stone steps, in the night, alone and exhausted. No food. No money. No brothers. The poor kid had walked on past the turnoff and had just kept going, thinking his brothers were just another kilometre or two up ahead. Patrick was so happy.

I left my bed and found the bunk with the twin brother who had stayed behind. In probably the worst German I have ever attempted, I woke up twin number two and told him his other half had been found and that both brothers were okay. In the dark, he nodded sleepily that he understood. My smile and calm communicated more to him than my butchered German words ever could.

By the time Patrick had reunited with his brother in Santiago, it was nearing midnight, and the albergues would have been closed and locked for the evening. I crawled back into my own bed, wondering if those two would have to sleep outside again after all of that walking and worry.

I fell asleep thinking how this final night had cupped a contrast of experiences for each of us: Patrick had been exhausted, worried, and was now no doubt sleeping on stone outside; Haley had sought solitude in her bunk; and then there was my night, joining in the camaraderie with strangers, and stepping into the lightness and jovial energy shared amongst the travellers I had met.

16.2 KM

Pedrouzo to Santiago

As PER USUAL, AND for the last time in the Camino spirit, I awoke early to the sound of bags rustling, alarms beeping, and flashlights bobbing. Haley wanted to stroll into Santiago, to take her time, to dreamily and presently allow herself space to finish her Pilgrimage in her own way.

But I was ready to get there.

With everything stuffed hurriedly in my pack, I struck out on what would be my very last morning of striking out towards the Compostela de Santiago. On this dark morning, the sun was a long way off from rising. My flashlight had failed for good long ago, and I had failed to replace it. With no light of my own, I began my last day's walk, listening to the steps of other pilgrims on their way, and fell in line behind them.

Leaving the albergue, I followed the painted yellow arrows, barely visible in the crisp dark. They took me up a slightly steep, woody hill and around a shadowy bend. Here, the yellow Camino arrows led off the main road and took each of its pilgrims down a narrow footpath instead.

The trees were so tall.

This path crept deeper into dense woodland, the oaks closing in on sleepy-eyed pilgrims. Trees in the night, while beautiful and majestic, are still creepy in the dark. All my life, a magical, calming daytime forest has slid into the realm of the sinister at nightfall. Something about the absence of daylight, the removal of sounds sparked by life awakened. What remains amongst the trees is an ominous, humbling, and sometimes frightening feeling I never can shake. Unlike how I've long felt when arriving at a location under the cover of darkness warmed with the romance and mystery of the evening lights' glow, while crossing through the dark mornings on the Camino, I couldn't help but feel like I was the unwelcome and invasive intruder. There's a stark difference between arriving in a mysterious place after nightfall, so much of its wonder veiled and awaiting exploration, and having to journey through its darkness, with no lamplight or street glow. A nighttime arrival is the loveliest tease—a peek behind the curtain of all that a place has to offer. A nighttime journey bears a heavy load of trespass. No matter how many of my days along the Camino had begun so early in the purple, sleeping mornings, with or without companions, I always responded to the dark with a feeling of being unsettled, of feeling unnerved. As I walked, I thought of Patrick, of the faster twin brother who'd had to carry on alone, through the trees in the night, unsure whether they would find each other or how far they would have to walk. I wonder if they might have felt the same, walking in the dark, carrying their fear, travelling unfamiliar trails while shrouded in the night.

I moved deeper into my morning walk. Leading the way ahead were the silhouettes and dim headlamps of two small, young Italian guys. They were too far ahead for their lights to be of any help to light my path. But their distant voices and pleasant human sounds helped me remember that I was not alone in the Spanish woods and brought some comfort—even if they were strangers.

After a few minutes of trailing a safe distance behind them, I began to sense that they were a little scared of the dark as well, these two young men. I couldn't understand their Italian words, but they seemed a little edgy in tone, and their rapid banter was speckled with nervous laughter.

I suppose I could have taken comfort or self-awareness of my own bravery, hearing these two grown men displaying that they were just as fearful of the dark woods as I was. From my perspective, they had no reason to be scared of the night. There were two of them, and they were using their headlamps to light the way; freeing their hands for self-defence would be simple, should it come to that. I was a lone woman, travelling without a light.

Some people, in times of fright, begin to pray. Some call for help. Some panic and shift into fight mode. These two Italians? They battled their fear with song. Not even the morning lark was awake, but through the shadows between their steps and mine, through the still of the woods, I could hear the poorly harmonised tune:

Nella giungla, giungla possente, il leone dorme stasera!

While I couldn't understand the words exactly, the tune was unmistakable. These two grown Italian men were walking through the quiet forest singing to themselves, "In the jungle, the mighty jungle, the lion sleeps tonight."

Perhaps I joined in, singing aloud, or perhaps I sang along in my head in English. Either way, the song helped us shift our minds from fearing the dark into feeling silly and cheerful. And it was that tune and those thoughts that accompanied each of our steps, unbeknownst to each other, and walked us safely through the woods together. Even if we never met.

It was a solo walk for me all the way to the gates of the city. My mind rattled with so many moving pieces, travelling back into the past and projecting into the future, then returning to the present as I stepped, blistered foot in front of blistered foot, forward along the trail.

The sun began to glow behind me. The woods became fields, the fields became hills. The hills sloped down into the outskirts. The outskirts crept up against family houses and fruit stalls, and the dirt path became concrete sidewalk stained with old chewing gum and tar. Road signs and stop signs and traffic lights rose from street corners. The sun shone from high and poured hot light on my tired shoulders as I walked the last kilometre. I had arrived.

From the centre of the city, the Catedral de Santiago loomed. Medieval, Romanesque in structure, Gothic and Baroque, it eyed the arrival of present-day pilgrims solemnly.

Surrounded by a wide plaza on every side, dotted with aching, tired pilgrims, refreshed pilgrims, sorrowful pilgrims, joyous pilgrims, pilgrims flashing camera bulbs, and pilgrims writing postcards. Pilgrims whose faces were stained with tears.

Even the Camino dog could be seen sniffing the ground, wagging his tail, and making friends with those who tossed him a chunk of a baguette.

The Catedral de Santiago held mass every day at noon for the pilgrims who had arrived, finishing the Pilgrimage, no matter where they had begun their journey. The priests would read off a list of nations that represented each of the pilgrims who had arrived that morning.

The cathedral, immense and breathtaking, was detailed with stories from the Bible or mythology or history carved into every stone. The stone steps leading up to the large wooden doors had been worn down and grooved in the centre from hundreds of thousands of weary pilgrims' footsteps finishing hundreds of thousands of journeys.

A large stone pillar framing the entry had become smoothly indented and grooved from hundreds of thousands of weary pilgrims leaning their hands against it as they steadied themselves and gratefully entered the cathedral. What stories that pillar would tell—the endless number of pilgrims' burdens, carrying their walking sticks and their shells, following the yellow arrows for weeks and weeks, and finally arriving so that they could lean, sit, cry, and pray.

The reasons that pilgrims would walk were many. Pilgrims would walk to Santiago to ask forgiveness. They would walk seeking blessings. They would carry their sick and their dying for hundreds of kilometres for the blessing of St. James, so strong was their faith in the healing power of blessings they received from the cathedral. And blessings received from paying alms. If they could, they would take these blessings and this forgiveness back to the life they had left behind. They would return home and carry hope and lightness. They would carry a belief that something had changed for them. That their lives would now be better in some significant way, that only a Pilgrimage such as this could change for them.

Forgiveness and blessings must be two of our most costly needs. When I finally reached the Catedral de Santiago, after journeying hundreds of kilometres, when I entered the city alone on my blistered, torn feet, my aching shoulders and sweaty, tired everything, all I wanted to do was sit on those stone steps and cry.

Cry because I had finally arrived.

Cry because it was so beautiful.

Cry because I was weary.

Cry for the other pilgrims who had travelled much further than I with their burdens.

Cry because I missed Lenny.

Cry because it was over.

Cry because of all the sadness of leaving and saying good-bye to so many of my treasured people in so many unforgettable ways.

I wanted to open myself fully and cascade cries out from my

heart—all of the heavy steps I had taken to arrive at this moment, sitting on the smooth cathedral stones.

~

IT WASN'T TOO LONG after I arrived, taking in my thoughts and the sights surrounding the cathedral, before I spotted Markus, the quiet German and his trademark straw farmer's hat, standing just outside the facade. One of the twins was nearby too. I am not sure if he was the lost, quick twin who'd finished the Pilgrimage alone in the night, or the unlost, slower twin, who had slept and arrived in daylight, well-fed.

The cathedral was crowded. Was it Sunday? I couldn't be sure, but some people were dressed up for the service while most of us pilgrims were as dirty as was to be expected, still carrying walking sticks and backpacks. Some were limping. I think I might have been limping, too. My dirty bag weighed on my back. I entered the nave, and partook in mass, delivered in Latin, sitting amongst the Germans in the medieval, Spanish cathedral. I had attended mass a few times before, and some even in so grand a cathedral as the one I shakily stood in now, but never had I been to a ceremony that was populated by such a multitude of international people, and people from every walk of life.

There were pilgrims, tourists, worshipers, the young, the old, the very old; some were cleaned up, others, like me, attended grubby and wounded. We could have been from every country on every continent. I spent as much time gawking at the architecture and cathedral itself as I did the immense and diverse spread of people. There were so many of us, cameras clicking or heads bowed. Or both.

At the peak mass and the highlight of the ceremony was the lighting of the incense burner. In other cathedrals, during mass, a priest walks down the aisle, swinging incense that billows out from a small burner, dangling on a chain from his hands, left to right, spreading its smoky fragrance amongst the congregation.

In Santiago, the musical and visual highlight of the mass was the synchronisation of the beautiful "Hymn to Christ" with the spectacular swinging of the huge Botafumeiro, which is what the swinging incense burner is formally called. Here, the incense burner was not small enough to dangle from hands, but was as tall as a man;

it took two or three priests to pull thick ropes attached to the top of the burner and swing it as you would ring a large bell. The Botafumeiro hung from a thick, twisted rope suspended from the centre of the ceiling directly over the altar. From here, it was lowered and, with the priests pulling it back to one side as much as they could, they released it and let it sail.

The incense billowed out from the top of the gold-covered burner and over the upturned heads of the pilgrim worshipers who flashed away with their cameras. The Botafumeiro did not swing over the transepts or at the front of the Catedral, as one might expect, but longways down the centre of the cathedral and over the pews of pilgrims. Reaching as high as its chain would allow, the burner dropped back down, swinging back over across heads and arching over down the other side to the nave. The smoky incense was heavy and perfumed and thickly filled the cathedral. Back and forth, it swung, billowing out its blessings, blessing those of us who were sorry, those of us who were saddened, those of us who were grateful, those of us who felt relief, those who finally felt joy. The blessings and the Latin hymns heavily rolled above us, over us, and amongst our tired faces, worn-out bodies, and each of our beating hearts.

Santiago de Compostela

FROM HERE ON OUT, the spirit of the Camino begins to splinter.

Along the trail, either with companions or solo, in pain or light-footed, present in my surroundings or my mind miles away, the Camino spirit had shaped the journey.

I never knew exactly how far or how long I would walk each day, where my food would come from, what kind of food it would be, or if I would even have a bed that night. But I gave no thought to any of these things. I never knew who was in the bed next to me, who was trailing me in the dark, or how much the entire trip would cost me in the end.

Still, the spirit of the Camino was such that it took my mind away from these things. They became trivial. Better to engage in friendly banter with a new friend. Better to reflect on my past and dream of my friends in the life I'd just left. Better to anticipate the surprises of the future and where the next bend in life's road could take me. Strangers on the path were honest and friendly and trustworthy. There was an unspoken code amongst the pilgrims.

Somewhere after Sarria several days back and walking down yet another dirt road in the middle of nowhere, we came across a wooden table set up on the side of the path. Placed on this table were two or three dozen small boxes of fresh-picked raspberries. They must have been picked somewhere close by just that morning and set out for passing pilgrims. Alongside the open boxes of berries on the table, locked up with a small slit in the lid, was a money box, and hand-drawn on the side were the words "€1 each."

Haley and I had dug into our pockets, dropped a few €1 coins in the makeshift cash register, chose a punnet of berries, and carried on our way. A little bit later, we passed a trash can where I went to throw away my empty berry basket. I could hardly fit our basket in the bin because the bin was full to the brim with empty berry baskets.

I'm not good at math, but that's a lot of Euros that the berry picker had earned that day. But this demonstrates the honest nature of the Camino spirit. Someone had gathered the berries, set up the table, and gone on about whatever other chores they had still to do, or perhaps wandered off for a well-earned nap and left a cash box for honest pilgrims to pay into. It wasn't an empty box, nor was it tied down, and our coins rattled amongst others. This left us with a good feeling in our bellies towards other humans and the unspoken trust between the pilgrims and the unseen berry picker.

~

AFTER MASS HAD FINISHED, and the last prayer was lifted, we went our separate ways. Me and the Germans, me and the other pilgrims as we had known each other on the trail, we said farewell.

In the city, I lined up to present my pilgrim passport, where I had collected a stamp from every albergue I had stayed in along The Way. Pilgrims had to walk at least 100 km in order to receive their official Compostela. I had walked about 300 km. The Compostela is a certificate of accomplishment given to pilgrims on completing The Way. It's written in Latin and reads:

> The Chapter of this Holy Apostolic Metropolitan Cathedral of St. James, custodian of the seal of St. James' Altar, to all faithful and pilgrims who come from everywhere over the world as an act of devotion, under vow or promise to the Apostle's Tomb, our Patron, and Protector of Spain, witnesses in the sight of all who read this document, that: Mr.....................
> has visited devoutly this Sacred Church in a religious sense (pietatis causa).

> Witness whereof I hand this document over to him, authenticated by the seal of this Sacred Church.

> Given in St. James de Compostela on the (day)......(month)......
> A.D. ....Chapter Secretary

I eventually caught up with Haley, and we made our way to our post-Camino albergue. It wasn't very nice. This albergue was more dormitory than monastery. Since I had left my pyjamas in the albergue the night before, I had to sleep in the sheets and just my bikini. Pilgrims shushed each other in the night, showers were cold, and iPods were stolen. The honest spirit of the Pilgrimage and its pilgrims displayed days ago by the berry basket table seemed to have faded with the journey's end.

My feet were still blistered, still breaking open on occasion, and oozing beneath my feet. I limped through the plaza, over cobbled passages, and allowed the weariness to settle as I mildly explored the winding, historic alleys and buildings of Santiago.

I had not planned to spend many days in Santiago. The day after my arrival, I had booked a long, overnight train journey to Lyon, France. From there, I would travel to Paris and catch a flight to Toronto for a week to enjoy the company of a few very good friends. A few good friends, but minus one. Lenny would no longer meet me at the end of my journey.

After a week in Canada reconnecting with some of my Castle friends, I would board my final flight from Toronto to Southern California and join my family. From there, I wasn't too sure where my life would go.

The train left early the next morning, less than 24 hours after I had arrived in Santiago. I boarded it by myself. I had woken up to a cold shower, hungry, having slept in dirty sheets with 50 other strangers. Now, I was travelling solo towards a delicious breakfast at a café in Paris.

As I took my seat by a window and looked out over the Spanish city, I wished I was still on the trail, waking up and heading out. I was already nostalgic of the Camino and envious of those who were still on their Pilgrimage. On the trail still, days behind me, were Johan and Casey, the Russian soldier, and so many other pilgrims I had connected with in some meaningful way.

They knew what to do with their day when they awoke, and where to go.

The train rolled along the rails, leaving Santiago and moving away from the cathedral I had spent so many days trying to reach. It swiftly rolled past forests and cities, crossing back over the trail I had just walked. Swiftly, swiftly, stopping, changing, then rolling again.

At one stop somewhere near the border of France, I stepped off the train for a moment to buy a coffee at the café in the station. A middle-aged Spanish man with a cane sat near me and noticed my bandaged feet and heavy pack, and struck up a conversation.

He said he had done the entire Camino 27 times in his life. Twenty-six of these Pilgrimages were by bike, and only once he had completed the entire Camino by foot. Now, he laughed tapping his legs with his cane, now his knees were broken.

Back on the rails, I thought about that man and his many journeys. Did he carry the same burdens each time? I thought about my own journey, watching from my window as Spain passed by and eventually became France.

That night on the train, I bunked in a small sleeper cabin with six other people. My train seat was a couchette, perched at the top of the triple-stacked, narrow beds.

Within arms' length lay an older Belgian man. Even though he was laying horizontal, he seemed short to me, and stocky, his shaggy grey hair and unkempt beard framing his pudgy, weathered, and kind face.

He also had just finished the Camino and was on his way home. He was weary, but his journey was over. He told me how much he had missed his wife during the weeks he had been gone and how he couldn't wait to see her. Then he rolled over and went to sleep, snoring peacefully.

The way time unfolds while travelling never fails to astound me. The Camino, in many ways, felt like a lifetime in itself. Now, in less than a day, I would travel worlds away from the Pilgrimage that had journeyed me between where I had been, and where I would be.

I closed my eyes, listening to the sound of the rails against the night outside, and I let the dreams come.

Epilogue

EVENTUALLY, I MADE IT relatively unscathed back to southern California, but my stay didn't last long.

I fell in love with a man who was half-Australian, half-Kiwi (from New Zealand). Within a year, I had moved to Australia with him, obtained my permanent residency and settled down.

Kind of.

In the time leading up to my move to Australia, there were spontaneous travels to Colombia and Ecuador; cancelled return flights from Jamaica; treks through mountains and coasts in Mexico, summits up volcanoes in Guatemala, and terrifying bus rides throughout Honduras and El Salvador, journeying with new friends and old.

What came next? Even more.

Moving to Australia for an expat life amongst the big-hearted Aussies was a lifetime in itself: sipping local Pinot from glass tumblers, picnicking on hilltops, overlooking plains of kangaroos grazing below and watching the sun dip behind far off tree-lined ridges.

There was slipping and sliding across receding glaciers and road-tripping through New Zealand, or hopping on flights over the Pacific to indulge in the island life in Fiji.

While in Australia, teaching university-level leadership, I co-founded a company, EDventure International. For the next 5 years, my team and I created life-changing experiences overseas for students, combining my love of travel, learning, exploration and teaching.

I continued to travel extensively—both for work and for pleasure—with the aim of creating for others the same soul-shaping experiences from purposeful travel that have pivoted and shaped my own life.

These journeys took me and my fellow travellers and students to the ancient temples and bright green rice fields of heart-warming Cambodia, the muggy jungles and elephant rescue villages in Thailand, the villages, plains and beaches of South Africa and the mountainous and tropical "pura vida" vibe of Costa Rica.

Since the timeline of the stories in this book, the adventures have stacked exponentially, as have the life lessons.

And of course, there are more heart-warming and eye-opening stories with animals: Leatherback sea turtles, curious elephants, elusive manatees and black rhinos, just to name a few.

Within these threads of life, love, travel, business, and adventure are stories that may one day be spilt onto pages that become books that stack on bedside tables, or glow on screens.

Importantly, the purpose in sharing any of these tales, (or tails), is this:

Woven through this fabric of travel is the ever-possible inner lighting up of our souls, of who we really are. Of who we can be if we allow ourselves to dream big, and to expand the scope of what is possible.

It's the connection through travel, through momentary camaraderie with foreign faces and friendly strangers. It's the connection with ourselves, and all the raw beauty that each of us contains within.

I hope you each have a story to tell of the shaping of your soul—and if you don't yet, then I hope you re-chart the map of your own life so that you do.

CHRISTY NICHOLS IS AN educator, adventurer, Life Purpose professional coach, speaker, author, purposeful travel advocate, leadership and personal growth expert, seasoned traveler, and serial ex-pat. She has traveled extensively to more than 40 countries.

Today, Christy lives a full-time life in Nicaragua, where her travel with a purpose business "Venture Within" thrives, creating a fusion of immersive, purposeful, and life-changing experiences for others, and sunny adventures still continue to shape her soul.